DISCONTENTED MIRACLE

Growth, Conflict, and
Institutional Adaptations in China

Series on Contemporary China **(ISSN: 1793-0847)**

Published

Vol. 1 Legitimacy: Ambiguities of Political Success or Failure in East and Southeast Asia
edited by Lynn White

Vol. 2 China Under Hu Jintao: Opportunities, Dangers, and Dilemmas
edited by Tun-jen Cheng, Jacques deLisle & Deborah Brown

Vol. 3 China's Compliance in Global Affairs: Trade, Arms Control, Environmental Protection, Human Rights
by Gerald Chan

Vol. 4 Political Civilization and Modernization in China: The Political Context of China's Transformation
edited by Yang Zhong & Shiping Hua

Vol. 5 China into the Hu-Wen Era: Policy Initiatives and Challenges
edited by John Wong & Lai Hongyi

Vol. 6 Water and Development in China: The Political Economy of Shanghai Water Policy
by Seungho Lee

Vol. 7 De Facto Federalism in China: Reforms and Dynamics of Central-Local Relations
by Zheng Yongnian

Vol. 8 China's Elite Politics: Political Transition and Power Balancing
by Bo Zhiyue

Vol. 9 Economic Reform and Cross-Strait Relations: Taiwan and China in the WTO
edited by Julian Chang & Steven M Goldstein

Vol. 10 Discontented Miracle: Growth, Conflict, and Institutional Adaptations in China
edited by Dali L Yang

Series on Contemporary China – Vol. 10

DISCONTENTED MIRACLE

Growth, Conflict, and Institutional Adaptations in China

Edited by

Dali L Yang

University of Chicago, USA

World Scientific

NEW JERSEY • LONDON • SINGAPORE • BEIJING • SHANGHAI • HONG KONG • TAIPEI • CHENNAI

Published by

World Scientific Publishing Co. Pte. Ltd.
5 Toh Tuck Link, Singapore 596224
USA office: 27 Warren Street, Suite 401-402, Hackensack, NJ 07601
UK office: 57 Shelton Street, Covent Garden, London WC2H 9HE

Library of Congress Cataloging-in-Publication Data
Discontented miracle : growth, conflict, and institutional adaptations in China / edited by Dali L. Yang.
p. cm. -- (Series on contemporary China ; v. 10)
Includes bibliographical references and index.
ISBN 978-981-270-354-5 (alk. paper) -- ISBN 981-270-354-3 (alk. paper)
1. China--Economic conditions--2000. 2. China--Social conditions--2000. 3. China--Politics and government--2002.

HC427.95.D59 2007
330.951--dc22 2006048098

British Library Cataloguing-in-Publication Data
A catalogue record for this book is available from the British Library.

Typeset by Stallion Press
Email: enquiries@stallionpress.com

Printed in Singapore by World Scientific Printers (S) Pte Ltd

Preface and Acknowledgments

China has enjoyed stellar economic growth for more than a quarter of a century. That growth, following the era of Maoist misrule, has been known as the China Miracle.[1] Yet the rapid growth amid market-oriented reforms has not been an unalloyed blessing. It has been accompanied by soaring income inequality and rising social tensions.[2] It has also over-taxed China's resource base and contributed to a crisis of the environment.[3] Meanwhile, despite the introduction of elections in villages and some urban neighborhoods, the improvement in political participation has lagged behind the substantial improvement in standard of living and other social indicators. Instead, China's leaders have, in the aftermath of the Tiananmen crackdown, steadfastly held back the opening up of the political system.

In this volume, contributors from the disciplines of economics, political science, and sociology consider the theme "Tensions,

---

[1] Justin Yifu Lin, Fang Cai, Zhou Li, *The China Miracle: Development Strategy and Economic Reform* (Hong Kong: The Chinese University Press, 2003); Alvin Y. So, *China's Developmental Miracle: Origins, Transformations, and Challenges* (Armonk, NY: M.E. Sharpe, 2003).

[2] For a survey of the literature, see Dali L. Yang, "Economic Transformation and Its Political Discontents in China: Authoritarianism, Unequal Growth, and the Dilemmas of Political Development," *Annual Review of Political Science*, no. 9 (2006): 150–158.

[3] Elizabeth C. Economy, *The River Runs Black: The Environmental Challenge to China's Future* (Ithaca, NY: Cornell University Press, 2004); Vaclav Smil, *China's Environmental Crisis: An Inquiry into the Limits of National Development* (Armonk, NY: M.E. Sharpe, 1993).

Conflicts, and Institutions in China." The chapters examine how existing institutions, broadly defined, might have exacerbated tensions in China's evolving economy, society, and polity as well as how institutional developments have been introduced to deal with existing or emerging conflicts and tensions.

We begin with two classic topics, the regulation of the media and the evolving role of the *hukou* or household registration system. In "Cornering the Market (Chap. 1)," Ashley Esarey sheds interesting light on the dilemmas facing China's censors and publishers in the age of the market and the Internet. While the Propaganda czars continue to rein in the media sector politically, they have nonetheless introduced market incentives to encourage the increasingly diverse media outlets to be both politically acceptable and commercially relevant. In response to these competing demands, the Chinese media industry tends to exhibit symptoms of a sort of schizophrenia. On a broad range of contents the media has become increasingly competitive and open. But, when push comes to shove, the Party-state continues to wield enormous clout over the media industry. Meanwhile, Fei-ling Wang (Chap. 2) zeroes in on the complicated functions of the *hukou* or household registration system. Though its importance has declined in the reform era, the *hukou* continues to be a key social and political institution in China. According to Wang, while the *hukou* system has helped the ruling elite gain socio-political control, it has also generated substantial tensions and is ripe for further reforms.

Chapters 3–5 examine three issue areas that have gained growing prominence in recent years as China's economic boom has engendered more property rights disputes and increased concerns about the environment and consumer safety. In "Resources and Strategies (Chap. 3)," Tianfu Wang and Bobai Li dissect the tensions and conflicts between real estate developers and property buyers that have emerged with the commercialization of residential housing. For Wang and Li, these tensions and conflicts are both a reflection of China's changing social structure and a contributor to the formation of a new social structure. In "Multifaceted State and Fragmented Society (Chap. 4)," Yanfei Sun and Dingxin Zhao examine three environmental campaigns to illuminate the complexities of China's environmental movement. On the basis of detailed case studies, Sun and Zhao discuss the conditions under which such campaigns are more likely to succeed. In Chap. 5, Waikeung Tam and Dali Yang draw attention to a scandal involving the sale of fake and substandard milk powder and elucidate the challenges in China's regulatory development. The chapter highlights some of the deficiencies of the food safety regulatory regime and addresses some salient issues concerning the regulatory state building, including the regulatory chasm between urban and rural areas, the appropriate role of the state in socioeconomic regulation, the uncertainties created by government reforms, and the conflict between food safety and employment.

As income inequality has risen, the treatment of the disadvantaged has been high on the policy agenda. Although China in the reform era has sharply reduced the number of people in poverty, it has become more difficult to make further progress in poverty reduction in recent years. In their assessment of China's anti-poverty strategy and policies, Ran Tao and Mingxing Liu (Chap. 6) point to the various disincentives and weaknesses in the current system of spatially defined anti-poverty programs. Their analysis of poverty reduction policies not only points to the need for the adjustment of anti-poverty policies but also raises interesting questions about decentralization and governance in China. Meanwhile, in "Grain for Green or Grain for Gain (Chap. 7)," Jintao Xu and Ran Tao draw on survey data to dissect the acclaimed Grain for Green Program, which the Chinese government introduced at the end of the 1990s to encourage farmers to convert farmland into forests and grassland. While the program has been credited for its beneficial ecological impact, Xu and Tao provide a skeptical view of the Program's political origins. Their discussion of the Program's limitations for environmental protection and for boosting farmers' income is sobering.

Partly to respond to the problems of governance in the localities, the Chinese authorities have introduced elections into the villages. In the final chapter, Su and Yang argue that the promotion of competitive elections at the village level should be complemented by simultaneous improvements in a number of other non-electoral areas to enhance the accountability of public officials. The Chinese leadership has paid some attention to these aspects in recent years through the introduction of diverse initiatives, including tax-for-fee reform, new accounting practices, village affairs disclosure, and institutionalized participation in democratic decision making. The interaction between local initiatives and central interventions will shape the future of village democracy and local governance in China.

Several individuals have played indispensable roles in the making of this volume. Mel Gurtov got the project started when he asked me to put together a special issue of *Asian Perspective*. I wish to thank him for his expert editing of several chapters that appeared in that issue and for his encouragement and good humor. I would like to gratefully acknowledge the permission of *Asian Perspective* to use materials previously published in vol. 29, no. 4 (chapters 1–3, 5, 8).

Cheong Chean Chian of World Scientific Publishing has been a wonderfully supportive editor. Chris Chhim and Joyce Juanjie Shen served as my able assistants during the editorial process and deserve special thanks. Ran Tao, co-author of Chapters 6–7, wishes to thank the National Science Foundation of China (Project 70303011) and the NSFC Matching Fund of the Institute of Geographical Sciences and Natural Resource Research, the Chinese Academy of Sciences for financial support.

Contents

Chapter

1

Cornering the Market: State Strategies for Controlling China's Commercial Media

Ashley Esarey

INTRODUCTION*

Beginning in the 1980s, the Chinese Communist Party (CCP) launched sweeping reforms of the media industry, which led to rapid proliferation of print and television news media and diversification of media content. The resulting transformation of the news media industry made local media content more difficult to be controlled and reduced the number of people reached

* The interview data used in this article were collected during more than 15 months of fieldwork in Beijing, Shanghai, Guangzhou, and Changsha from 2001 to 2005. Due to the sensitivity of the subject matter, interviewees were promised anonymity.

by propaganda produced by more easily controlled central media.[1]

In the 1980s, the CCP retained control of the burgeoning news media by reducing the absolute number of media organizations through media re-registration campaigns and through closure of media that produced politically controversial material. Due to the CCP's post-Tiananmen legitimacy crisis, the CCP adjusted its media management policy in the 1990s, utilizing corporate strategies employed by media conglomerates in the West.

Media reformers in China believed that private ownership determined the nature of news content in the West. Therefore, state ownership of commercial media in the PRC could create financially successful media without sacrificing regime control over news content.[2] Media reforms since the 1990s have given rise to a lucrative media industry, subject to central control over news content and capable of producing carefully crafted state propaganda that reaches more Chinese than ever before.

This chapter considers the effect of commercialization on news coverage by television stations and daily newspapers, the media available to the largest number of Chinese. It explains how decentralization of state ownership of the media and commercialization in the 1980s led to challenges to the state control of television and print media content. Then, it describes the regime's efforts to retain control of the media industry by eliminating the media operating outside the law, the media perceived as posing a political threat, due to support for the 1989 pro-democracy demonstrations, and the media deemed too weak

[1] The term "local" refers to the provincial level and below. Propaganda was operationalized as a report that contains only one perspective, with the state's opinion on the news clearly stated. For example, the report indicates the state's positive or negative evaluation of the news or the state's preference for a certain outcome. In propaganda, the state is interpreting the news for the citizens in an attempt to influence public opinion, a phenomenon very different from news content that presents an array of diverse and potentially oppositional viewpoints, which citizens are expected to consider and utilize in forming their own opinions.

[2] The term "state" throughout this study refers to government institutions, including the communist party and its various branches. For more on this view of the Chinese state, see Marc Blecher, *China Against the Tides: Restructuring through Revolution, Radicalism and Reform* (London: Pinter Press, 1997), 117, 139–140.

to resist central-led reforms. While similar tactics have been employed to reduce the absolute number of the media in recent years, the regime policy toward media management has shifted to provide media (and journalists) with financial incentives to comply with CCP requirements for censorship and the dissemination of propaganda.

The final section of the chapter tests the extent to which commercial media were controlled by the state during the Severe Acute Respiratory Syndrome (SARS) crisis in 2003. The SARS case demonstrates that the news media were largely compliant with state censorship and that commercialization of the media has done little to diminish party control of news content.[3] Rather than presenting a serious challenge to state control, the establishment of market incentives in the media industry has strengthened incentives for the media to propagate the party line.

LOCALIZING MEDIA MANAGEMENT POWERS IN THE 1980s

Decentralization

Encouragement for lower levels of the state apparatus to start their own news organizations can be traced to the air of openness and political reform following the Third Plenum of the Communist Party's 11th Central Committee in December 1978 when reformists led by Deng Xiaoping attempted to improve the economy and bolster party legitimacy battered by the effects of the Cultural Revolution.[4] The spirit of reform carried over into the "National News Work Meeting" held by the Central Propaganda Department on March 8, 1979. In his address, the then director of the Central Propaganda Department, Hu Yaobang, advocated lifting restrictions on intellectual inquiry and encouraged

---

[3] Noteworthy exceptions, such as *Southern Weekend* [*Nanfang zhoumo*], *21st Century World Herald* [*21 shiji huanqiu baodao*], the CCTV investigative program *News Probe* [*Xinwen diaocha*], and *Caijing Magazine* [*Caijing zazhi*], did produce reports that directly or indirectly criticized state handling of the epidemic. The SARS case discussed in these media and subsequent disciplinary actions imposed by the state are examined below.

[4] Richard Baum, *Burying Mao: Chinese Politics in the Age of Deng Xiaoping* (Princeton University Press, 1994), chaps. 3–4.

the media to be more proactive and original, while strengthening the centralization of the party leadership and unity in party ranks.[5] Party committees of provinces, autonomous regions, self-administered cities, cities, planned cities (*jihua danlie shi*), districts (*zhou*), counties, and county-level cities were urged to start newspapers to increase the flow of information for economic development and to rebuild the power of the propaganda system.[6] Beginning in 1980, the establishment of new "party papers" sparked the meteoric rise in the number of media outlets that led to a fivefold increase in the number of newspapers by 1985, and an eightfold increase in the number of newspapers by the end of the decade. From the perspective of the party committees, founding newspapers offered an excellent chance to promote the careers and policy priorities of local party leaders as well as to disseminate central party propaganda. With the legalization of the sale of advertisements in 1979, party papers and those founded by other state organizations could become profit-making ventures. After 1983, they were allowed to retain residual profits.[7]

A number of television stations experienced rapid growth after 1983 when the CCP Central Committee announced the goal of "four levels" of television and radio stations, that is, nationwide programming by central, provincial, municipal and county-level stations.

---

[5] Fang Hanqi et al., ed., *Zhongguo xinwen shiye tongshi*, vol. 3, 434–435, 505–506.

[6] Kenneth Lieberthal, citing A. Doak Barnett, defines a "system" or *xitong* in the Chinese government as a grouping of "bureaucracies that together deal with the broad task the top political leaders want performed." *Governing China: From Revolution Through Reform* (New York: W.W. Norton, 1995), 194. The media is part of the powerful propaganda and education system, which also governs health issues, and is responsible for shaping the "values and perspective of the entire population." (Ibid., 197.) A variety of institutions interact in this system to generate media policy and monitor media content. Of particular importance to the news media are the CCP's Central Propaganda Department and its local bureaus, the Thought Work Small Group [*Sixiang gongzuo xiaozu*], headed by President and CCP Chairman Hu Jintao, and two state administrative bodies: the General Administration of Press and Publication and the State Administration of Radio, Film and Television (SARFT), and their subordinate branches.

[7] Cao Peng, *Zhongguo baoye jituan fazhan yanjiu* [*China Newspaper Group Development Research*] (Beijing: Xinhua chubanshe, 1999), 198, 200.

The new television stations were placed under the "dual responsibility system" that gave management responsibilities to local governments as well as to the Ministry of Radio, Film and Television (MRFT). Local government was given primary authority over day-to-day operations.[8] Television stations could produce their own news reports in addition to carrying mandatory broadcasts of CCTV1, the national television station founded in 1978. With rising affluence, many Chinese were able to afford to purchase television sets by the late 1980s. The age of China "turned on" to television commenced.[9]

Decentralization of ownership and managing rights over newspapers and television to lower levels of the state hierarchy, and the resulting growth in the number of media organizations, rapidly created problems for party monitoring of media content. In the early 1980s, Deng Xiaoping among others criticized the participation of party cadres in the printing of illegal publications with content containing mistaken ideology that undermined stability.[10] Party leaders bemoaned the inadequate training of top editors but also of copy editors and journalists due to the closure of schools and universities during the Cultural Revolution and the sharp rise in demand for media personnel.

Monitoring the television industry caused more headaches for the leaders of national state institutions. In 1983, China had 52 television stations, a number that by 1990 climbed to 509. The vast majority of the new stations were at the municipal and county level.[11]

---

[8] *Zhongguo guangbo dianshi nianjian* [*China Radio and Television Annual*], 1987, 38.

[9] For one of the earlier English-language studies of the evolving role of television in the Chinese society, see James Lull, *China Turned On: Television, Reform and Resistance* (New York: Routledge, 1991).

[10] Deng Xiaoping, "Dang de baokan yao chengwei guo anding tuanjie de sixiangshang de zhongxin" [Party Papers Must Become the Ideological Center of National Stability and Unity], transcript of speech on January 16, 1980. See a brief discussion of these views and the related political struggles at the time in Baum, *Burying Mao*, especially p. 89.

[11] The 1983 statistic is from Fang Hanqi, *Zhongguo xinwen shiye tongshi*, vol. 3, 570; the 1990 statistic is from *China News Annual*, 1991, appendix 3.2.

Staffed by inexperienced personnel and virtually unmonitored by the Central Propaganda Department, municipal and county stations broadcast a diverse and chaotic combination of programs related to local and national news, agricultural affairs, travel, arts and leisure, business, and a great deal of unauthorized content from overseas. The high viewership of city and county television posed a challenge to the viewers of CCTV and provincial stations, clear evidence that the appeal of the party's main outlets for propaganda was weakening.[12]

After a 1986 meeting attended by the leadership of the MRFT and the directors of the MRFT bureaus nationwide, the ministry admitted that its directives concerning the party's propaganda priorities for municipal and county television stations had been insufficient and issued a resolution for change. The resolution called for administrators to prevent stations without adequate standards from broadcasting. It also appealed for greater assistance from party committees to correct the "professional guiding thought" (*yewu zhidao sixiang*) of existing stations to improve management and programming quality. The document was a stern reminder that the foremost duty of these stations was to broadcast the programming of the national television channel CCTV1 without any interruption, even of CCTV advertisements, despite the fact that the local stations got no share of advertising revenue.[13]

The Rise, Decline, and Proliferation of Media

Significant outcomes of decentralization policies in the early 1980s included an explosion in the number of news media outlets, an increase in the value of media advertising revenues, a heightened competition for advertising revenue, and the expansion of media

---

[12] Fang Hanqi, *Zhongguo xinwen shiye tongshi*, vol. 3, 570.

[13] See *Zhongguo guangbo dianshi nianjian*, discussing the contents of the "National Village Radio and Television Bureau Directors Meeting," p. 35. Complaints by local television interests about the CCTV monopoly on the national television advertising market have intensified over time. Local broadcast media groups see the inability to alter the CCTV programming and insert local advertisements as the loss of a valuable opportunity to earn revenue.

freedom to report the news as opposed to party propaganda. Central government-sponsored policies empowered lower levels of the party-state to license news media organizations, encouraged the news media to "walk on their own two feet" by selling advertisements, and slashed state subsidies.[14] The resulting competition, a function of media commercialization and proliferation, forced media organizations to distinguish themselves from their competitors. This heightened competition prompted a rise in investigative reporting, exposés of environmental degradation, open confrontations between media and government regulatory institutions, and sensational coverage of official malfeasance.[15]

Media most defiant were at the provincial level and below, although higher placement in China's bureaucratic hierarchy at times afforded greater journalistic freedom.[16] The decentralized system of territorial state "ownership" of the Chinese media had the

[14] Daniel C. Lynch, *After the Propaganda State: Media, Politics and "Thought Work" in Reformed China* (Stanford, CA.: Stanford University Press, 1999), 31.

[15] Examples of sensational reporting of politically sensitive topics abound. A few prominent examples are *Caijing Magazine*'s coverage of the SARS outbreak in April 2003, *Southern Metropolitan Daily* reports on the prison murder of Sun Zhigang in September 2003, and the newspaper *Football*'s [*Zuqiubao*] bitter criticism of the Chinese Football Association's defense of government enterprises involvement in the Chinese Football League. See *Southern Weekend*, January 15, 2004, 3.

[16] Lee Chin-chuan, "Chinese Communication: Prisms, Trajectories and Modes of Understanding," *Power, Money, and Media: Communication Patterns and Bureaucratic Control in Cultural China* (DeKalb, IL: Northwestern University Press, 2000), 13; Zhao Yuezhi, *Media, Market and Democracy in China: Between the Party Line and the Bottom Line* (Champagne, IL: University of Illinois Press, 1998); and Lynch, *After the Propaganda State*. All these sources provide accounts of the freedom of "local" media, or media defined here as corresponding to the province, city, and county levels. Lee Chin-chuan argues (p. 13) that the CCP views press conglomeration as a "panacea for resolving many difficult problems" concerning "small papers" that have defied state orders. Central-level news organizations such as *News Probe* [*Xinwen diaocha*] at CCTV 1, Focus [*Jiaodian fangtan*], or *Renminwang* are often afforded considerable freedom in reporting on local news, largely because local governments have no administrative means to pressure these organizations to censor reports through the nomenklatura system, which can only be done at higher bureaucratic levels, i.e., by the Central Propaganda Department.

effect of rooting control over media content to the place of registration, which made cross-regional attempts to "correct" or suppress unflattering news coverage more difficult. The news media of different cities or provinces found lucrative news material by joyfully sniping at the travails of other areas, so long as doing so increased circulation, viewership, and advertisement revenue. By the mid-1980s, the number of news media rose to an extent that compromised the party's ability to monitor and dictate media content.

The first major step taken by the central leadership to reduce the growth of media and control the concomitant institutional pluralism was a national re-registration drive conducted jointly by the Central Propaganda Department and the State Press and Publication Administration (SPPA) in 1987.[17] Re-registration was intended as a vehicle for analyzing the status and conduct of all media organizations prior to approving continued operations. The issuing of Central Document No. 4 allowed the government to "suppress further publication of those newspapers and periodicals that have committed political mistakes or which contain material not on a high level."[18] According to government statistics, the 1987 re-registration drive to eliminate or consolidate illegally operating print media cut back the number of daily newspapers from 1,776 at the beginning of the year to 1,482 by early 1988, a 15 percent decrease.[19] These

---

[17] The term "institutional pluralism" describes the diversity of opinion within the state structure in Soviet-style regimes. For a classic discussion of institutional pluralism in communist party regimes, see the contribution of Archie Brown, "Pluralism, Power and the Soviet Political System: A Comparative Perspective," in *Pluralism in the Soviet Union: Essays in Honor of H. Gordon Skilling,* ed. Susan Gross Solomon (New York: St. Martin's Press, 1983), 61–107.

[18] Richard Baum, *Burying Mao*, 210, citing domestic Chinese sources and a BBC survey of World Broadcasts, Far East Report. This point is corroborated in the "1987 National Newspaper Rectification Report," *Zhongguo xinwen nianjian* [*China News Annual*], 1988, 30.

[19] *Zhongguo xinwen nianjian*, 1990, 3 and *Zhongguo xinwen nianjian*, 1988, 30. Subsequent data collected in 1999 showed that the decrease in the number of newspapers as a result of the crackdown was much less than originally believed. The 2000 edition of the same yearbook showed that the number of newspapers in 1987 was 1,611, which is the number used in Fig. 4.1. *Zhongguo xinwen nianjian*, 2000, 567.

government statistics stating full and complete implementation of the re-registration campaign are probably exaggerated. Moreover, the number of newspapers increased again in 1989, driven upward by yearly increases in national advertising revenue of more than 20 percent as well as by the profits made by government and party agencies that managed print media through subscription revenues. (See Figs. 1–6; for information on data sources see Tables 1 and 2.)[20]

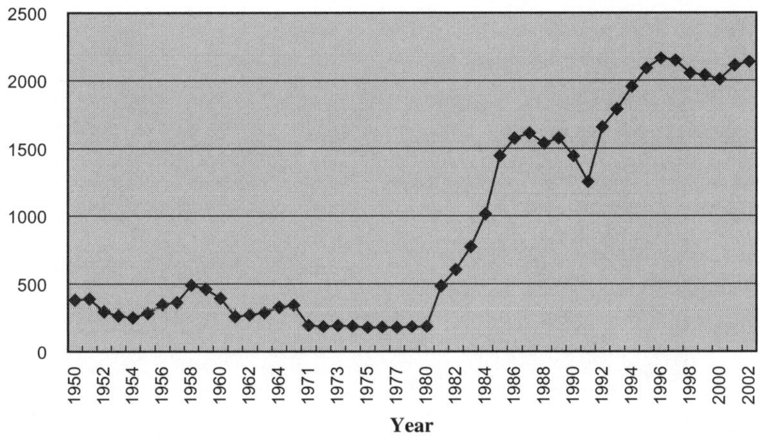

Fig. 1: Newspapers in China

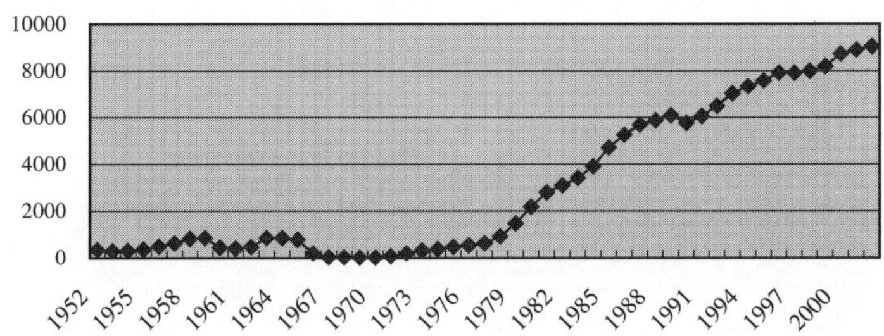

Fig. 2: Magazines in China

[20] The data in Figs. 1–4 reflect an amalgamation of official sources, representing all available data. For many years, data are simply not available; for this reason, the year entries in these charts, corresponding to data points, are not listed in regular intervals.

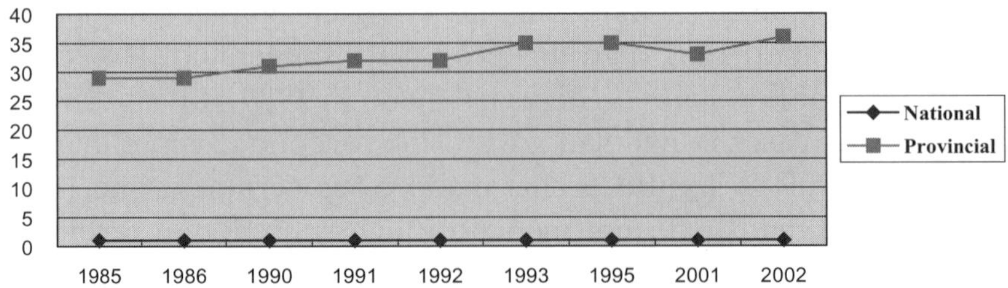

Fig. 3: National and Provincial Television Stations

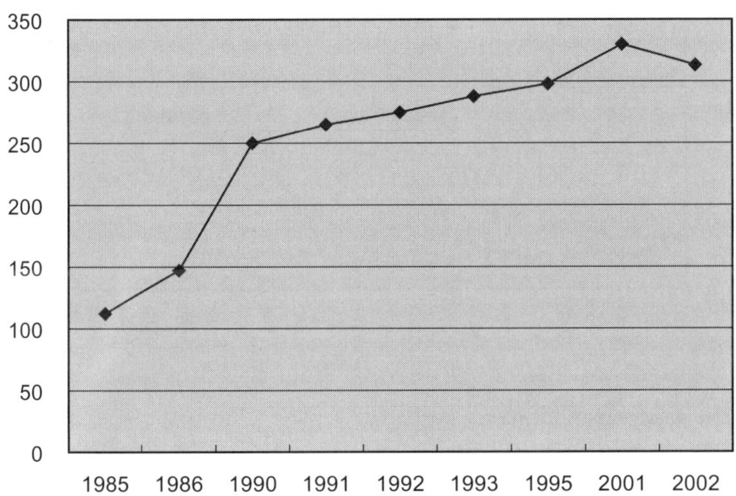

Fig. 4: City Television Stations

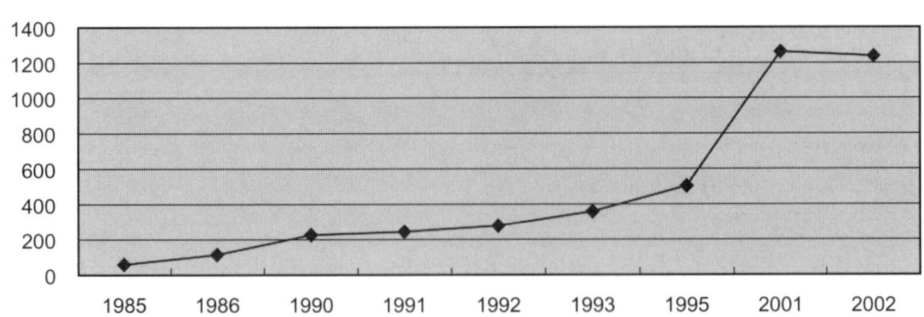

Fig. 5: County Television Stations

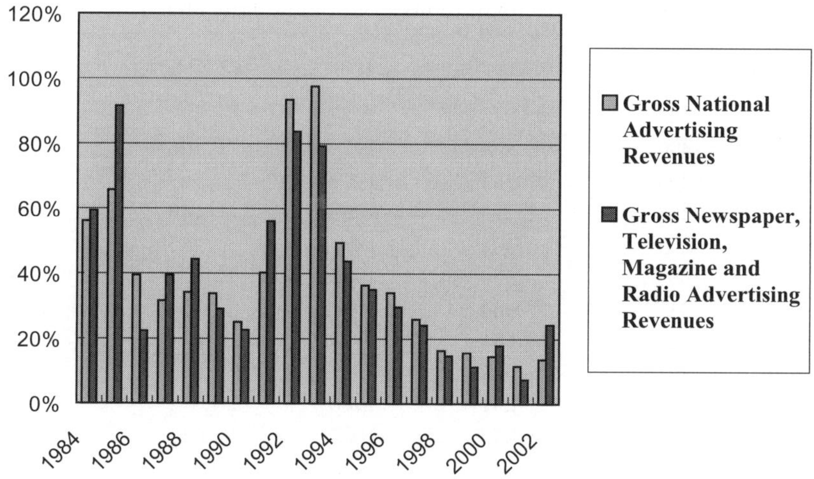

Fig. 6: Yearly Percentage Growth for Gross National Advertising Revenues and Gross Newspaper, Television, Magazines and Radio Advertising Revenues

Party support for greater media autonomy in the late 1980s, most notably by CCP General Secretary Zhao Ziyang in 1987, increased the confidence of the news media to run stories critical of the state and to report more objectively on the social and economic problems resulting from the semi-planned economy.[21] In his speech at the 13th Party Congress in October 1987, Zhao Ziyang said the party should foster "public opinion supervision" (*yulun jiandu*),

[21] A study of critical news reports in the *Zhongguo qingnianbao* [*China Youth Daily*] conducted by Sun Xupei shows that the number of critical reports rose in 1988 when compared to the number of critical reports in the same paper in 1985. The number of critical reports went from 17 in 1985 to 22 in 1988. Sun's measuring scheme calculates the number of new critical stories introduced rather than the total number of critical news reports. If one assumes that critical news reports in *China Youth Daily* are indicative of a larger national trend, then Sun's findings support the assertion that print media were more willing to publish critical stories in the year following Zhao's address at the 13th Party Congress. See Sun Xupei, *Zhongguo chuanmei de huodong kongjian* [*Chinese Broadcast Media's Area of Activity*] (Beijing: Renmin chubanshi, 2004), 373–377.

Table 1: The Total Number of Chinese Print Media

Year	Newspapers	Magazines	Year	Newspapers	Magazines
1950	382	N/A	1977	180	628
1951	390	N/A	1978	186	930
1952	296	354	1979	69*	1,470
1953	265	295	1980	188	2,191
1954	253	304	1981	485	2,801
1955	285	370	1982	606	3,100
1956	347	484	1983	773	3,415
1957	364	634	1984	1,014	3,907
1958	491	822	1985	1,445	4,705
1959	463	851	1986	1,574	5,248
1960	396	442	1987	1,611	5,687
1961	260	410	1988	1,537	5,865
1962	273	483	1989	1,576	6,078
1963	289	861	1990	1,444	5,751
1964	329	856	1991	1,254	6,056
1965	343	790	1992	1,657	6,486
1966	49*	191	1993	1,788	7,011
1967	43*	27	1994	1,953	7,325
1968	42*	22	1995	2,089	7,583
1969	42*	20	1996	2,163	7,916
1970	42*	21	1997	2,149	7,918
1971	195	72	1998	2,053	7,999
1972	185	194	1999	2,038	8,187
1973	192	320	2000	2,007	8,725
1974	189	382	2001	2,111	8,889
1975	180	476	2002	2,137	9,029
1976	182	542			

Sources: Data for Hong Kong, Macao, and Taiwan (Fig. 1) are not included. Newspaper data from 1950 to 1979 are cited from *China Journalism Yearbook*, 1982 ed. The figures marked with an asterisk in 1966–1970 and 1979 exclude the number of newspapers below the provincial level. The data from 1980 to 1995 are cited from *China Journalism Yearbook,* 2000 ed. Data from 1996 to 2002 are from *Statistical Materials Regarding China Journalism and Publication*, 1997–2003 eds. (Beijing: *Xinwen Chubanshu Jihua Caiwusi Tongjichu* or the Central News and Publication Economic Statistical Center). The data for magazines from 1952 to 1999 are cited from *China Journalism Yearbook*, 2000, pp. 566–567. Magazine data from 2000 to 2002 are cited from *Compilation of Statistical Materials of China Journalism and Publication*, 2001–2003.

Table 2: Number of TV Stations

Year	Television Station				
	Total	National	Provincial	City	County
1985	202	1	29	112	60
1986	292	1	29	147	115
1987	366	1	N/A	N/A	N/A
1988	422	1	N/A	N/A	N/A
1989	469	1	N/A	N/A	N/A
1990	509	1	31	250	227
1991	543	1	32	265	245
1992	586	1	32	275	278
1993	684	1	35	288	360
1994	766	1	N/A	N/A	N/A
1995	837	1	35	298	503
1996	880	1	N/A	N/A	N/A
1997	923	1	N/A	N/A	N/A
1998	1,283	1	N/A	N/A	N/A
1999	352*	1	N/A	N/A	N/A
2000	354*	1	N/A	N/A	N/A
2001	1,627	1	33	330	1,263
2002	1,588	1	36	313	1,238

Sources: In Fig. 2, data for Hong Kong, Macao, and Taiwan are excluded. All data of television stations exclude the number of educational television stations and cable television stations in China. Data for 1998 are from *China Advertisement Yearbook*, 1999 ed. Data asterisked in 1999 and 2000 are from *China Statistical Yearbook*, 2000 and 2001 eds. The source of all other data is *China Radio and Television Yearbook*, 1986–2002 eds. For the years 1987 to 1989, 1994, and 1996–2000 data on the number of provincial, city, and county television stations are not available.

Note: Advertising revenue data — The data used to generate Fig. 3 excludes that of Hong Kong, Macao, and Taiwan. National advertisement statistics include advertisement company revenue, and advertisement revenue for television, radio, newspapers, magazines, cable television, radio stations, and other related industries. The data of 1981–2001 is from the *China Advertisement Yearbook*, 1999 ed. and *The Operation and Management of Media Groups*, 2003. The figure of 2002 is cited from *China Journalism Yearbook*, 2003 ed., pp. 71–73.

inform people of important matters, and allow people to participate in debates on key matters.[22] The blush of media freedom in the late 1980s, of course, faced a radical reversal when the military violently dispersed protests and the party subsequently reeducated hundreds of journalists. In order to regain control of the mass media, the party forced many managers of major media into retirement, fired them, or transferred them outside Beijing.[23] So-called party conservatives Li Peng and Chen Yun had considerable influence following the 1989 purge of Zhao Ziyang. The media was swiftly cowed by repression.

The proliferation of newspapers in the 1980s reached a peak of 1,611 in 1987, growing by a factor of eight in less than one decade.[24] Deng's crackdown on media support for widespread demonstrations in 1989 led to massive closures among newspapers and magazines believed to have supported the demonstrations. From 1989 to 1991, the total number of daily and weekly newspapers in China dropped from 1,576 to 1,254 — a decrease of 20 percent of the national total; from 1989 to 1990, the number of magazines fell from 6,078 to 5,751, a 5 percent decrease. The downward slopes appearing in Figs.1 and 2 from 1989 to 1990 illustrate this effect.[25]

Statistics on the growth of the number of television stations in China are presented in Figs. 3–5. For the last 25 years, CCTV

---

[22] Zhao Yuezhi, *Media, Market and Democracy in China*, 35–36.

[23] Allison Liu Jernow, *"Don't Force Us to Lie": The Struggle of Chinese Journalists in the Reform Era* (New York: Committee to Protect Journalists, 1991), 139.

[24] Some studies show the number of newspapers as 1,761 prior to the registration campaign. The number cited here is from the more recent study in *Zhongguo xinwen nianjian,* 2000, 567.

[25] Figure 1 also reflects the extent to which political events have strongly impacted the number of newspapers in China over time. In the mid-1950s the decrease in the number of newspapers is related to nationalization of privately owned newspapers, a process that led to closures. Interview 2004 — #6. During the Great Leap Forward, a number of newspapers declined until the political moderation of the 1960s. The closure of most newspapers due to the Cultural Revolution can be observed in the drop in the number of newspapers after 1966 when the Cultural Revolution commenced.

has been the only national television station by which the central government disseminates propaganda to the vast majority of Chinese.[26] The number of provincial television stations has grown from 29 to 36, a slight increase, although the number of channels and programs these stations produce has increased within the framework of television media groups. The great explosion in Chinese television media occurred at the city and county levels, with the number of city television stations rising from 112 in 1985 (the first year for which reliable data is available) to 313 in 2001 and county stations from 60 in 1985 to a peak of 1,263 in 2001. County television stations, which were subject to less monitoring, became the primary source of competition for the vastly less numerous and more carefully monitored national station and provincial stations.[27]

Figure 6 indicates the incentive for profit maximization among the media due to sky-rocketing growth values of the Chinese advertising market in the 1980s and 1990s.[28] In many years, thc growth rate of the advertising market nationally exceeded 20 percent annually, sometimes rising as high as 90 percent a year. This growth became a powerful financial motivation for the mass media to cater to popular preferences. Considering the rate of media proliferation and the pressures of commercialization, competition drove the media to make media content more consumer-driven. Changes in content included more investigative journalism and news stories critical of social problems and political corruption as well as racy

---

[26] CCTV broadcasts programming on 16 channels. Since the 1980s, local stations have been required to rebroadcast CCTV1, which has the nation's largest viewership.

[27] In the 1980s, television programming from CCTV was available throughout much of the country. Provincial television from neighboring provinces could be received via a terrestrial signal. In recent years, provincial stations have become widely available through reciprocal exchanges between different provinces via station signals (uplink) to a shared satellite, cable networks, and terrestrial broadcast.

[28] In Fig. 6, the important difference between gross advertising revenue and gross revenue from mainstream media is that the former statistic contains revenue from advertising agencies, which do not produce news content.

stories related to crime and sex, and the use of unauthorized foreign news sources.[29]

In the television industry, the central leadership waited until the late 1990s to centralize political control over television stations through the formation of broadcast media conglomerates. (This topic is considered in detail below.) In 2002, the central leadership pulled the plug on county television autonomy by promulgating a regulation that canceled the right of county-level television stations to produce their own programming, effectively forcing all county stations to re-broadcast municipal, provincial, and central television programs.[30]

Reduction of the number of print media has occurred three times since the 1980s: during the 1985 re-registration that cut the number of print publications by 270; as a result of media closures following the 1989 crackdown on pro-democracy protests affecting 322 media; and in 2004, with the closure of 677 publications that were not financially self-supporting or were suspected of using executive powers to maintain high circulation levels.[31]

---

[29] For a study on the Chinese tabloid press see Zhao Yuezhi, "The Rich, the Laid-off, and the Criminal in Tabloid Tales: Read All about It!" in *Popular China: Unofficial Culture in a Globalizing Society*, eds. Perry Link, Richard P. Madsen, and Paul G. Pickowicz (New York: Rowman and Littlefield, 2002), 111–135. Zhao argues that tabloids are not the "carriers of opposition political consciousness," just commercial entities interested in profits that look unfavorably upon political risk-taking.

[30] When faced with the imposition of these regulations, county television stations have engaged in noncompliance to an extent. During a visit to the rural Hunan Province in July 2002, I found county television stations operating normally. One county station manager, who also headed the county Bureau of Radio and Television [*Guangdianjü*], said he had no plans to cease operations because the television station had the support of the county government, which also owned the local cable network, and could therefore insert county television programming at will. Government statistics no longer reflect county television stations. See *Zhongguo dianshi shoushi nianjian* [*China TV Rating Yearbook*], 2004, 3. These statistics are almost certainly wrong.

[31] *Renminwang*, December 1, 2003, www.people.com.cn/GB/14677/14737/22036/2217149.html.

"CORPORATIZING" THE STATE-OWNED MEDIA

After Tiananmen, Deng Xiaoping and Li Ruihuan, the Politburo member in charge of the mass media, were forced to consider the question of how to improve the effectiveness of the mass media as a tool for disseminating party propaganda. By early 1992, Deng became frustrated with the unwillingness of bureaucratic interests to support his economic reform agenda. In a style reminiscent of Mao Zedong, Deng went around top party leadership to make his case directly to the public in a widely publicized "Southern Tour," propounding the virtues of market economics. The effect of the Southern Tour on the media industry was to ignite enthusiasm to expand and improve content in the interest of higher profits. New strategies for commercialization of the media became possible and were even encouraged by central and provincial party leaders, because they had come to the opinion that commercialization of the state-owned media, if properly managed, was the best means for improving the effectiveness of party propaganda and regime legitimacy. The rationale for this marked departure from the past strategy reflected the practical considerations of media managers who wanted to raise profits, without changing party control over news content. Media managers began to focus on changing the way the media had delivered its messages. They exchanged the old dogmatic style of the Mao era for flashy advertising and polished presentation akin to corporate advertising in the West.[32]

The "re-packaging" of media products, while present in the print media, was especially apparent in television, where a new wave of advertising encouraged Chinese to take pride in consumerism. A leading advocate of commercializing the television industry, Shanghai Party Secretary Gong Xueping served as the principal architect of mid-1990s development of the Shanghai broadcast media. As a man with experience in both running and managing the broadcast media, Gong had served in Shanghai as television editor,

[32] Geremie R. Barme, "CCP TM and ADCULT PRC," *The China Journal* no. 41 (January 1999), 1–23.

television station manager, deputy director, and director of the Shanghai Bureau of Radio, Television and Film (*Guangdian zongju*). He argued that China did not have to choose between either Soviet-style state-funded media or Western-style private media. The weakness of the Soviet model was that media only sought the approbation of their superiors and cared little about public opinion. Western media were very popular and profitable but, due to total marketization, cared little about the social effects of their content, engaging in a race to the bottom with programming on crime, sex, and corruption.[33] Instead of choosing one of these two models, Gong suggested that China could create its own "socialist" mass media with "Chinese characteristics," that combined the characteristics of both styles. From the Soviet model, China adopted party control of content; from the Western media, China could adopt management techniques designed to make mass media popular and financially self-supporting. The type of commercial media advocated by Gong Xueping could thus satisfy popular demand for more modern media content as well as party priorities for transmitting propaganda.

According to one of Gong Xueping's colleagues in the Shanghai Bureau of Radio, Television and Film at the time, the slogan describing the media's new commercialized role was "The media is the [party] mouthpiece as well as an industry" (*meiti jishi houshe you shi chanye*).[34] A second related slogan for party media managers was "You must manage the news firmly but not manage it to death" (*xinwen yao guanzhu buyao guansi*).[35] In other words, the media had to have enough freedom to create products attractive to consumers but not so much freedom as to damage the party's legitimacy through potentially embarrassing news or exposés. Especially

---

[33] The difference between commercialization and marketization is the autonomy-increasing component implied in the latter. Thus, commercial media operate like a business while remaining state-owned enterprises.

[34] Interview 2005 — #2.

[35] Ibid.

in terms of radio and television, the Shanghai media proved both commercially successful and under firm control concerning news content and propaganda, and served as an example that other media were encouraged to emulate.[36]

The CCP's new strategy for managing the mass media in the 1990s had four principal components: commercialization of media operations to allow the use of market resources to "re-package" media content and party propaganda; introduction of Western-style management techniques concerning personnel and advertising; centralization of political control over the management of the media; and continued elimination and consolidation of media that were difficult to control or those deemed politically vulnerable and easiest to shut down.

Commercialization of media operations meant not only bringing in greater revenue necessary for media to upgrade production capabilities, such as buying foreign-made printing presses, television cameras, and editing facilities but also pitching party propaganda in a manner more appealing to people through a melding of consumerism and the party message. As President and CCP Chairman Jiang Zemin put it in a speech to the staff of the *People's Daily*, journalists had to "make their propaganda reports closer to the [public's] lifestyle, closer to their readers and more delightful to the majority of readers."[37] The Chinese news media has typically had difficulty in generating reports that accurately portray the lives of most Chinese citizens, due primarily to an administrative hierarchy that has incentives to suppress unfavorable information. However, the media under Jiang Zemin proved much more successful at generating news that was popular with consumers.

---

[36] Chin Yu, "Gong Xueping zonglun guangbo dianshi gaige jishi houshe youshi chanye" [Gong Xueping Speaking about Television Reform: Party Mouthpiece and a Business], *The Journalist* [*Xinwen jizhe*] 1 (1993), 5.

[37] "Jiang Zemin tongzhi shicha renmin ribaoshe shi de jianghua" [Comrade Jiang Zemin's Speech during a Visit to *People's Daily*], *Renmin ribao* [*People's Daily*, Beijing], October 21, 1996.

EVALUATING COMMERCIALIZATION

The commercialization of the Chinese news media, in general, demonstrates two liberalizing effects and one effect mitigating liberalization. The first liberalizing effect is the shifting of the media's loyalty from the party to advertisers, who through a media organization's appeal to consumers, provide the bulk of revenue. The second effect of commercialization is to change the incentives of the local state vis-à-vis the news media. As the case of county television illustrates, county governments received tax revenue and direct profit from media that faced closure and therefore demonstrated willingness to oppose the closures. Due to access to tax revenue and informal levies, the local state's role is that of protector of, and advocate for, the media it oversees, compromising its role as enforcer of central party priorities. Implementation of policies from higher levels of the state hierarchy is, however, difficult to oppose. When forced to choose between heeding the wishes of the central party leadership and supporting media ventures, including financially lucrative levels of media freedom, the local state has typically chosen the former because nomenklatura links the career prospects of cadres to their loyalty to the party apparatus and because of an array of coercive tools available to those enforcing central policies.

Chinese media operate within the state structure. Barring greater privatization of the news media, which is occurring gradually through the stock-market-listed companies affiliated with media groups, commercial media organizations are unlikely to struggle for greater autonomy in the near future.[38] Another form of "creeping" privatization is occurring as media allow operations to be managed by private corporations.[39] These arrangements are illegal but increasingly prevalent. The reason is the incentive of earning fast

[38] To the present, the Chinese stock markets have been a relatively poor source of wealth generation due to regulations that restrict listings by private enterprises and, in most cases, require state interests own the majority of shares.

[39] Interview 2004 — #26.

returns on investments due to the high annual growth rate of the Chinese media sector.

In addition to creating the obligation to please consumers, a powerful third effect of commercialization is to provide incentives for media managers and journalists to be risk averse. Top-level managers are appointed by the Propaganda Department in consultation with the CCP Organization Department.[40] The career prospects of media managers are tied to their effectiveness, i.e., producing media content that is both attractive to consumers and politically controlled. Media managers are quite well paid in comparison with average incomes. The publisher (*shezhang*) of a top Shanghai newspaper, for example, makes roughly $35,000 per year, a huge sum even in China's rich coastal cities, where the average per capita income is estimated as $3,000 per year. The editor-in-chief makes slightly less, around $30,000, and the deputy editor-in-chief earns $28,000.[41]

Underneath the party-appointed leadership of the news media are lesser managers, senior editors, copyeditors, and journalists. These positions are filled by employees under contract, typically working on a yearly basis. Therefore, employees are under constant pressure to increase viewership and profits. Some contracts with managers require them to achieve annual revenue increases of 15 percent or risk demotion.[42]

Many media organizations make attempts to quantify the quality of employee performance and link performance to the amount of salary an employee receives. The performance of television producers, for example, is evaluated in part by the ACNielsen ratings of the programming they oversee. Their bonuses are determined by upper-level managers within the television station. Data from my interviews suggest that the bonuses make up roughly 20 percent of the total salary for producers and editors.

---

[40] Interview 2004 — #6. Unlike appointments for other state positions, the Propaganda Department typically dominates the appointment process for the media.

[41] Interview 2004 — #17; Interview 2004 — #26.

[42] Interview 2002 — #22; Interview 2004 — #26.

Typically, a much greater percentage of a journalist's salary is derived from performance bonuses. One criterion for evaluating performance that is not usually quantified is the popularity of their reports based predominantly upon readers' response. If readers are happy with a journalist's article, they may write letters to the newspaper or send emails or text messages with favorable comments. A positive (or negative) response from a reader is seen as an indicator of consumer preference that drives circulation levels. Circulation, in turn, is often used to justify advertising space. In general, newspapers with high circulation can charge high advertising prices.

Since the early 1990s, journalists' pay has also been tied to the number and length of stories that are broadcast or published. If a report is considered too sensational to print, most journalists do not receive payment and risk losing performance bonuses, which amount to more than half of their salary.[43] Therefore, journalists who fall out of favor with their superiors, or whose work is frequently censored, find themselves quickly out of money. They can even be made to pay the production costs out of their pockets for the censored material.[44]

At *Southern Weekend*, a major weekly operating in Guangdong Province, the monthly base salary for journalists in 2003 was $340 (before taxes), or approximately the same amount as an average farmer's annual income.[45] Performance bonuses at *Southern Weekend* increased a journalist's *monthly* salary to a ceiling of around $2,430, an amount almost double the *yearly* average for per capita income in China.[46] *Southern Weekend* journalists, by all accounts, are exceptionally well paid compared to most

---

[43] Interview 2004 — #24.

[44] Ibid.

[45] By comparison, the average yearly farming income in 2004 was $353. Joseph Kahn, "China Pledges to Lift Wealth of Its Peasants," *International Herald Tribune*, February 3, 2005.

[46] The average per capita income in China in 2005 is around $1,230. See "China Sets 2020 Growth Goal," *CNN.com*, May 17, 2005.

print journalists in China and are held to strict standards for professionalism.[47]

Journalists in the Shanghai Media Group receive a base salary that is 15–20 percent of the total. Monthly performance ratings determine 75–80 percent of the total. A yearly bonus amounts to another 10 percent. The disparity between the top and the bottom of the salary scale, based on the amounts of bonuses, can be as much as a factor of 10.[48] At the CCTV Channel 1 investigative news program, *News Probe*, each editor works on about four stories a year; each reporter does roughly 15 stories a year. Bonuses for both positions vary widely, as they are based both on an internal evaluation and on ACNielsen ratings after the program is aired. Members of an advisory board, of senior media professionals, scholars, and the producer, give each report a score that is adjusted based upon viewer ratings by ACNielsen for the time slot in which the program is broadcast.[49] These two factors are used to calculate performance bonuses for every report. Variation between the lowest score for a report and the highest can lead to differences in performance bonus equaling a factor of 18.[50]

The desire to win performance bonuses tends to result in journalism that steers well clear of dangerous political controversy and meets the party's propaganda requirements. One factor that mitigates this effect is fierce competition among media for superior employees.

---

[47] According to a 2002 statistical survey of print and broadcast journalists in Shanghai, the average monthly salary for print journalists was $473 and the average salary for broadcast journalists was $416. Lu Ye and Yu Weidong, "Shehui zhuanxing guochengzhong xinwen congyezhe de gongzuo zhuangkuang he zhiye lixiang: 2002 nian Shanghai xinwen congyezhe diaocha baogao" [The Professional Ideals of News Media Workers During the Process of Social Transformation: 2002 Shanghai News Worker Report], *Xinwen Jizhe* [*The Journalist Magazine*], 1 (2003). Performance bonuses included, most journalists at *Southern Weekend* earned a higher average salary ($850–$972) than did print journalists in Shanghai, a city with high salaries for journalists compared to most other areas in China. Interview 2003 — #10.

[48] Ibid.

[49] The score of each report is adjusted based upon three rating categories: high (top 15 percent), medium (middle 70 percent) and low (bottom 15 percent) viewership.

[50] Interview 2004 — #12.

If a journalist strikes out at one media organization, it is possible to work for a competitor. [51] A second strategy employed by media that value hard-hitting news coverage is to offer partial performance bonuses for journalists even if their material is censored for political reasons. For example, when *Southern Weekend* journalists write material too sensitive to print, they receive 50–70 percent of the amount they would have received if the story had been published.[52]

THE RISE OF PRINT MEDIA GROUPS: TWO CASES

Under Jiang Zemin's leadership in the mid- to late-1990s, media management strategies became even more sophisticated, with the formation of media conglomerates intended to strengthen the media industry financially, and place it under more politically reliable leadership. After initial experimentation with media conglomerates, the Propaganda Department and SPPA decided to reorganize print media at the city, provincial, and central level into media conglomerates or media "groups" as designated in China. The officially stated motivation for creating media groups was that they would eliminate unnecessary waste of resources by having too many media organizations. However, it is more likely that the motivation for the central party leadership was that forming news groups would vastly simplify the task of appointing media managers and would provide market incentive for the media to comply with party priorities for content by reducing competition for advertisement revenues.

Guangzhou Daily

Initial experimentation began in south China when a mid-level cadre in the Guangzhou Municipal Propaganda Department, Li Yuanjiang, was given permission by the central government in 1996 to adopt a strategy for the creation of a state-owned and party-run

[51] Interview 2004 — #14.

[52] Payment of 70 percent has become the norm according to one source. Interview 2003 — #11.

media conglomerate. Li's success was to have lasting implications for the reorganization of the media industry. As the editor-in-chief of the *Guangzhou Daily*, the mouthpiece of the Guangzhou Party Committee, Li Yuanjiang published breaking news stories, re-wrote international stories to reduce their political sensitivity, upgraded newsroom facilities, imported new printing presses, added subsidiary publications, and strengthened editorial control.[53] The Guangzhou Daily Press Group was successful in consolidating financial assets as well as furthering propaganda objectives by increasing readership. In organizing the Guangzhou Daily Press Group, Li consciously emulated international media conglomerates. Indeed, he noted at a Time Warner-sponsored forum in Shanghai that, "the most efficient way to boost circulation is to form a press group according to the practice of the international media."[54]

With the diversification of news content to attract more consumers, one might anticipate a reduction in the number of propaganda pieces, and the publication of many more stories related to non-controversial topics, such as fashion, arts and leisure, and sport. While one study shows that the ratio of propaganda stories to news stories decreased after the group's formation, the *Guangzhou Daily* strategy probably fits nicely with the CCP's objective of broadening the reach of propaganda by re-packaging propaganda articles in an attractive manner and by including propaganda pieces with articles favored by young urban readers.[55]

The effect of Li's efforts was to create a thick and attractively printed newspaper with numerous sections that appealed to a broad

---

[53] Zhao Yuezhi, "From Commercialization to Conglomeration: The Transformation of the Chinese Press within the Orbit of the Party State," *Journal of Communication* 50, no. 2 (2000): 16.

[54] Ibid.

[55] Ernest Yuyan Zhang, "A Study of the Conglomeration of China's Newspaper Industry," M.A. thesis, University of Missouri-Columbia, December 2001, 94. Zhang conducted content analysis on news appearing on the *Guangzhou Daily*'s front page for a "constructed week" of news coverage in 1994 and 2000. He concluded that the ratio of "party journalism" to "non-party journalism" has decreased since conglomeration.

segment of the population. The paper had mass appeal, not only in Guangzhou, but also throughout south China more generally. By 1998, the *Guangzhou Daily* had a large circulation and the highest advertising revenues of any newspaper in China.[56] Municipal party leadership over the newspaper was excellent. As a reward for Li Yuanjiang's successful management of the *Guangzhou Daily*, he was promoted to head of the Guangzhou Municipal Propaganda Department, a position from which he would guide all media under the supervision of the Guangzhou Municipal Party Committee.[57]

Southern Daily

After a careful study of the Guangzhou Daily Group, the central government pronounced it a success.[58] In 1998, the SPPA approved the formation of other newspaper conglomerates in 1998 under the leadership of party papers with high political prominence, circulation levels, or a combination of the two.[59] In Guangdong Province, the Southern Daily Press Group was created along similar lines as the *Guangzhou Daily*, but with very different results. The nominal head of the press conglomerate was the party paper, the *Southern Daily* (*Nanfang ribao*), the party-appointed managers of which were in charge of the operations of four other newspapers, including the *Southern Metropolitan Post* (*Nanfang dushibao*) and *Southern Weekend* (*Nanfang zhoumo*).

Rather than, serving as the flagship of the group in terms of providing popular content, designed to increase circulation, the *Southern*

[56] *Zhongguo guanggao nianjian* [*China Advertising Annual*], 1999, 53.

[57] Zhao Yuezhi, "From Commercialization to Conglomeration," 18.

[58] Ibid.

[59] An example of a party-initiated union of two newspapers with high political prominence and high circulation was the formation of Wenxin Press Group in Shanghai, which brought together the elite-focused *Wenhui Daily* [*Wenhuibao*] and the mass circulation *Xinmin Evening Paper* [*Xinmin wanbao*]. For an early study on the formation of China's press groups, see Cao Peng, *Zhongguo baoye jituan fazhan yanjiu* [*China's Press Groups*] (Beijing: Xinhua Publishing Company, 1999).

Daily continued to publish what might be called old-fashioned propaganda pieces related to the activities of the Guangdong Provincial Party leadership and the provincial government. The *Southern Metropolitan Post* and *Southern Weekend* offered very different fare. The *Southern Metropolitan Post* adopted the presentation of Hong Kong-style tabloid papers, with sensational photos and pages filled with advertisements. News content focused largely on matters of local concern: crime, corruption, pollution, abuse of power (especially in Guangzhou), and sport. *Southern Weekend*, originally an insert for the *Southern Daily* featuring art, literature, and leisure, had by the late 1990s established itself as the most important voice challenging the central party leadership in China's official press and, due in part to national distribution, proved to be a great commercial success.

Instead of providing both popular news and party propaganda in one newspaper, as was the case in the Guangzhou Daily Press Group, in the Southern Daily Press Group, propaganda was printed in the party paper as before, and commercially valuable and sensational content appeared in subsidiary publications, including such newspapers as *Southern Athletics* (*Nanfang Tiyu*), *21st Century Economic Report* (*Ershiyishiji jingjibaodao*), *21st Century World Herald* (*Ershiyishiji huanqiu baodao*), *Southern Village News* (*Nanfang nongcun bao*), *City Pictoral Newspaper* (*Chengshi huabao*), *Namebrand Magazine* (*Mingpai zazhi*), and *Southern Profiles Weekly* (*Nanfang renwu zhoukan*). Profits from commercially successful arms of the Southern Daily Group subsidized the expansion of the group and proved especially useful when new publications started up.

One result of the rising popularity of newspapers such as the *Southern Metropolitan Post* and *Southern Weekend* is that circulation for central and provincial party papers has declined precipitously.[60] (The *Guangzhou Daily* is a municipal party paper and an exception to the general trend.) A very visible indicator of this trend is the

[60] Zhao Yuezhi, "From Commercialization to Conglomeration," 6–7, 9–10.

falling circulation of the mouthpiece of the CCP Central Committee, the *People's Daily*. Once the newspaper with the highest national circulation, *People's Daily* now has a "reliable" circulation of 200,000, far less than that of many commercial papers, and is no longer sold at newsstands.[61] It is difficult to obtain reliable statistics on the circulation of the *People's Daily*, because the central party leadership has incentives to exaggerate the reach of its newspaper. If the *People's Daily*'s circulation was reported accurately, the low number would indicate the weakness of this historically important propaganda organ and embarrass the Central Committee. Therefore, the official count for the paper's circulation is officially listed as averaging more than 1.8 million per edition.[62] However, even assuming that the official statistics are accurate, circulation has declined considerably from an average of 5 million copies per edition in the 1980s.[63]

As advertising revenue is typically linked to circulation, low advertising revenue would indicate that official statistics for the *People's Daily's* circulation are greatly inflated. According to Zhao Yuezhi, the *People's Daily* ranked first among newspapers in advertising revenue in 1990[64]; but by 1998, the *People's Daily* slipped to number 13 and has fallen further subsequently.[65] By 2002, the *People's Daily* was ranked 42nd in a list of China's top media in terms of advertising revenue and 16th among print media.[66] In terms of assuring that central propaganda is disseminated to the population, the decline in the circulation of party papers has made retaining control of popular, more commercial newspapers more important for the Propaganda Department.

[61] Interview 2003 — #16.

[62] *Zhongguo xinwen nianjian* [*China News Annual*], 2004, 624.

[63] In 1983, 1985, and 1987 the circulation of *People's Daily* was recorded as 5 million per edition. *Zhongguo xinwen nianjian* [*China News Annual*], 1984, 564; *Zhongguo xinwen nianjian*, 1986, 296; *Zhongguo xinwen nianjian*, 1988, 412.

[64] Zhao, From Commercialization to Conglomeration," 10.

[65] *Zhongguo guangbo nianjian* [*China Advertising Annual*], 1999, 53.

[66] *Meiti* [*Media*], September 2003, 57.

BROADCAST MEDIA GROUPS: HUNAN MEDIA GROUP AND SHANGHAI MEDIA GROUP

The CCP's strategy for consolidating the broadcast media into media groups began in late 2000 with the State Administration of Radio Film and Television's (SARFT) approval of the formation of Hunan Media Group (HMG), an arrangement that brought all the television, radio, Internet, music, and film studios as well as television-related print media in Hunan Province under the party-appointed management.[67] HMG also included a stock-listed company, which acted as a means of raising investment capital. Hunan television stations have the reputation for highly innovative and politically harmless programming. The activities of various arms of HMG are highly commercialized; employees work on a yearly contractual basis, and individual television programs operate largely independently of party-appointed HMG Chairman Wei Wenbin, who has reportedly said that the secret to Hunan Economic Television's success is that he "barely manages" it (*shaoguan*).[68] There has been little centralization of advertising sales or even advertising prices because individual programs operate their own advertising departments, creating a dynamic of internal competition for advertising revenues. Producers of individual programs have considerable autonomy. After 50 percent of program revenues is paid to HMG, the producer determines employee salaries and bonuses and distributes 20–30 percent of the program's annual profits to employees.[69] The remaining funds are retained by the program for future use.[70] Since its formation, HMG has been lauded for investigative reports concerning economic affairs and innovative entertainment programming,

[67] Huang Shenmin, ed., *Zhongguo guangdian meijie jituanhua yanjiu* [*Research Concerning the Conglomeration of China's Broadcast Media*] (Beijing: China Consumer Prices Publishing Company, 2001), 155.

[68] Sun Jitie, *Zhongguo chuanmei dangdai zuijü yingxiang de chuangmeiren fangtan lu* [*China's Mass Media: Interviews with the Most Influential Media People of Our Time*] (Zhuhai: Zhuhai Chubanshe, 2002), 37.

[69] Ibid., 43.

[70] Interview 2002 — #19.

including the first Chinese imitation of "Survivor" set in a luxurious apartment complex in Hunan Province.[71]

As is common in China as elsewhere, local news receives the highest audience ratings. News of major events in China is taken from CCTV or Xinhua wire reports.[72] The unwillingness of Chinese broadcast journalists working at local media organizations, whether due to the cost of doing so or political restrictions, to report on major national news stories in effect increases central control over important news content. This reduces competition in the national media market and, thereby, the likelihood that broadcast media will produce politically controversial news reports.

Another model broadcast media conglomerate, from the perspective of the Central Propaganda Department, is Shanghai Media and Entertainment Group (SMEG), which due to the dominance of its television and radio stations is the second most profitable media group in China behind the national CCTV Broadcast Group.[73] Owned by the Propaganda Department of the Shanghai Municipal Party Committee, SMEG and its sub-group, Shanghai Media Group (SMG), are organizational behemoths. At its founding, SMEG included two radio stations, 11 television channels, a popular website, newspapers and magazines, film production facilities, professional sports teams, dance troupes, the Shanghai Opera House, an international conference center, and one stock-listed company. In 2001, the group's assets were estimated to be worth more than $17 billion.[74] SMG's popular "Comprehensive News Channel" (*Xinwen zonghe pingdao*) is watched by 1.28 million Shanghai residents

---

[71] Interview 2002 — #15 and Interview 2002 — #17. The challenge to this game show was to see who would crack when contestants were denied the freedom to leave the apartment complex and prevented from having any contact with the outside world.

[72] Interview 2002 — #19.

[73] In 2001, SMEG's revenue were more than $210 million and CCTV's earnings were nearly $659 million. "2001 nian guanggao meijie danwei yingye e paixu" [2001 Annual Media Advertising Ranking by Revenue], *Chuanmei* [*Broadcast Media*], 2002.

[74] *China Broadcast Yearbook* [*Zhongguo guangbo dianshi nianjian*], 2002, 34.

every day.[75] After obtaining approval from the Central Propaganda Department, two managers appointed by the Shanghai Municipal Party Committee, Ye Zhikang, head of SMEG, and Li Ruigang, CEO of SMG, were made responsible for the operations and content of the entire group. Their appointments at least nominally gave the center supervision over key management positions. Ye and Li then selected managers of television and radio stations — who were nearly all party members — for their ability to produce popular programming that was not politically sensitive in nature.[76] Thus far, the formation of print and broadcast media conglomerates has simplified appointments of key management personnel and, by reducing competition in local markets, provided considerable incentive for media groups to offer the public entertainment and party propaganda, but not with news reports challenging the regime legitimacy.

CASE STUDY: THE 2003 SARS EPIDEMIC

This section tests the extent to which media complied with party directives on news content concerning a crisis that posed a severe threat to the CCP legitimacy: the 2003 Severe Acute Respiratory Syndrome (SARS) epidemic. At issue is the extent to which mass media accepted party control when they had extremely high incentive to accurately report news of the epidemic in the interest of saving lives. The SARS case provides the opportunity for us to determine, with a single case study, whether the commercialized Chinese media either suppressed information and endangered the lives of media consumers or rejected the state censorship.[77]

While much of the coverage appearing in daily newspapers was published in the form of Xinhua wire stories, central and local

---

[75] ACNielsen 2003 report as cited on SMG's website, March 8, 2005.

[76] Interview 2003 — #1, #2, #3; Interview 2004 — #24.

[77] The SARS case represents what Harry Eckstein has called a "crucial" case study capable of confirming (or disconfirming) a theory. Harry Eckstein, "Case Study and Theory in Political Science," in *Handbook of Political Science*, vol. 7, eds. Fred I. Greenstein and Nelson W. Polsby (Reading, MA: Addison-Wesley Publishing Company, 1975), 113–132.

media filed hundreds, if not thousands, of their own reports, making it imperative to consider reporting by a broad range of sources. For this reason, this case study considers the coverage of the epidemic by print media in Guangdong, where the epidemic was first discovered, as well as coverage by daily newspapers in Beijing and Shanghai and weekly newspapers with national circulation. It also examines coverage by *Caijing Magazine*, a highly professional weekly, and, to a limited degree, reportage by CCTV's investigative program *News Probe*.

Damage Control

According to the World Health Organization statistics issued on June 9, 2003, from November 2002 to June 2003, the SARS epidemic affected 32 countries, including Taiwan and Hong Kong. A total of 8,421 people were infected worldwide, of whom 784 eventually died. In China, the death toll was 44 percent of the world total or 340.[78] The disease was hitherto unknown prior to its appearance in Guangdong Province in November 2003. Because the symptoms of SARS are similar to those of a very severe pneumonia — inflammation of the lungs and high fever — the danger posed by the highly contagious virus was not well understood until SARS had spread beyond China's borders. Indeed, at an early stage, the chief virologist at the Chinese Center of Disease Control announced that SARS was caused by Chlamydia.[79]

The political sensitivity of the succession of the then relatively unknown Hu Jintao to the post of CCP general secretary and PRC president is the main reason why the Chinese media avoided coverage of SARS cases. When the first SARS cases appeared in Guangdong Province in mid-November 2002, the CCP was selecting the new

---

[78] Yanzhong Huang quoted a source at the Chinese Health Ministry indicating the death toll in China was 349, instead of the 340 noted by the WHO. Huang Yanzhong, "The Politics of China's SARS Crisis," *Harvard Asia Quarterly* 7, no. 4 (Autumn 2003): 9.

[79] Ibid., 11.

leaders of the Politburo Standing Committee (Table 3). At the time, Hu Jintao had no large popular following; few Chinese knew much about his political views, career, or private life. Hu's lack of popular support made the Propaganda Department unwilling to subject his leadership to major challenges early in his term as president. At the time, one official in the Propaganda Department observed, "the state of the epidemic is not frightening, the media is frightening."[80]

Table 3: Major SARS-Related Events[81]

Date	Description
Mid-November 2002	First SARS cases appeared in Foshan, Guangdong Province, during the meeting of the 16th Party Congress to select the new members of the Politburo Standing Committee.
January 27	A report on the unknown virus was sent to the Guangdong Province Health Bureau by a team of experts from the Ministry of Health.
February 11	Guangdong print media began to publish the first wave of reports on SARS in China.
Late February	Propaganda Department ordered a halt to the SARS coverage after media reports questioned the government's handling of the epidemic.
Mid-March	Media black out on SARS continued during election of President Hu Jintao as president by the National People's Congress. As a result, many people assumed the epidemic had run its course. The *21st Century World Herald*, the Guangdong newspaper with the most aggressive SARS reporting was shut down; Xiang Xi, editor-in-chief of the *Southern Weekend*, a newspaper that questioned the government handling of SARS, was removed from his post and replaced by Propaganda Department official Zhang Dongming.

(*Continued*)

[80] Huang Li, "SARS weiji yu dalu de chuanbo meiti" [SARS Crisis and the Mainland Broadcast Media], *Disanjie Xinshijie yulunjiandu yanjiu huiyi xuanbian* [*New Century Media Supervision Research Meeting Collected Volume, Third Session*] (Zhongguo qingnian zhengzhi xueyuan, 2003), 177.

[81] Principal source for the chart is Yanzhong Huang, "The Politics of China's SARS Crisis," 9–16.

Table 3: *(Continued)*

Date	Description
March 15	The WHO issued first global warning about the threat of SARS.
April 2	The WHO recommended travelers postpone all non-essential travel to Guangdong because of the risk of contracting SARS.
April 3	Health Minister Zhang Wenkang held a press conference and announced that SARS had been "effectively controlled" in the China region. He said, "In China, it's safe to work, live and travel!"
April 14	*Time* magazine exposé of hidden SARS cases in Beijing military hospitals fueled panic in the capital.
April 20	Health Minister Zhang Wenkang and Beijing Mayor Meng Xuenong were removed from their posts.
May 7	According to the *People's Daily Overseas Edition*, 80 million people were mobilized to clean houses and streets in Guangdong Province.
May 8	Official media reported 120 officials had been dismissed or punished for lax handling of the epidemic.
June 2	Shanghai lifted 10-day quarantine on people from SARS-afflicted areas.
June 24	The WHO lifted advisory against travel to Beijing.
August 16	Last two SARS patients discharged from Beijing Ditan Hospital. China declared free of SARS cases.

As the number of SARS cases began to rise, on February 7, the Guangdong Party Committee's Propaganda Department ordered the media to unify all content and statistics in the SARS coverage.[82] On February 8, cell phone text messages announcing the outbreak were circulated among thousands of Guangzhou users, and panic ensued as Guangzhou residents rushed to stores to stockpile groceries and medical supplies.[83] As evidence of party restrictions on the SARS

[82] Huang Li, "SARS Crisis and the Mainland Broadcast Media," 177. Even news of the ban on unauthorized publication of information on SARS victims could not be printed.
[83] Lu Ye, "'Feidian' baodao: fansi yu qianzhan" [SARS Reports: Reflection and Prospects], unpublished manuscript received from the author, a television producer and professor of journalism at Fudan University, 2003.

reporting, the *Guangzhou Daily* ran an article with the headline "305 Cases of SARS Discovered in Guangdong." However, the report did not discuss any details of the disease in Guangzhou.[84]

On February 11, the Guangzhou Municipal Government's Health Department and the Guangdong Province Health Bureau held press conferences at which officials announced that Guangdong Province had 305 cases of SARS, of which 105 cases were medical personnel. According to government sources, SARS led to five deaths, none of which were medical personnel, a point stressed in many news reports. Guangzhou's Health Department Director, Huang Jionglie, assured media at the press conference that, although the number of cases would continue to rise, SARS was under control. He said all victims were well cared for; for the majority, symptoms were under control, and a number of people had already been released from the hospital.[85]

In the days to follow, the Guangdong print media succeeded in publishing several controversial articles on SARS. Due to restrictions imposed by the Propaganda Department, journalists could not write about the rapid spread of the disease or interview those affected. They did, however, criticize governmental suppression of information (indirectly), and they reported on the public's panicked response to the threat of SARS.[86]

On February 13, the *21st Century Economic Report*, a provincial weekly, wrote a comprehensive account of the spread of the disease in Guangdong Province since the discovery of the first case in late December. The article, "Everyone Mobilized to Fight Pneumonia," provided an explanation of SARS symptoms and mentioned that scientists had not yet determined if it was viral or bacterial. The report mentioned that hospitals across the country had established emergency SARS treatment units. It noted that in Guangdong, medical

---

[84] Huang Li, "SARS Crisis and the Mainland Broadcast Media," 177.

[85] Cai Yifei and Chen Jibao, "Kangji feiyan zong dongyuan" [Everyone Mobilized to Fight Pneumonia], *21st Century Economic Report*, 5.

[86] *Southern Metropolitan Post* ran two editorials indirectly criticizing state suppression of information on SARS and questioning the government's position that the outbreak was under control.

staff had begun to wear quarantine uniforms and guards had been placed outside hospitals.[87]

On February 17, the *21st Century World Herald*, a weekly with a reputation for pushing the limits of party tolerance, printed a far more detailed account of the spread of the disease in a series of articles. The *Herald* documented the appearance of SARS in Guangzhou as early as late November, reported the public's frightened reaction to this unknown malady, and speculated about the political fall out of the crisis. Quoting Li Xiguang of Qinghua University, one article indicated that officials in Guangdong had suppressed information on the spread of SARS in Guangzhou out of fear that it would lead to widespread public concern, a decision that ultimately contributed to rising infections and rumors.[88] This was one of the articles to directly attribute responsibility for the spread of SARS to suppression of information by the Guangdong leadership and almost certainly contributed to the Provincial Propaganda Department's decision to shut down the *21st Century World Herald* without warning in March.[89] As if to distance itself from the hard line taken by the *Herald*, the *21st Century Economic Report* published an editorial on February 17 entitled, "Rumors Worse than Pneumonia, Stop Rumors to Save the Public," which argued that SARS in Guangdong was under control. But persistent rumors, due in part to the lack of timely information, were aggravating the situation.[90] The little freedom available to write about SARS in Guangdong Province ceased after reports by the *Nanfang Metropolitan Post* on February 19, "Dispute over the Origins of the Disease," and on March 6, "Guangdong Asks for International Assistance with SARS

---

[87] Cai Yifei and Chen Jibao, "Kangji feiyan zong dongyuan," 5.

[88] Duan Ninghong, "Feidianxingfeiyan jubu liuxing Guangdong qingkuang huibao hehu jizhi" [The Relationship between the Spread of SARS and the System of Reporting in Guangdong], *21st Century World Herald*, 6.

[89] The "warning system" created in 2000 was not used prior to the closure of the *21st Century World Herald*. Interview 2004 — #16.

[90] "Rumors Worse than Pneumonia, Stop Rumors to Save the Public," editorial, *21st Century Economic Report*, 2.

and Seeks Experts to Join Research," encountered severe party criticism.[91]

After initially publishing relatively "free" investigative reports, *Southern Weekend* was notably subdued during the latter stages of the SARS crisis. On February 13, *Southern Weekend* published an investigative piece, relying on identified sources in the national Center for Disease Control, that implied that local government agencies were responsible for the poor handling of the epidemic. A second story entitled, "Guangzhou Fights an Unknown Disease," described the explosion in communication by text messages and Internet users as Guangzhou residents attempted to understand the epidemic and considered measures to prevent infection.[92] On February 20, the *Weekend* published another controversial piece about the question of whether information should be suppressed or openly discussed, citing the chaotic public reaction to SARS. The article concluded that suppression of information would be "counter-productive."[93] However, the *Weekend's* editors misjudged the limit of party tolerance.[94] In March, *Weekend's* editor-in-chief, Xiang Xi, was demoted and put in charge of a monthly magazine.[95] Several journalists at *Weekend* subsequently protested by resigning or refusing to write articles. A senior cadre at the Guangdong Propaganda Department, Zhang Dongming, took control of the

---

91 Lu Ye, "Weiji chuanbo: cong SARS baodao kan Zhongguo gonggong weisheng shijian yu jiankang chuanbo jizhi de chuishi" [Crisis Communication: Using SARS Reports to Examine the Failings of the PRC's Public Sanitation Incidents and Health Institutions], *Disanjie Xinshijie yulunjiandu yanjiu huiyi xuanbian* [*New Century Media Supervision Research Meeting Collected Volume, Third Session*] (Zhongguo qingnian zhengzhi xueyuan, 2003), 175.

92 Wu Zhenguang, "Zhongda tufa gonggong weisheng shijian ruhe chuli?" [How Should the Sudden Appearance of Major Health Issues by Handled?]; Chen Hai and Jiang Hua, "Guangzhou kangji buming bingdu" [Guangzhou Fights Unknown Disease], *Southern Weekend*, February 13, 2003.

93 Yan Lieshan, "Xinxi gongkai guannian de yushe" [Preparing a Perspective on Information Transparency: Citizens' Debate], *Southern Weekend*, February 20, 2003.

94 Interview 2003 — #9.

95 Interview 2003 — #11.

paper with the effect of temporarily muzzling the paper's trademark investigative journalism.

From early March to the first half of April, when the epidemic had already spread overseas, there were almost no reports on SARS by the Chinese media.[96] In March, the National People's Congress was scheduled to elect CCP General Secretary Hu Jintao to a five-year term as president, appoint Wen Jiabao as premier, and confirm Wen's selections for a reshuffled State Council.[97] A challenge to party legitimacy posed by a serious health crisis was threatening because the "fourth generation" of leaders due to take power in China lacked the experience of Jiang Zemin, the popularity of Zhu Rongji, or the revolutionary credentials of Deng Xiaoping. Coverage of SARS was so infrequent during the month of March that many journalists believed the epidemic had ended. The editor of *Cajing Magazine*, Hu Shuli, recalls remarking to a journalist from Guangdong: "This disaster was treated with greater openness and handled quite well." "How so?" the journalist replied, "Guangdong still has SARS. It's impossible to report on it." Hu Shuli concluded that this was one of the many clues that SARS required closer examination.[98]

On April 2, the World Health Organization recommended that travelers postpone all non-essential travel to Guangdong because of the risk of contracting SARS.[99] On the same day, CCTV broadcast an interview with Health Minister Zhang Wenkang in which he

---

[96] This point is demonstrated very convincingly by Shanghai University media scholar Dai Yuanguang, who charted the reports on SARS in late March and April for *People's Daily*, *Liberation Daily*, *Yangcheng Evening News* [*Yangcheng Wanbao*], and *Yunnan Daily*. *"New Century Media Supervision" Research Meeting Collected Volume, Third Session*, 148–151.

[97] In 2003, the State Council included four vice premiers, five state councilors, and 26 ministers and heads of national commissions. "People in Power: China," *Janet Matthews Information Services*, November 30, 2003.

[98] Hu Shuli, "SARS Reports: Caijing's (News) Selection and Thoughts," notes from her lecture given at the China Youth Political Institute in Beijing, December 10, 2003.

[99] This was the first such advisory in the WHO's 55-year history. Keith Bradsher, "WHO Issues Travel Warning over Respiratory Disease," *New York Times*, April 2, 2003.

admitted in his first nationally televised address on the outbreak that China had 46 SARS fatalities and 1,190 SARS cases, 934 of which had already been released from care.[100] On April 3, Zhang held a press conference in Beijing to proclaim that SARS had been "effectively controlled" in the China region. "In China, it's safe to work, live and travel!" he said. Zhang Wenkang noted the low number of SARS cases in Beijing (12 victims and three fatalities) and announced that the WHO had removed Beijing from the list of SARS stricken areas.[101] The confidence of the health minister was echoed several days later in Guangdong Province when provincial governor Huang Huahua told members of a WHO evaluation team that he had confidence that the "battle against SARS would be won."

> Since the outbreak of SARS, under the leadership of the Central Committee and the State Council, and with the great support of related ministries, the Guangdong Provincial Party Committee and the Provincial Government have resolutely guided and united the people of the province to take beneficial measures that have yielded excellent results in a short period of time. Now the spread of the disease has been effectively controlled. As of April 5, 82.2 percent of cases have left the hospital and the rate of new infections has decreased.[102]

By mid-March, SARS had spread to Hong Kong, Taiwan, Vietnam, Singapore, and soon thereafter to Canada and Switzerland. Quarantine measures were put in place in Hong Kong, Taiwan, Vietnam, and Singapore. In China, the absence of reliable news fueled a rumor mill that generated an environment of near hysteria. Lack of faith in official media reports prompted the public to turn to other sources of information. An opinion poll conducted by communications scholar Du Junfei revealed that the majority of residents

---

[100] Lou Yi, "Beijing ershi tian" [20 Days in Beijing], *Caijing Magazine*, April 20, 2003, 43.

[101] Lu Ye, "SARS Reports: Reflection and Prospects," 2.

[102] Duan Gongwei and Zeng Xi, "Guangdong you xinxin zhansheng feidianxing feiyan" [Guangdong Has Confidence To Beat SARS], *Southern Daily*, April 8, 2003; see also Joseph Kahn, "Chinese Official Says Disease Is Controlled in City of Origin," *New York Times*, April 8, 2003.

in five Chinese cities relied upon "word of mouth" for information about SARS. In Beijing, this percentage was the highest: 64.2 percent. The second most important source of information was telephone conversations, followed by the Internet.[103]

For a tiny majority, information on the spread of the disease came through foreign news reports and websites available only to the Chinese capable of reading foreign languages. One frequently updated source was the WHO website. The data available on the website, while later recognized to be unreliable, informed editors at *Caijing Magazine* that the number of SARS cases had continued to rise in Guangdong and that government-sponsored explanations concerning the nature of the illness differed from those of international scientists. The discrepancies between the information released by the WHO and the low profile and incomplete reports in the local Chinese media prompted the *Caijing* editors to decide that the truth about the spread of SARS "could not and should not be concealed."[104]

In early April, 72–year-old physician Jiang Yanyong, who worked in the 301 People's Liberation Army Hospital in Beijing, sent an email to CCTV and Hong Kong's Phoenix Television suggesting that the true number of SARS patients in Beijing had been suppressed.[105] Neither television station investigated Jiang's claims. However, *Time* magazine published an interview with Jiang Yanyong, including his account that SARS cases were being concealed in Beijing.[106] Although *Time* was not distributed in China

---

[103] The ranking for the importance of telephone conversations and the Internet is based on survey results in four out of the five cities measured. Du Junfei, *"New Century Media Supervision" Research Meeting Collected Volume, Third Session*, 186.

[104] *Caijing* editor Hu Shuli said that friends expressed concern at the time about her decision to assign in-depth reporting on SARS because few media were reporting on it in the comprehensive manner of the Guangdong media in mid-February. Xinhua had also not issued an internal report offering "guidance" on how to proceed with reporting on the subject. Hu Shuli, "SARS Reports: *Caijing*'s (News) Selection and Thoughts."

[105] Lu Ye, "SARS Reports: Reflection and Prospects," 2.

[106] Hanna Beech, "Unmasking a Crisis," *Time*, April 14, 2003.

due to the state's dissatisfaction with the previous content, versions of the article were emailed back to China and it was widely read among intellectuals.[107] The editor of the earliest Chinese media to resume comprehensive SARS reporting, Hu Shuli of *Caijing Magazine*, noted that she subsequently decided to prepare the critical report "Beijing Case" for publication on April 20.[108] That edition of *Caijing* featured 18 pages of articles and a commentary on the SARS epidemic in what proved to be a journalistic *tour de force*, revealing the spread of SARS internationally and considering the negative economic effects of the epidemic.[109] *Caijing* could not include an interview with Jiang Yanyong because he had "been instructed" not to grant interviews.[110] On the same day, *Caijing's* in-depth reports appeared, the CCP Central Committee announced via a short Xinhua news report that Health Minister Zhang Wenkang and Beijing Mayor Meng Xuenong had been relieved of their official duties.[111]

---

[107] Chinese media professionals were very quickly discussing the article, the effect of which was mentioned in numerous Chinese studies on communications during the SARS crisis.

[108] Hu Shuli, "SARS Reports: *Caijing's* (News) Selection and Thoughts."

[109] Zhu Xiaochao and Cao Haili, "Weixian laizi hefang?" [Where Is the Danger Coming From?], 34–42 and Ye Weiqiang et al., "Touzi yinhang de yuce yu caice" [The Estimates and Guesses of Investment Banks], 54–57, *Caijing Magazine*, April, 20, 2003.

[110] Ibid.

[111] "Zhonggong zhongyang tiaozheng weisheng bu he Beijingshi zhuyao fuzeren" [Party Central Adjusts Health Ministry and Major Leaders in Beijing], Xinhua News wire as published in *China Youth Daily* [*Zhongguo qingnianbao*], April 21, 2003, 1. Health Minister Zhang Wenkang and the mayor of Beijing, Meng Xuenong, were soon appointed to other important posts, an indication that their removals were a response to public pressure rather than represented party censure for dereliction of duty. Zhang Wenkang was named to head the Song Qingling Association, a charitable organization of considerable prestige. Meng Xuenong, who had only been in office about a month prior to his removal, was transferred to a position running the North-South Water Diversion Project — an influential post. I am grateful to comments from Associated Press Shanghai correspondent Christopher Bodeen for pointing this out.

The Government Response to the Crisis

On April 21, a Xinhua article published in the *China Youth Daily* presented an account of a press conference held by Vice Health Minister Gao Qiang, who said that the number of SARS cases in China had risen to 1,807, including 339 cases in Beijing, 108 in Shanxi, 25 in Inner Mongolia, 12 in Guangxi, six in Hunan, five in Sichuan, three in Fujian, two in Shanghai, two in Henan, and one in Ningxia. Gao Qiang reported 79 SARS-related deaths and advised citizens not to travel during the week-long holiday beginning May 1. In a response to a question by a CNN journalist, Gao Qiang attributed the inaccuracies of the previous reporting of SARS cases in Beijing to the decentralized nature of China's medical system.[112] The CCP had begun to admit the gravity of the situation. To mollify the domestic and international public opinion, Gao Qiang took a number of questions from the international media; his answers were published by Xinhua in the question-and-answer format.

For the Chinese news media, the sacking of Zhang and Meng and the health ministry's admission of the presence of hundreds of additional SARS cases in Beijing signaled the government's intention to handle the epidemic with greater transparency.[113] After April 20, hundreds of reports emerged on various aspects of the SARS epidemic. Yet in spite of the relative openness, *Caijing Magazine* reporters complained of the extreme difficulty in gaining access to the doctors who were treating SARS patients or hospital records. Similar sentiment was echoed by Zhang Jie, producer of *News Probe*, which broadcast the first images from inside Beijing hospitals. The program's footage was filmed by a resourceful team of journalists using a concealed camera. After the *News Probe* report was aired, Zhang Jie was told by the Propaganda Department officials, "One such report is enough. No other television program will be allowed to broadcast this kind

[112] "Weile kongzhi yiqing, hua duoshao qian ye zai suobuxi" [In Order to Control the Epidemic, the Amount of Money Spent Does Not Matter], Xinhua News wire as published in *China Youth Daily*, April 21, 2003, 2.

[113] Ibid.

of material."[114] Nearly one month after other countries had implemented quarantines on SARS patients, Beijing publicly announced quarantine policies.

The SARS epidemic, which affected at least 25 provinces and cities in China, represented a tremendous challenge for journalists seeking to "get the story out" for the good of the society, and for profit-maximizing media managers to boost sales. However, the gravity of the epidemic and the insecurity of the CCP's new leadership placed tremendous pressure on the media not to report freely. In February, the news media's strategy was to test the water with initial coverage on the epidemic. However, the communist party pressure forced the media to retreat, while rumors of the epidemic worsened. In March and early April, information found its way to China's elite via the Internet, international organizations, and the foreign media, creating pressure for greater transparency in the government's handling of the epidemic and renewed reporting by the Chinese media. The floodgate for reporting in China opened after the announcement of the resignation of the health minister and the mayor of Beijing.

The media had been waiting for a political cue that greater openness was possible without the risk of repression. Once the SARS reportage entered the mainstream, the risk for sensational, even critical, reporting on the epidemic was reduced considerably. By late April and early May, news coverage of SARS once again took on the tone of party propaganda, imploring the country to support medical personnel, take care of SARS orphans, and join together in the fight against SARS. The tone of these reports was not unlike that of the enthusiasm generated during Mao-era political campaigns.[115]

---

[114] Interview with Zhang Jie, Producer, *News Probe*, February 2004.

[115] See, for example, "Rang women shouqianshou jianqi kangji 'feidian' de qingchun changcheng" [Let's Join Hands to Create a Great Wall of Spring to Fight 'SARS'], *China Youth Daily* [*Zhongguo qingnian bao*], April 25, 2003, 1; Wang Pan, "'Feidian' jianmiezhan, women gai xiang shei zhijing," ("Who We Should Salute in the War to Annihilate SARS"), and Qu Yujie, "Jianyi wei 'feidian' sizhe jiangbanqi," [Recommendation that the Flag Should Be Lowered Halfway in Honor of SARS Dead], *China Youth Daily*, April 25, 2003, 7.

Case Summary

The appearance of SARS represented an unanticipated crisis for the CCP at a very delicate political moment. Nevertheless, the Chinese media's handling of the SARS epidemic revealed the effectiveness of the CCP's mechanisms for suppressing information. The Chinese media issued few accurate reports or reports critical of the government handling of the SARS crisis. It engaged in little investigative journalism until it received a political cue in the form of the resignations of two high-ranking officials that SARS reporting might not have dangerous repercussions. Most reports parroted the party line that SARS was under control.

The lack of free reporting should be seen as indicative of the considerable extent to which China's ruling party determines when and what type of information can be released to the public through the commercial news media. Further, the public's reliance on word of mouth and telephone communication illustrated the media's failure to provide trusted information. Yet, brave exceptions that provided excellent news coverage should be noted. News organizations such as *Southern Metropolitan Daily*, *Southern Weekend*, *21st Century World Herald*, *China Youth Daily*, *Caijing Magazine*, and *News Probe* weighed the risk of writing reports critical of the state against the benefits and decided to proceed to the extent possible. These media set examples for other media to emulate in the future and demonstrated the difficulty that a post-totalitarian state faces in forcing the commercial media to issue propaganda in the face of public pressure for real news.

Unfortunately, state repression severely affected four of these organizations. Some repression occurred during the SARS crisis and other moves to strengthen party control occurred subsequently. The *21st Century World Economic Herald* was closed down in March after publishing the most critical SARS news as well as articles related to democratization in China and Taiwan. *Southern Weekend* was forced to withdraw an edition already sent to publishers for the last minute revision,[116] and Editor-in-Chief Xiang Xi was removed

[116] See various reports in *Yazhou zhoukan* [*Asia Weekly*], April 28 and May 4, 2003.

from his post, demoralizing many of the paper's journalists with reputations for courageous journalism.[117] The *Southern Metropolitan Post* got its "payback" the following year with the arrests of senior managers and the editor-in-chief on corruption charges, which was related to the paper's aggressive SARS coverage as well as articles published on the murder of Sun Zhigang during the SARS media blackout.[118] The editor-in-chief at the *China Youth Daily*, which published editorials highly critical of the state after April 20, was removed in late 2004.[119] His successor subsequently attempted to create a system of bonuses that would provide incentive for journalists to engage in outright flattery of central party leaders and self-censorship.[120]

Caijing Magazine strategically timed its in-depth coverage of SARS to coincide with official announcements of the removal of Zhang Wenkang and Meng Xuenong, a decision that reduced the risk of reprimand. It is also to *Caijing*'s advantage that the magazine has a relatively small circulation of 80,000 to 100,000,[121] compared to the much higher circulations of *Southern Weekend* and the *Southern Metropolitan Post*.[122] Newspapers with high circulations are read by

[117] Interview 2003 — #7, #10, #11.

[118] For extensive analysis on the *Southern Metropolitan Post* coverage of the Sun Zhigang case, see Benjamin Liebman, "Watchdog or Demagogue? The Media in the Chinese Legal System," *Columbia Law Review* 105, no. 1 (January 2005): 45.

[119] While many media professionals have expressed admiration for editorials published by *China Youth Daily* on the SARS epidemic, it is unclear if the paper's SARS reporting was responsible for the change of its top management, or whether the appointment of Li Erliang as editor-in-chief reflected a general tightening of state control over the media under the leadership of President Hu Jintao. The management at *News Probe* has not changed. However, the freedom of *News Probe* reporters has visibly decreased since 2004. According to one *News Probe* staffer, the program is now "experiencing its winter."

[120] Kristine Kwok, "Freedom Row at China Youth Daily," *South China Morning Post*, August 16, 2005.

[121] Interview 2003 — #9.

[122] The circulation at *Southern Weekend* is between 700,000 and 800,000. Interview 2003 — #7. Circulation at *Southern Metropolitan Post* is over one million. See "2002nian bufen dushilei baozhi zhuyao jingji zhibiao" [2002 Major Economic Statistics for Metro Papers], *Chuanmei* [*Commuications Magazine*], October 2003, 30.

more people and have a greater effect in the formation of public opinion. Thus, newspapers' or magazines' high circulations are potentially more threatening to party legitimacy, because they influence the views of more readers.[123]

Much of the news coverage of SARS in major publications consisted of Xinhua wire reports. Benjamin Liebman quoted a journalist in Beijing saying that 50 percent of his local paper's SARS coverage relied on Xinhua news.[124] This indicates two dynamics at work. First, by mandating that newspapers use Xinhua news stories, the party can standardize and control news content. Second, the inability of newspapers to write their own coverage reduces the effect of competition for the simple reason that media have no incentive to differentiate content from competitors to win consumers. For media such as *Caijing* that succeeded in reporting on SARS more freely without encountering repression, the effects of globalization were empowering. Foreign media reports and access to online information were clearly crucial for Chinese journalists seeking the opportunity, if not the excuse, to issue accurate reports. (In other words, if the information is on the WHO website and in news reports outside China, why can't I write about it?) In this sense, global information flows placed arrows in the quivers, so to speak, of the Chinese journalists seeking to report the truth.

In the case of the SARS coverage, media that misjudged the limits of party tolerance paid a price, and the frequent use of the Xinhua coverage reduced the opportunities for journalists to write innovative reports. However, in the case of SARS reporting, free and professionalized reporting appeared, indicating that party control over news content was considerable but not complete.

---

[123] With its broad reach, television news coverage is the most potentially delegitimizing news source. CCTV reaches nearly 95 percent of the Chinese population or 1.3 billion people. See *Zhongguo guangbo nianjian* [*China Broadcast Yearbook*], 2004, 504–507. Not surprisingly, television is the most tightly controlled of all Chinese media.

[124] Benjamin Liebman, "Watchdog or Demagogue?" 45.

CONCLUSION

In the 1980s, decentralization and commercialization of the media industry in the 1980s gave rise to "slippery rocks" as the CCP leadership negotiated its way across the "river" of reform. Following Deng's Southern Tour, subsequent innovations in the media industry made the process of commercialization serve state interests for media control, at the level of both media organizations and individual journalists. In addition, centralization strategies similar to those applied to the reform of China's stock markets, the People's Bank of China, and other sectors of the economy reduced the power of the local state and increased that of the center through the creation of print and broadcast media groups. As the analysis of the SARS case demonstrated, when forced to choose between serving the interests of state and society, the commercial media chose the former even though it depended upon the latter for revenue. This was in large measure due to the party's introduction of market incentives that supplemented the threat of coercion, which by itself had proven ineffective.

Chapter

2

Brewing Tensions while Maintaining Stabilities: The Dual Role of the *Hukou* System in Contemporary China

Fei-Ling Wang

THE *HUKOU* SYSTEM

Few other institutions have been more important than the *hukou* (household registration) system in defining and conditioning the politics, social life, and economic development of the People's Republic of China (PRC). Few other Chinese institutions have more complicated functions, both positive and negative, that defy a clear-cut normative assessment. In the early 21st century, this long-lasting and highly peculiar Chinese institution continues its crucial functions while demonstrating significant changes. At this historical juncture when there is a widely shared expectation for an epic rise of China's economic power on the international stage, the *hukou* system deserves special attention as it reveals some key characteristics of the PRC and explains much of the dynamics and tendencies in China today.

This chapter briefly describes the current status of the *hukou* system, especially its leading functions. Facilitating a rapid but uneven economic growth that creates significant social and regional disparities, the *hukou* system helps greatly to stabilize the PRC sociopolitical order through an effective police control of an increasingly mobile populace. But the system also generates powerful tensions in the areas of human rights, equity of citizenship, and simple ethics. It is in need of further reform to continue its role in the Chinese political economy; yet, a withering or abolishing of the *hukou* system may seriously challenge China's sociopolitical stability and economic growth.[1] The dual-role of the *hukou* system makes it both an easy target of political action and an indispensable pillar of political stability that is required for a peaceful political reform. Brewing tensions while stabilizing the society, the *hukou* system continues to be a key institution in the PRC.[2]

THE *HUKOU* SYSTEM IN THE 2000s: A SKETCH

Formally adopted in the 1950s, the *hukou* system can actually be traced back to the fifth century B.C., during the Warring States period. It was institutionalized and adopted with varied degrees of effectiveness and extensiveness as an important part of the Chinese imperial political system by the dynasties from the Qin (third century B.C.) to

---

[1] For a comprehensive study of the *hukou* system, see Fei-Ling Wang, *Organizing through Division and Exclusion: China's Hukou System* (Stanford, CA: Stanford University Press, 2005).

[2] On the reform of the *hukou* system, see Fei-Ling Wang, "Reformed Migration Control and New List of the Targeted People: China's *Hukou* System in the 2000s," *China Quarterly* no. 181 (March 2004): 115–132. For earlier studies of the system, see Tiejun Cheng, *Dialectics of Control: The Household Registration (Hukou) System in Contemporary China*, Ph.D. dissertation, State University of New York, Binghamton, 1991; Tiejun Cheng and Mark Selden, "The Origins and Social Consequences of China's *Hukou* System," *China Quarterly* no. 139 (1994): 644–668; Dorothy J. Solinger, *Contesting Citizenship in Urban China: Peasant Migrants, the State, and the Logic of the Market* (Berkeley, Calif.: University of California Press, 1999); and the special issue (guest edited by Zhang Tingting) of *Chinese Law and Government*, May–June, 2001.

the Qing (1644–1911). The Republic of China (ROC) and the PRC both established a national *hukou* system. However, the *hukou* system achieved an unprecedented level of uniformity, extensiveness, effectiveness, and rigidity only in the PRC beginning in the 1950s.[3]

On January 9, 1958, Mao Zedong promulgated *The Regulation on Hukou Registration of the People's Republic of China*, formally creating the PRC national *hukou* system. Twenty-seven years later, on September 6, 1985, Beijing adopted its *Regulation on Resident's Personal Identification Card in the People's Republic of China*. These two regulations and their implementation procedures are the main legal basis for the PRC *hukou* system. Every Chinese citizen knows and is affected by the *hukou* system; yet the system has remained an administrative system, highly nontransparent and not mentioned in the PRC constitution or its civil codes.

The PRC State Council and its ministries and bureaus have issued numerous, often ad hoc, regulations, provisional regulations, directives, decrees, and documents that have substantiated and fine-tuned the *hukou* system. The majority of those "state documents," estimated to be over 600 from 1958 to 2005, have been the ever-changing criteria and mechanisms of control of internal migration, especially *qianyi* (permanent migration with *hukou* relocation). The Ministry of Public Security and the local public security bureaus and police stations are the administrators of the *hukou* system. Specialized *hukou* police officers are assigned to be in charge of *hukou* matters in each *hukou* zone: a neighborhood, street, *danwei* (unit), or township. With the authorization of the central government, provincial and municipal governments may make marginal

---

3 Solinger, *Contesting Citizenship*; Delia Davin, *Internal Migration in Contemporary China* (New York: Palgrave, 1999); Michael R. Dutton, *Policing and Punishment in China: From Patriarchy to "The People"* (New York: Cambridge University Press, 1992); Lei Guang, "Reconstructing the Rural-Urban Divide: Peasant Migration and the Rise of 'Orderly Migration' in Contemporary China," *Journal of Contemporary China* 10, no. 28 (2001): 471–493; Jianhong Liu, Lening Zhang, and Steven F. Messner, ed., *Crime and Social Control in a Changing China* (Westport, CT: Greenwood, 2001); Hein Mallee, "China's Household Registration System under Reform," *Development and Change* 26, no. 1 (January 1995): 1–29.

changes and experimental modifications to the *hukou* system in their respective jurisdictions.

The *hukou* system requires every Chinese citizen to be officially and constantly registered with the *hukou* authority (the *hukou* police) at birth. This registration is the legal basis for personal identification. The categories of non-agricultural (urban) or agricultural (rural), the legal address and location, the unit affiliation (employment), and a host of other personal and family information, including religious belief and physical features, are documented and verified, and these become the person's permanent *hukou* record. Until 1998, a person's *hukou* location and categorization or type were determined by the mother's *hukou* location and type rather than birthplace when a child was allowed to inherit the father's *or* mother's *hukou* location and categorization.

One cannot acquire a legal permanent residence and the numerous community-based rights, opportunities benefits, and privileges in places other than where his *hukou* is. Only through proper authorization of the government can one permanently change his *hukou* location and especially his *hukou* categorization from the rural type to the urban one. Travelers, visitors, and temporary migrants must be registered with the *hukou* police for extended stay (longer than three days) in a locality. For longer than a one-month stay and especially when seeking local employment, one must apply and be approved for a temporary residential permit. Violators are subject to fines, detention, forced repatriation, and criminal prosecution and even jail sentences. *Hukou* files are routinely used by the police for investigation, social control, and crime-fighting purposes.

Functions of the System

The semi-secretive PRC *hukou* system performs three leading functions. First, it is the basis for resource allocation and subsidization for selected groups of the population (mainly the residents of major urban centers). This function has shaped much of China's economic development in the past half century by politically affecting the movement of capital and human resources. The government has traditionally heavily favored the urban centers since the 1950s with investment and subsidies. Second, the *hukou* system allows the government to control and regulate internal migration, especially the rural-to-urban migration. The basic principles of the PRC's migration control have been to restrict the rural-to-urban and small-city-to-large-city migration but to encourage migration in the reverse direction. China's urbanization, as a consequence, is relatively small and slow compared to its economic development level. China's urban slums are also relatively small and less serious compared to those in many other developing nations such as Brazil or India.

Third, the *hukou* system has a less well-known but very powerful role of social control, especially the management of the so-called targeted people (*zhongdian renkou*). Based on *hukou* files, the police in each community maintain a confidential list of targeted people to be specially monitored and controlled. Such a focused monitoring and control of selected segments of the population have contributed significantly and effectively to the political stability of China's one-party authoritarian regime.

In the 2000s, the *hukou* system still enjoys a strong institutional legitimacy in China, perhaps largely because the divisions along familial and locational lines are more "natural" and prevalent than most other human differentiations. Unlike the similar but now disgraced and disintegrated *propiska* (residential permit) system in the former Soviet Union, the PRC *hukou* system is still both legal and strong. With only a few reform attempts and limited alterations, the *hukou* system continues to be a backbone of the Chinese institutional structure and fundamentally contributes to the seemingly puzzling coexistence of China's rapidly developing market economy and the remarkable stability of the Chinese Communist Party's (CCP's) political monopoly.

The *hukou* system's much examined function of resource allocation and subsidization to the urbanites has now been reduced and even replaced by the advancing market forces, as the urban rations of food and many other supplies have now either disappeared or become insignificant.[4] The administration of the well-known function of internal migration control is now reformed, relaxed, and localized, giving rise to increased mobility of the population in general and of rural laborers in particular.[5] The other leading, albeit much less known but highly crucial, function of the *hukou* system, the management of targeted people, however, continues to be highly centralized, rigid, and forceful, although its effectiveness has been declining steadily.

Since 1997 and especially since 2001, there has been a so-called "deep reform" of the *hukou* system. However, the migration-control function of the *hukou* system still demonstrates its remarkable continuity as the governing principles of internal migration regulation remain fundamentally unchanged. The changes in the management of targeted people so far are mainly technical and marginal. There actually is a tendency for this sociopolitical control function to be improved and enhanced in the early 2000s.

CHANGES, REFORMS, AND IMPROVEMENTS

Managing the System

Internally, the PRC *hukou* system is designed to perform one common governance duty (to collect and manage information concerning citizens' personal identification, kinship, and legal residence) and two "unique missions": to control internal migration through managing temporary residents/visitors and to have a tiered management of targeted people in the population.[6]

---

[4] Urban *hukou* holders in major cities, however, still enjoy significant state subsidies in housing, healthcare, employment, and especially education. In 2001, for example, a Beijing resident can get into college with a minimum admission score 140 points (or 28 percent of the national average score) lower than that in Shangdong Province. *Zhongguo qingnian bao* [*Chinese Youth Daily*], July–August 2001.

[5] Kam Wing Chan and Li Zhang, "The *Hukou* System and Rural-Urban Migration in China: Processes and Changes," *China Quarterly* no. 160 (1999): 831–840.

[6] Jiang Xianjin and Luo Feng, ed., *Jingcha yewu shiyong quanshu — jian guanli juan* [*Complete Guide of Police Work — Volume on Public Security Management*] (Beijing: Quinzhong Press, 1996), 218, 220; BPT-MPS (Bureau of Personnel and Training, Ministry of Public Security), *Huzheng guanli jiaocheng* [*Textbook on Hukou Management*] (Beijing: Qunzhong Press, 2000), 5, 161–173.

The *hukou* system has been an administrative system with sketchy legal foundations. Other than the 1958 *Regulation on the* Hukou *Registration of the People's Republic of China* and the 1985 *Regulation on Resident's Personal Identification Card in the PRC*, the system has been governed and regulated mostly by "internal" decrees and directives.[7] There have been talks in Beijing since the 1980s about making a PRC *Hukou* Law to firmly ground this important system in "modern legal languages."[8] Yet, by 2005, this effort is still at a very early stage with no date of completion in sight.

The administrators of the *hukou* system remain the Ministry of Public Security (MPS) and the local police stations (*paichusuo*). Administrative localization has increasingly taken place in the reform era, as exemplified by the so-called "blue stamp" *hukou* schemes that have various qualifications and implementation procedures in different localities to allow the migration of selected groups of people.[9] In April 2002, Shanghai suspended granting the blue-stamp *hukou* to those who have purchased a "commercial" housing unit in the city, due to "too much pressure from the new residents." But neighboring cities such as Nanjing continue to lure the rich to buy their apartments with their blue-stamp *hukou* quotas. Some other cities have simply replaced the blue-stamp *hukou* with the entry-condition based permanent *hukou*.[10]

To manage the massive files of the *hukou* system, the MPS started to establish an electronic *hukou* database in 1986 and got special funding for national computerization of the *hukou* system in 1992. By 2002, almost all (more than 30,000) police stations had

---

[7] Wang Huaian et al., ed., *Zhonghua Renmin Gongheguo fali quanshu* [*Complete Collection of the Laws of the People's Republic of China*] (Changchun: Jilin Renmin Press, 1989).

[8] One Chinese National People's Congress (NPC) deputy did propose a bill for a *hukou* law in March 2001. (Beijing: Associated Press, March 15, 2001). But it had no chance even to be included in the legislative agenda. Such symbolic actions have been made annually in March at meetings of the NPC since 2002.

[9] Kam Wing Chan and Li Zhang, "The *Hukou* System and Rural-Urban Migration," 836–840. Blue-stamp *hukou* is so named because instead of the regular red seal applied on the *hukou* form and booklet, the *hukou* police apply a blue seal.

[10] Author's interviews in Beijing, Shanghai, and Jiangsu, summer 2002.

computerized their *hukou* management. Some 1,180 cities and counties joined regional computer networks for file-sharing of the *hukou* records of a total of 1.07 billion people (about 83 percent of the total population), and 250 cities joined one single national *hukou* computer network to allow for instantaneous verification of *hukou* information covering 650 million people (about half of the total population).[11] In 2002, the MPS further required all hotels with 50 or more beds to have computer links to instantaneously transmit the photos of all guests to local police stations.[12]

Starting in the late 1990s, many Chinese have openly criticized the *hukou* system for creating population immobility, economic irrationality, and market segmentation and retardation.[13] Others have increasingly questioned the morality and ethics of the incomplete citizenship of the excluded rural residents, the uneven regional development, and the horizontal stratification in the nation.[14] External factors, such as China's accession to the World Trade Organization (WTO) in 2001 and the call for "conformity with international standards" — especially "national citizen [equal] treatment

[11] DOP-MPS (Department of Politics, Ministry of Public Security), *Gongan yewu jichu zhishii* [*Basic Knowledge of Public Security Work*] (Beijing: Qunzhong Press, 1999), 75–76; *Zhongguo qingnian bao* [*China Youth Daily*, Beijing], January 5, 2002.

[12] "E jingcha kaishi liangxian, huji dangan jiang dianzihua" [E-police Starts To Emerge and *Hukou* Files will Be Electronic], www.news.china.com (accessed February 19, 2002). The police believed that several high profile criminal cases in 2002 were solved due to the *hukou* police's routine but faster gathering and monitoring of hotel registration information. Author's interviews in Beijing and Shanghai, 2002.

[13] Wu Pengsen, "Mingongchao dui Zhongguo xibu diqu fazhan chaju de fumian yingxiang" [The Negative Impact of the Tide of Migrant Peasant Workers on the Economic Backwardness in the Western Regions], *Shehui* [*Society*], Shanghai no. 7 (2001): 4–6; "Yiwei zhe shenfen butong? tequan? jiedu hukou zhenshi yiyi" [Does It Mean Different Identity? Privileges? To Understand the Real Meaning of *Hukou*], *Zhongguo qingnian bao*, Beijing, August 12, 2001.

[14] Liu Juhua, "Zhuanjia cheng huji zhidu youliyu xianfa zhiwai jibupingdeng" [Experts Say That the *Hukou* System Is Floating Outside the Constitution and Is Extremely Unfair], *Renmin ribao* [*People's Daily*, Beijing], September 4, 2001; *Zhongguo qingnian bao*, Beijing, July 26, 2001.

of foreign investors and businessmen" — have highlighted and energized those criticisms. So far, talk of reforming the *hukou* system has focused exclusively on the system's function of restricting internal migration.[15] The *hukou*-based monitoring and control of targeted people, however, has never even been mentioned in open publications. Internally, the general opinion in discussions has actually been to advocate more effective measures for sociopolitical control under the *hukou* system, primarily in the name of public security and fighting crime.[16]

"Deep Reform"

The PRC launched a new round of "deep" reform of the *hukou* system on June 10, 1997, when the State Council approved the MPS's *Experimental Plans on Reforming the* Hukou *System in Small Cities and Towns* and *Suggestions on Improving Rural* Hukou *Management*. The experimental stage was replaced with nationwide implementation of the reform on March 30, 2001.

This deep reform of the *hukou* system includes four aspects. First, there is a general relaxation of internal migration restrictions, especially for selected groups of people such as elderly parents, children, and highly educated "talents" and skilled workers. A streamlining of internal migration procedures for temporary or permanent migration (*qianyi*) has also taken place nationwide.[17]

Second, on October 1, 2001, the government began to abolish the decade-old rural-to-urban migration quota system in all small cities and towns (defined as county-level cities, county seats, and established

[15] For an extensive collection of the "internal" but dominant views on the *hukou* system and its necessity, see Wang Taiyuan, *Huzheng yu renkou guanli lilun yanjiu zhongshu* [*Comprehensive Summary on the Theoretical Study of the Hukou System and Population Management*] (Beijing: Qunzhong Press, 1997).

[16] For examples, see ibid. and Li Zhongxin, *Zhongguo shequ jingwu yanjiu* [*Study on China's Community Policing*] (Beijing: Qunzhong Press, 1999).

[17] Many of these relaxations have already been reported and documented in English. See Kam Wing Chan and Li Zhang, "The *Hukou* System and Rural-Urban Migration," and the special issue of *Chinese Law and Government*, May–June 2001.

towns).[18] Anyone who has a stable non-agricultural income and permanent residence in a small city or town for at least two years will automatically qualify to have an urban *hukou* and become a permanent local resident.[19] Some medium and even large cities are also authorized to do the same, with a higher and more specific income, employment, and residence requirement.[20] The government plans to take five years to complete this reform in part of the country, to "establish an integrated labor market for urban and rural residents in eastern China . . . in order to eliminate market segmentation there."[21]

Third, the localized practice of selective migration to the major cities, nicknamed "*hukou* for talents and investments," has been repackaged and nationally adopted. Under the new regulations, major urban centers openly set high prices for their much sought-after *hukou*.[22] Highly educated workers with at least a college degree hired by local employers can now easily get a local *hukou* in most Chinese cities.[23] The going rate for a set of three Beijing urban *hukou* (self, spouse, and one child) is no less than being a multi-millionaire investor or a foreign educated "talent."[24] Alternatively, one

---

[18] *Renmin ribao*, September 24, 2001; *South China Morning Post* (Hong Kong), September 29, 2001; *Nanfang dushibao* [*Southern Metro Daily*, Guangzhou], September 8, 2001; and *China New Agency News Dispatch* (Guangzhou), September 24, 2001.

[19] But "all the migration registration procedures are still to be followed strictly." *Zhongguo minzhen* [*China Civil Affairs*], Beijing no. 11 (November 2001): 57.

[20] *Renmin ribao*, September 4, 2001.

[21] Shen Wenmin, "Guanyu huji zhidu gaige de wenda" [Q&A on the *Hukou* System Reforms], *Renmin Ribao — huadongban* [*People's Daily — Eastern China* ed., Shanghai], August 29, 2001, 3.

[22] Chinese Central TV, *Jingji banxiaoshi* [*Half Hour on the Economy*], Beijing, August 9, 2001.

[23] Beijing Municipal Government's *Regulations on Encouraging Chinese Who Studied Overseas To Work or Open Business in Beijing*, May 1, 2000; *Shengzhou xueren* [*Chinese Scholars*], Beijing (June 2000), 47.

[24] According to one calculation, to live in Beijing and own a business that qualifies for Beijing *hukou* under the new regulations (employing 100 workers and paying 800,000 yuan tax a year), one must have a net worth of from 8 to 16 million yuan. See www.news.china.com (accessed January 19, 2002). However, the average asset size of private businesses in China was only 530,000 yuan in the late 1990s. *China News Agency*, Beijing, October 1, 2001.

can purchase a high-end "commercial" unit of an apartment to qualify as a local *hukou* applicant — a one-time cost of at least 500,000 yuan in cash, or 30 times the average annual wage in Beijing.[25] Similar schemes exist in Shanghai, with a slightly lower price tag.[26] To "purchase" a major city's urban *hukou* this way is still subject to the available moving-in quota. Furthermore, openly showing off huge wealth is not very wise socially or safety-wise in a society that is increasingly polarized in income distribution.[27] In Beijing, a city that had at least 2.37 million temporary *hukou* holders in 1999, only 715 families acquired the local urban *hukou* through housing purchases.[28] Other than the needed skilled labor and the super-rich, China's major urban centers want few "outsiders."

Finally, a national wave of "erasing" the rural/urban distinction in the *hukou* system took place in 2001 and 2002. Some better-developed provinces such as Fujian, Guangdong, Jiangsu, and Zhejiang simply abolished the legal distinction between the agricultural and non-agricultural *hukou* and started to register people as

---

[25] The "commercial" units are different from "cost-priced" or economy [*anju*] housing that is subsidized for local urban residents only. (*Business China*, Hong Kong, August 30, 1999, 4 and *China Daily*, Beijing, April 24, 2001) Since only the local *hukou* holders can apply for mortgage loans and borrow from their pension plans to make the down-payment, "outsiders" must purchase these *hukou*-qualifying apartments with one-time cash payments. Chinese People's Bank, *Provisional Measure on the Management of Individual Housing Loans*, April 28, 1997.

[26] To create a "new" image, Shanghai changed the name of its *hukou* system to "residential location" [*juzhudi*] system in its propaganda materials in 2001. But the legal name of "*hukou* system" was still used in late 2002. The 1993 (revised in 1998) blue-stamp *hukou* measure was also updated to enhance the strategy to attract talent and money. The required price for getting a Shanghai *hukou* through purchasing an apartment is lower than that in Beijing. A "low" price has attracted "too many" outsiders to the booming city; so in April 2002, the Shanghai government stopped issuing blue-stamp *hukou* to those who purchased a commercial housing unit while still allowing the "talents" and investors to come in.

[27] Mark O'Neil, "Dislike Grows for Incomers as Wealth Casts Shadow on City," *South China Morning Post*, June 25, 2001; author's interviews in Beijing and Shanghai, 1999–2002.

[28] "Jiujing shui caishi zuixuyao Beijing hukou de ren?" [Exactly Who Needs a Beijing *Hukou* the Most?], www.news.china.com (accessed January 6, 2002).

either local residents or temporary residents. To acquire a local *hukou* and thus become a full member of the local community still requires the applicant to meet locally set "entry conditions" that usually include a stable and officially sanctioned local job (with varied minimum pay) and a local legal residence for at least two years.[29] Some provinces ventured further. Guizhou, one of the poorest provinces, decided to give a small city/town urban *hukou* immediately to anyone who met the income and residence requirements, waiving the usual two-year waiting period. Shanxi, another less developed province, used the urban *hukou* to reward migrant rural people who had moved to those remote regions to reclaim desert land through tree-planting.[30] However, merely eight months into the reform, in mid-2002, this national wave to rename the rural/urban distinction was halted by Beijing, pending "further instructions." The suspension seems to be primarily the result of the lack of funding and infrastructure to quickly accommodate new urban residents' massive needs in education, health care, and social welfare.[31]

This round of "deep" reform, hence, was largely put on hold nationally in mid-2002 so as to secure a "stable and united environment" for the CCP's leadership change in 2002–2004. The new leadership of Hu Jintao and Wen Jiabao since 2003 has shown signs of considering the negatives of the *hukou* system as a political liability and trying in certain way to ease further some of the rough edges of the system. However, the 2001 reform of the *hukou* system remains very much unaccomplished six years later, especially above the level of small towns and cities, and has encountered significant regional discrepancies. By 2007, the PRC *hukou* system has in fact developed an even stronger degree of regionalization.

---

[29] *Hunan Ribao* [*Hunan Daily*, Changsha], January 20, 2002; *Renmin Ribao — huadongban,* January 9, 2002; *Nanfang dushi bao* [*Southern Urban Daily*, Guangzhou], September 8, 2001; *Xinhua Daily Telegraph*, Beijing, December 24, 2001.

[30] *Xinhua Daily Telegraph*, August 9, 2001.

[31] *China News Weekly* (Beijing) and *Huaxi dushi bao* [*Western China Metro News*, Chengdu], September 5, 2002.

On March 17, 2003, a young migrant from Wuhan of Hubei Province named Sun Zhigang was arrested by the police in Guangzhou for having no identification papers, where he was actually lawfully employed. He was in typical manner abused by the police, and was brutally beaten to death three days later by fellow inmates during the repatriation process. The case was reported by influential Chinese news outlets and led directly to a public outcry against the irrationality and injustice generated by the *hukou* system, especially the practice of forced repatriation. A dozen perpetrators, including several police officers, were sentenced to death or long jail terms. As a result, the PRC State Council canceled the 1982 "Measures of Detaining and Repatriating Floating and Begging People in the Cities" and issued "Measures on Repatriation of Urban Homeless Beggars" on June 18, 2003, and "Measures on Managing and Assisting Urban Homeless Beggars without Income" on June 20, 2003, establishing new rules governing the handling and assisting of destitute migrants. Many cities, including the most controlled Beijing municipality, decided soon afterwards that *hukou*-less migrants must be dealt with more carefully; they are no longer automatically subject to detention, fines, or forced repatriation unless they have become homeless, paupers, or criminals.[32]

This change of repatriation policy was a much needed reform and has been widely praised as a humane move under the "new politics" of the Hu–Wen era. However, as an interesting twist that vividly revealed the political reality in the PRC, the editor and the reporter of the newspaper, *Nanfang dushi bao* (*Southern Urban News*), that broke the Sun Zhigang story were soon arrested and sentenced to prison for multiple years under trumped up charges of bribery and corruption in 2004–2005. Furthermore, empirically, perhaps as a sign of the dual and complicated role of the *hukou* system, the relaxed measures of forced repatriation have seemed to

[32] Zhang Yinghong, "Sun Zhigang zhisi yu zhidu zhier" [The Death of Sun Zhigang and the Evil of the [*Hukou*] System], April 28, 2003, www.mlcool.com; *Caijing shibao* [*Financial and Economic Times*, Beijing], June 15, 2003; *Changsha wanbao* [*Changsha Evening News*], June 13, 2003; *Xinhua Daily Telegraph*, June 21, 2004.

cause a surge in the number of paupers and street people in places like Beijing's Tiananmen Square in the two years afterwards. Hence, discussion of a "Latin Americanization" of China's cities and concern about decay of the Chinese urban business environment emerged in the PRC's relatively free cyber space by mid-2005.[33]

To be sure, the latest *hukou* reform has relaxed and decentralized internal migration control mechanisms, mainly in small cities and towns; but it has not touched the sociopolitical control functions of the system. A majority of the over 100 million migrants or "floating population" still appear to be unable to change the location of their *hukou* permanently. In Ningbo of Zhejiang Province, a national model of the *hukou* reform, only about 30,000 migrants — less than two percent of the two million migrants from the countryside (who constitute one-third of the city's total population) — we are expected to qualify for the local *hukou* during the reform.[34] In Shijiazhuang of Hebei Province, only about 11,000 migrant workers (out of about 300,000 in the city) were qualified to apply for the local *hukou* in 2001. A key problem had been the difficulty for a migrant to find a stable job in the city, which had already been plagued by high unemployment for years.[35]

Limited and controlled, the latest *hukou* reform has started to change the unsightly and discriminatory legal distinction between rural and urban *hukou* holders. It is a major albeit highly symbolic victory of the advancing market institutions and new norms of citizenship and human rights in China. However, "the *hukou* system has not been abolished but only enhanced and improved with scientific means," declared a *hukou* expert associated with the MPS. The universal residential registration, the basic principles of internal

---

[33] Zheng Binwen, "China Should Carefully Prevent Latin Americanization," May 29, 2005, www.yannan.cn/data/detail.php?id=5889.

[34] "Ningbo hukou bilei hongran daota" [The *Hukou* Barriers Collapsing], *Nanfang zhoumu* [*Southern Weekend*, Guangzhou], August 31, 2001; *Zhongguo qingnianbao*, September 17, 2001.

[35] Josephine Ma, "Farmers Turn Noses Up at Life in the City," *South China Morning Post*, October 17, 2001.

migration control, and the uniquely Chinese style of sociopolitical control through the management of targeted people all continue and will be further "strengthened." The *hukou* reforms are to be "well-synchronized, and must consider the rational flow and allocation of talents and labor, and guarantee the stability of socioeconomic order."[36]

THE USEFULNESS OF THE *HUKOU* SYSTEM: GROWTH AND STABILITY

The PRC *hukou* system has been playing profound and complex roles in the Chinese political economy. It has contributed significantly to China's sociopolitical stability by creating an environment that is conducive to the perpetuation of an authoritarian regime, albeit still leaving some room for a possible elite democracy to develop. It has allowed the PRC to circumvent the so-called Lewis Transition and hence to enjoy rapid economic growth and technological sophistication in a dual economy with the existence of a massive surplus labor while producing tremendous irrationalities, imbalances, and waste and barriers to further development of the Chinese market. Finally, the PRC *hukou* system has created clear horizontal stratification, regional gaps, and personal discrimination that not only directly challenge social justice and equity but also potentially call China's political cohesion and national unity into question.[37]

There are positive institutional and policy aspects of this otherwise ethically questionable system. These positive functions of the *hukou* system will be outlined in this section. In the next section, the main negative consequences of the *hukou* system in order to convey the point that this system has a dual role in contemporary

---

[36] Wang Taiyuan's interview with *People's Net News* on October 1, 2001 (accessed January 19, 2002).

[37] The discussions in this and the next section draw heavily from my book, *Organizing through Division and Exclusion: China's Hukou System* (Stanford, CA: Stanford University Press, 2005), especially 129–165.

China that makes its reform highly difficult and complicated will be described.

The usefulness of the *hukou* system is especially seen in economic growth. The system has perpetuated the duality of the Chinese economy and economic irrationalities and inefficiency associated with low labor mobility. But overall, the *hukou* system has so far allowed the PRC to have rapid economic growth and a significant technological sophistication in a nation that has the world's largest unskilled labor force and one of the world's lowest per-capita resource and capital endowments.

Like other developing nations with nearly unlimited supplies of unskilled labor, China faces the narrow, arduous, and precarious Lewis Transition.[38] In the late 1990s, China had nearly 500 million rural laborers (people aged 16–55), about 150–240 million of whom were estimated to be surplus. Meanwhile, the rural population was still growing by more than 10 million every year. Moreover, only about 5 percent of rural laborers had any professional training or industrial skills by the early 2000s.[39] A normal Lewis Transition model of development would take too long and inevitably become impractical and unacceptable. With the *hukou*-based institutional exclusion, however, the PRC so far appears to have circumvented if not replaced the Lewis Transition. Instead of being impeded by a seemingly endless process of absorbing hundreds of millions of unskilled rural laborers before achieving economic take-off and eradicating dreaded poverty and backwardness, the Chinese economy has sustained a high rate of growth (8–9 percent annually) for

---

[38] Named after the developmental economist W. Arthur Lewis, this transition refers to the "necessary" process of transferring the unskilled rural labor to be industrial employees before a developing economy can truly take off. See W. Arthur Lewis, *The Theory of Economic Growth* (London: George Allen & Irwin, 1954, 1956) and *Dynamic Factors in Economic Growth* (New York: Advent Books, 1974).

[39] State Statistical Bureau, *Zhongguo tongji nianjian* [*China Statistical Yearbook*], 2000, 2001, and 2002 (Beijing: China Tongji Press, 2001); Hong Ma and Wang Mengkui, ed., *Zhongguo shichang fazhan baogao, 2000–2001* [*China Market Development Report 2000–2001*] (Beijing: Zhongguo Fazhan Press, 2001), 190.

more than two decades,[40] a duration and scale rarely seen and more than twice the average growth rate of other developing countries, basically bypassing this process while perpetuating its economic duality.

The exclusive and discriminatory nature of the PRC *hukou* system enables easy and fast capital accumulation in the urban sector and in the hands of the state (and gradually among the new, so-called Red Capitalists too), through naked massive extraction of value from the excluded rural population, and to a lesser extent from the smaller cities as well.[41] It also allows for easy prioritization of resource allocation in education and social development in the "in" areas and sectors, modernizing them quickly and well ahead of the rest of the country. Together, these efforts provide the basis for a state-led or -guided economic development strategy to proceed. A prosperous, protected, and privileged urban China is effective in reducing capital flight, a common occurrence that has plagued so many developing nations. These positive functions of the PRC *hukou* system have been especially obvious since the early 1980s when the market was finally introduced to replace the failed central-planning system as the main economic institution in China.

It takes the right kind of politics (a developmental commitment) and economic institution (the market system and norms) for the *hukou*-based institutional exclusion to function positively in a sea of unskilled labor. Conversely, this positive potential of the *hukou* system could not be well realized in a nonmarket economy such as the PRC's before the 1980s. A combination of market forces and the *hukou* system appears to be an effective way to circumvent the Lewis Transition.

---

[40] Estimates of China's growth rate vary, but most agree that the Chinese economy has grown at an average annual rate of above 8 percent for the past two decades. Nicholas R. Lardy, *Integrating China into the Global Economy* (Washington, DC: Brookings Institution, 2002), 11–13.

[41] Hu Angang, Yang Fan et al., *Daguo zhanlue: Zhongguo liyi yu shiming* [*A Great Power's Strategy: China's Interest and Mission*] (Shenyang: Liaoning Renmin Press, 2000), 294–295.

In China's case, an artificial environment has been created in which unskilled labor is administratively, cheaply, yet effectively excluded rather than genuinely but exorbitantly absorbed. Despite low and diminished income in the agricultural sector, the *hukou* system contributes immensely to the stable retention of millions of surplus rural laborers,[42] assisted by the widespread family-based but labor-holding agrarian moral economy in the countryside. The excluded rural sector functions as an artificial reservoir of fresh workers, conditioned by the ups and downs of the urban sector.[43] The Chinese socioeconomic duality is thus stabilized, even when a market economy is rapidly advancing. The drag effect commonly seen in large developing nations of a dual economy on the economic and technological progress in the modern or urban sector is hence minimized and controlled, at least so far. As a consequence, China's economic development has been able to maintain high-speed growth in a stable dual economy for many years, made possible by the constant and continued sacrifice of the excluded majority in the Chinese villages.

The *hukou* system allows for selective internal migration. It thus provides the talented or educated and the rich with a de facto cross-regional and cross-sector mobility so that skilled labor can achieve quasinational circulation and allocation. The regulated and restricted rural-to-urban migration also allows for a limited but steady supply of low-skilled but very hard-working labor that can be forced to work long hours with minimum pay and protection. The *liudong* (migrant) rural laborers are highly mobile and responsive to market demands for cheap labor. They create only temporary, minimal burdens for the cities and usually have no means of raising their own demands for benefits, promotion, job security, or the right to get the promised pay. Lacking organization and even a stable legal status, the migrant rural people who work in the cities are politically powerless and generally peaceful

[42] Susan Cook and Margaret Maurer-Fazio, ed., *The Workers' State Meets the Market: Labor in China's Transition* (London: Frank Cass, 1999).

[43] Solinger, *Contesting Citizenship*, 37, 54.

as a group.[44] As a consequence, the Chinese urban economy, especially in the metropolitan centers and state-designated special economic zones, has experienced spectacular development since the early 1980s. Capital-intensive and technology-intensive industries have achieved considerable scale and sophistication in a short period of time. More remarkably, this has taken place in a nation that still has between 150 million and 240 million unemployed, underemployed, or surplus laborers.

Controlled labor allocation in China provides the government with the means to distribute human resources and the economy with protected zones in which high salaries draw talent and nourish new commercial demands as well as entrepreneurship to facilitate the growth of the new market economy. At the same time, controlled labor mobility under the *hukou* system helps to ensure that the fast-developing urban centers have a continuous supply of cheap, able, willing labor with only minimal problems of massive relocation from rural areas. The PRC's slower urbanization, about half the average rate of developing nations after World War II but roughly comparable to that before 1900 in what are today's developed nations,[45] may indeed hold an important explanation for China's sociopolitical stability and economic success.

Major urban centers such as Shanghai and Beijing have now achieved a per-capita GDP equivalent to that of some European nations and the general technological and cultural sophistication of world-class metropolises. The first step in Deng Xiaoping's development strategy of letting some people and some places get rich first

[44] For example, in the increasingly common demonstrations and riots that sometimes stopped railway and highway traffic for many hours in the Lower Yangtze River Delta region, the "outside" or migrant workers who suffered most actually participated least, out of the six social groups of residents identified. Ding Yuanzhu, "Tiaozhan yu jiyu: WTO xia Zhongguo shehui fazhan de ruogan wenti" [Challenge and Opportunity: Several Issues in China's Social Development Under WTO], *Zhongguo shehui kexue jikan* [*Chinese Social Science Quarterly*], Hong Kong no. 32 (Winter 2000): 136.

[45] Harry Xiaoying Wu, "Rural to Urban Migration in the People's Republic of China," *China Quarterly* no. 139 (1994): 691–692.

and then pulling and pushing the whole nation into common prosperity was indeed well carried out in the Chinese cities, especially those in eastern and coastal China.[46] The *Hukou*-based institutional exclusion provided the basis for the urban-first rapid growth in a sea of unskilled and surplus labor. Of course, whether the second step of this strategy, a common prosperity, can take place extensively and quickly enough in China remains to be seen. It appears that the entire success or eventual failure of this two-step development model rests heavily on the future existence and function of the PRC *hukou* system.

In addition, the *hukou* system allows the PRC to utilize its limited resources of capital and talent to pursue state-of-the-art technology in selected sectors and industries. The *hukou* system hence contributes to the unusually rapid development of the Chinese economy in geographically designated areas and chosen industrial sectors. Focused efforts have transformed China from a near-autarkic economy to the sixth-largest trading nation (with increasing technology exports) and the second-largest recipient of foreign direct investment in the world in less than 20 years. As a result, China's foreign currency reserve ballooned from $10 billion in 1990 to more than one trillion US dollars in 2007, overtaking Japan as the world's largest holder of foreign currency reserves. Manipulation or creative use of the *hukou* system is seen by some Chinese scholars as an effective way to relocate people for the purpose of environmental protection.[47]

Another economic effect of the PRC *hukou* system is equally important, even critical, in the era of increasing globalization: helping

[46] Deng Xiaoping, *Deng Xiaoping wenxuan 1975–1982* [*Selected Works of Deng Xiaoping 1975–1982*] (Beijing: Renmin Press, 1983), 222; Jiang Zemin's speech at the celebration of the 80th anniversary of the CCP on July 1, 2001 — Jiang Zemin, *Lun sange daibiao* [*On the "Three Represents"*] (Beijing: Zhongyang Wenxian Press, 2001), 179.

[47] For example, Zhang Shanyu et al., *Renkou chuizhe fenbu guilu he Zhongguo shanqu renkou heli zaifenbu yanjiu* [*Study on Vertical Distribution of Population and Rational Redistribution of Population in Mountainous Areas*] (Shanghai: Huadong Normal University Press, 1996), 124–138.

to minimize the capital flight that has plagued so many developing nations. The artificially maintained tranquility, safety, and profitability in the urban centers, at the expense of the excluded rural majority under the *hukou* system, have made Chinese cities highly attractive for retaining nationally accumulated capital and for attracting significant foreign investment. Consistently since the mid-1990s, China has been second only to the United States in luring foreign direct investment.[48] Most foreign capital has gone to China's "in" urban sector. Despite Beijing's tight control of its domestic capital market, China nonetheless started to have its own capital-flight problem in the late 1980s. A decade later, by the end of the 20th century, even the official media started to report that China had the fourth-largest capital flight in the world, behind such well-known victims of capital flight as Venezuela, Mexico, and Argentina. In 1998 alone, at least $35 billion of capital illegally flowed out of China.[49] It is no exaggeration to argue that, without the *hukou*-based institutional exclusion, Chinese cities would be much less attractive to native and foreign investors, and China might indeed quickly have become Latin Americanized.

China's rapid economic development and industrialization have been relatively orderly, with limited problems of urban slums, urban poverty, and homelessness that have plagued many other developing nations. Massive slums have been deemed "an inevitable and expanding feature of cities in the developing countries."[50] Yet so far, in the Chinese cities, the urban slums are generally small, temporary, and insignificant,[51] as many of them are often forced to close down and their residents repatriated. For example, in the first half of 2001, in the Dongfeng township in the Chaoyang district of Beijing,

---

[48] An A. T. Keaney study in 2002 concluded that China replaced the United States as the most "attractive" place for foreign investors. Chris Giles, "China Attracts More Investors than the U.S.," *Financial Times*, September 23, 2002.

[49] *Dadi* [*Earth*], Beijing no. 96 (December 1999): 50–52.

[50] A. R. Desai and S. Devada Pillai, ed., *Slums and Urbanization* (London: Sangam Books, 1990), 2.

[51] Solinger, *Contesting Citizenship*, 231–234, 249–256; *Fazhi ribao* [*Legal Daily*, Beijing], November 21, 2001.

the authorities forcibly demolished illegally constructed rental housing in 66 residential compounds to enhance the management of floating people. For some more developed settlements of sojourning ruralites, such as Zhejiang Village in Beijing, the local government has invested in and even taken over the management to upgrade the settlement and integrate it.

In a way, the "positive" economic impact of the *hukou* system in China may be viewed as similar to that of the Westphalia international political system in the world economy since the end of the Middle Ages. Under the Westphalia system, there was a political division of the sovereign nations, a citizenship-based division of humankind, and an exclusion of foreigners maintained by the regulation and restriction of international migration. These may have indispensably contributed to the development of the modern capitalist market economy that has brought unprecedented economic growth and technological sophistication to the "in" parts of the world, primarily the nations that today form the Organization of Economic Cooperation and Development (OECD). The world economy has developed spectacularly in the past few centuries, but in the 2000s, 80 percent of humankind have been living in the less developed nations, excluded from most of the world's achievements.[52] China's prosperous urban centers in its eastern and coastal regions, compared with the country as a whole, may be functionally viewed as roughly equivalent to the OECD nations in comparison with the world. A key difference, however, is that the citizenship-based institutional divide between the OECD nations and the rest of the world is much more rigidly defined and forceful, hence more effectively enforced, than the *hukou* barriers that separate the urbanites in Shanghai and Beijing from the ruralites in the inland Chinese provinces. Furthermore, a central government in Beijing that regulates the *hukou* system and provides some cross-regional resource reallocation may have made the *hukou* system more humane and more tolerable to the excluded than the Westphalia system did.

---

[52] United Nations Development Program, *Human Development Report 2001* (New York: Oxford University Press, 2001), 144, 157.

THE NEGATIVES: BREWING PROBLEMS AND TENSIONS

A leading consequence of the PRC's *hukou* system has been, not surprisingly, a relatively small and slow urbanization in China. "Affected by the strict *hukou* management and the policy restricting rural-to-urban migration," concluded one Chinese scholar, "our urbanization has always fallen behind our industrialization and developed slowly . . . [hence] hundreds of millions of peasants who should have been in the cities are still kept away."[53] China's urbanization has been small and very slow ever since the mid-19th century, compared with the world urbanization rate. It almost stopped and even decreased for about two decades under Mao Zedong. During the reform era, China's urbanization has been significantly slower than its economic growth and industrialization rate, even though the adaptive measures and the practical relaxation of the *hukou* system have accelerated urbanization since the late 1980s. By 2000, China's urbanization was still less than 30 percent, whereas countries in the same range of per-capita GDP ($500–$730 by standard method or $2,000–$3,800 by purchasing-power-parity method) had an urbanization of 42.5–50 percent. Although by some indicators China's economic development in the late 1990s was at the level that the United States attained from the 1950s through the 1970s, China's urbanization was comparable to that in the United States only in the 1880s and 1890s.[54] As a result, on the one hand the United States and other developed countries treated China largely as an industrialized nation during its arduous entry into the WTO between 1987 and 2001. On the other hand, the overwhelming majority (74 percent) of China's population are still institutionally characterized and organized as rural residents, even though they do not all live in the countryside and work in the agricultural sector.

[53] Wang Fang, "Chengshihua yu renkou xiandaihua de guanxi" [The Relationship Between Urbanization and Population Modernization], *Renkou yanjiu* [*Population Research*], Beijing 25, no. 1 (2001): 31.

[54] Robert W. Forgel, "Aspects of Economic Growth: A Comparison of the U.S. and China," conference paper, Chengdu, China, 1999, 1–2.

Slow urbanization perpetuates a stable dual economy featuring a rural majority of the population and a stable, large, ever-increasing rural–urban disparity of income and resource distribution. The gap in living standards and cultures of the urban and rural sectors has become increasingly wide in recent decades. Officially, the urban–rural income gap was about 2.2 in 1964, 2.6 in 1978, 2.7 in 1995, and 2.8 in 2000. Semiofficially, the urban–rural income gap was estimated to be about 4.0 in 1993.[55] Including indirect income in the form of state subsidies, the gap stood at a staggering 5.0–6.0 by 2001.[56] Furthermore, while per-capita income for urbanites grew at 8.5 percent annually between 1999 and 2001, rural per-capita income increased barely 2 percent each year.[57] Per-capita government spending on social welfare for urban residents in the 1990s was some 30 times greater than for rural areas.[58] In 2000, Zhejiang Province, one of the three administrative units (along with Shanghai and Guangdong) that had experimented with a uniform social welfare program called "minimum living-standard protection" guaranteed poor urban *hukou* holders a minimum living standard of 240 yuan each per month while assuring poor holders of the rural *hukou* only 67 yuan.[59]

A rigid and stable dual economy based on the exclusion of the rural population has systematically and artificially suppressed the rural Chinese market and may have severely limited the growth potential for the Chinese economy as a whole, which needs domestic demand to increase continually. Nationally, per-capita consumer

---

[55] Zhong Yicai, "Chengxiang eyuan shehui de yonghe yu yingnong jingcheng" [*The Merging of the Dual Urban-Rural Societies and the Pulling of the Peasants into the Cities*], *Shehui kexue* [Social Sciences], Shanghai no. 1 (1995): 55–58.

[56] State Statistical Bureau, "Cong gini xishu kan pingfu chaju" [The Gap Between Rich and Poor Based on the Gini Index], *Zhongguo guoqing guoli* [*China's National Conditions and Strength*], Beijing no. 97 (January, 2001): 29.

[57] PRC State Statistical Bureau data, ibid., 28.

[58] Liu Cuixiao, "*Zhongguo nongmin de shehui baozhang wenti*" [*The Issue of Social Security for Chinese Peasants*], *Faxue yanjiu* [*Legal Studies*], Beijing no. 2 (2002).

[59] Among the 259,000 poor who were protected in 2001 in that city, 230,000 were rural *hukou* holders. *Nanfang zhoumu*, October 18, 2001, 2.

spending in the cities is 3.5 times as great as in the rural areas. The rural residents, more than two-thirds of the total population, consume less than one-third of the goods and services produced in the PRC.[60] Raising the purchasing power of the rural Chinese majority would probably provide the Chinese economy with a great push in the years ahead.

In addition to perpetuating a dual economy and retarding the rural consumer market, the *hukou* system has created significant irrationalities in labor allocation and utilization. A two-tier, well-segregated labor market for local urban *hukou* holders and outsiders exists in Chinese cities, leading to inequalities and inefficiencies within the same locality. There is often an oversupply of educated and skilled labor, especially professionals, in major urban centers while a chronic shortage of such labor plagues small cities, remote regions, and especially the rural areas. In order to continue living in the desirable urban centers to which they are socially accustomed, many of the highly educated have abandoned their acquired expertise and skills to take whatever jobs they can get, thus wasting tremendous educational resources. In almost every Chinese city, there are hundreds of thousands of surplus laborers, usually former state employees with the urban *hukou* who could not find or are not willing to take jobs outside their *hukou* zones. Meanwhile, millions of more rural workers are floating among the cities looking for any work at all.

Promoting Inequalities

An obviously negative impact of the *hukou* system has been that it brews regional disparities and inequality. As a high price of *hukou*-assisted rapid growth, China has had a very uneven economic development across regions. A group of influential Chinese scholars concluded that "there are three main disparities in contemporary Chinese society: the disparities between the peasants and the industrial

[60] *Zhongguo guoqing guoli* no. 97 (January 2001): 28.

workers, between the urban and rural areas, and among the regions."[61] The PRC *hukou* system is fundamentally responsible for all three.[62] In addition to the chronic and widening income and spending gaps between rural and urban residents, there is a clearly visible regional gap of per-capita income in China. In fact, the government in the late 1990s officially divided the country into three regions: the developed region of the 12 eastern and coastal provinces and metropolises, the less developed region of the nine central provinces, and the undeveloped region of the remaining nine western provinces.[63]

Despite official efforts to achieve a more balanced development, including the latest Grand Development of the West campaign, the major urban centers continue to get the lion's share of investment and government spending. Six provinces or metropolises in eastern China received 54 percent of all Chinese research and development funding in 1994; the 18 provinces in central and western China got only 35.9 percent.[64] In 1990, Beijing had the highest per-capita government spending at 633 yuan, about 2.7 times the lowest spending of 106 yuan in Henan Province, only a couple of hundred miles away. In 1996, Shanghai had the highest per-capita government spending of 2,348 yuan, 8.45 times the lowest, 278 yuan, also in Henan Province. In 1998, per-capita investment in the three metropolises (Shanghai, Beijing, and Tianjin) was 7.3, 5, and 3.1 times

---

[61] Hu Angang, Wang Shaoguang, and Kang Xiaoguang, *Zhongguo diqu chaju baogao* [*Report on China's Regional Disparities*] (Shenyang: Liaoning Renmin Press, 1995), 223.

[62] There are, naturally, many other factors responsible for the East-West gap in China. Dali Yang [*Beyond Beijing: Liberalization and the Regions in China* (London: Routledge, 1999)] described a Chinese political system in which the PRC has been led by an east coast "oligarchy" so that the interests of the east dominate.

[63] Lu Wenlong and Huang Minyou, "Qian fada diqu jingji fazhan qianyi" [Preliminary Discussion on Economic Development in the Less Developed Region], *Shehui kexuejia* [Social Scientist], Guilin no. 69 (January 1998): 21–26.

[64] Guo Tong, "Keji touru: Dongzhongxibu bupingheng" [R&D Investment: Uneven Among the East, Central and West], *Zhongguo xinxibao* [*China Journal of Information*], Beijing, August 3, 1995: 1.

higher, respectively, than the national average, while the like in Guizhou Province was only 33 percent of the national average.[65]

Not surprisingly, foreign investment is very unevenly concentrated. By 1998, 88 percent of foreign direct investment was in eastern and coastal China, and five provinces in this region received over 63 percent of China's total foreign direct investment. Dividing China's provincial-level administrative units into four regions, one recent study found great inequality in educational opportunities between the various regions. In the late 1990s, the illiteracy rate in region 1 (the metropolises) was as low as 4–14 percent, but it was 14–52 percent in region 4 (the western provinces and regions). The government spent on average 2,308 yuan per student in region 1 but only 340 yuan in region 4.[66] Another study showed that, by the late 1990s, the average education of the workers was eight to 10 years of schooling in the metropolises and provinces in eastern and coastal regions but only three to six years of schooling in the western provinces.[67]

At the end of the 1990s, per-capita annual GDP in Shanghai was over 28,000 yuan, 12 times higher than in Guizhou Province (merely 2,323 yuan).[68] The average annual urban wage in the eastern coastal provinces was 2,702 yuan, 35 percent (up from 29.2 percent in 1994) higher than in the central and western areas. The average annual wage in the same period in the coastal province of Guangdong was twice that in neighboring Jiangxi Province (3,595 versus 1,713 yuan). It is estimated that the east–west annual income

---

[65] State System Reform Commission, *Gaige neichan* [*Internal Reference on Economic Reform*], Beijing, internal publication, selected issues, no. 273 (1998): 22. Hu Angang and Zou Ping, *Shehui yu fazhan: Zhongguo shehui fazhan diqu chaju yanjiu* [*Society and Development: A Study of China's Regional Gap in Social Development*] (Hangzhou: Zhejiang Renmin Press, 2000), 5.

[66] Xue Lan Rong and Tianjian Shi, "Inequality in Chinese Education," *Journal of Contemporary China* 10, no. 26 (February, 2001): 117–121.

[67] Tan Youlin, "Zhongguo laodongli jiegou de quyu chayi yanjiu" [A Study on the Regional Difference of China's Labor Force], *Renkou yu jingji* [*Population and Economics*], Beijing no. 124 (January 2001): 57.

[68] Hu and Zou, *Shehui yu fazhan*, 3.

gap grew from 48 percent in 1986 to 52 percent in 1991 (2,283 yuan in the east and 1,095 in the west). In 2000, urban *hukou* holders' highest per-capita annual income was 11,802 yuan (in Shanghai); the lowest was only 4,745 yuan (in Shanxi). Rural *hukou* holders' highest per-capita annual income was 5,596 yuan (again in Shanghai), and the lowest was only 1,331 yuan (in Tibet). By 2001, the highest per-capita urban income was 4.8 times greater in eastern than in western China.[69] Some cities' average income of urban *hukou* holders was six to seven times higher than others'.[70] To accept the reality of regional disparity legally and politically, the PRC has set different pay scales for state employees in the different regions ever since the mid-1950s.[71]

By the 1990s, the government-mandated minimum wage in the PRC varied drastically across regions, separated by the *hukou* system and other community barriers. The state's urban poverty-relief scheme also varied across regions. Not only does there exist in China a huge income gap between urban and rural residents and between the eastern and coastal areas and the interior regions, but also the price of state-allocated resources is significantly different across the *hukou*-divided sectors and the layers of Chinese society. In 2001, for example, China's state-monopoly power companies charged residents living in the prosperous urban centers of Shanghai and Beijing only 0.5 yuan per kw. But they charged the residents of other large- and medium-sized cities about 0.78 yuan per kw, county towns 45 percent more, and rural areas still another 50 percent

---

[69] State Planning Commission figures in *Jingji gongzhuzhe xuexi ziliao* [*Study Materials for Economic Workers*], Beijing no. 68 (1994): 7; *Hunan Ribao* [*Hunan Daily*, Changsha], April 18, 2001.

[70] Li Rujian, "*Difang wailai renkou guanli fagui chubu tangtao*" [Preliminary Study on the Regulations of the Management of Migrant Population], *Renkou yu jingji* no. 128 (May 2001): 21.

[71] For the detailed state-mandated regional differentiation (by county) in pay and subsidies in the different regions from 1954 to 1977, see Ministry of Personnel, *Renshi gongzuo wenjian xuanbian* vol. 2. [*Selected Documents on Personnel Work*], multi-volumes, internal publication (Beijing: Laodong Renshi Press, 1986), 22–25, 86–126, and 478–487.

higher.[72] This regional gap in income and standard of living, associated with and compounded by the regional investment and development gap, imposes increasing pressure on the PRC *hukou* system by creating voluntary, spontaneous, massive, lasting migrations to the richer regions and forcing it to make adaptive changes.

Politically, the regional gap is contributing to the rise of regionalism and regional protectionism that have already become major destabilizing factors in China in the early 2000s.[73] Regional differentiation in production costs, especially labor costs, may lead to a segmented Chinese market.[74] A legal fragmentation seems to have emerged, facilitating local protectionism and agency protectionism to pervert and hinder reforms and development of the Chinese legal system.[75] In response, Beijing has issued numerous decrees to tear down economic barriers erected by the local corporatist and protectionist activity.[76] The central government's political stability and

---

[72] Data provided by Yang Fan, a senior researcher at the Institute of Economic Studies, Chinese Academy of Social Science, October 2001. Rural residents of the central province of Henan were commonly charged two to three times as much as urban residents for electricity. Cao Jinqing, *Huanghe biande Zhongguo: yige xuezhe dui xiangcun shehui de guancha yu sikao* [*China by the Yellow River: A Scholarly Observation and Reflection of the Rural Society*] (Shanghai: Shanghai Wenyi Press, 2000), 601, 744.

[73] Some provincial and prefecture governments set up and enforce quotas for shipping in goods from outside. Chen Dongyou, ed., *Zhongguo nongmin* [*China's Peasants*] (Nanchang: Jiangxi Gaoxiao Press, 1999), 206. Even the official journals start to list various "striking" cases of regional and local protectionism that damage law enforcement and market development. *Dadi* no. 101 (May 2001): 46–47.

[74] One author even estimates that by 2020, the "Greater Chinese Economy" may form up to 10 distinctive economic regions. C. W. Kenneth Keng, "China's Future Economic Regionalism," *Journal of Contemporary China* 10 no. 29 (November 2001): 607–610. In 2004, it was reported that the PRC government was planning to formally create eight relatively distinct economic regions in the country. *Jinghua shibao* [*Jinghua Times*, Beijing], June 6, 2004.

[75] Stanley B. Lubman, *Bird in a Cage: Legal Reform in China after Mao* (Stanford, CA: Stanford University Press, 1999).

[76] One early effort was the State Council's Directive on Breaking Down Regional Blockade of the Market, November 10, 1990. A later such effort was the almost identically titled State Council Decree 303 of April 12, 2001.

power and even the unity of the nation may be at stake.[77] In many ways, the Chinese economy is not just a dual economy of rural and urban sectors but more a collection of several regional economies that are at various stages of development, with hugely different degrees of economic prosperity, separated chiefly by the *hukou* system.

Utilizing its Human Development Index (HDI), the United Nations has sponsored studies to measure overall socioeconomic development throughout the world. In its reports of 1999 and 2001, the UN listed China's regional gaps in socioeconomic development as among the largest in the world. Out of 162 nations, China ranked number 98 in overall HDI in 1999 and number 87 in 2001, just above Jordan in the medium human development range. By the same measurement, however, China's most developed regions, Shanghai, Beijing, and Tianjin (all metropolises in eastern or coastal China), ranked 25th, 27th, and 30th, in the high human development range, equivalent to Greece, Singapore, and Malta, respectively. China's least developed regions, Qinghai, Guizhou, and Tibet (all in western China), ranked 135th, 137th, and 147th, in the low human development range, equivalent to Haiti, the Sudan, and Angola, respectively.[78] In other words, developed societies and the poorest societies coexist within one nation not only vertically but also horizontally. This is indeed a mighty testament to the power of the *hukou* system.

A COUNTRY OF MANY LAYERS AND DIFFERENT SOCIETIES

Consequently, the *hukou* system has twisted Chinese social life to create a peculiar horizontal stratification. This system may have provided organization and social stability to a large nation, especially in

[77] Hu Angang, Wang Shaoguang, and Kang Xiaoguang, *Zhongguo diqu chaju baogao*, 27–31, 90–97, and 258–278; Minxin Pei, "China's Governance Crisis," *Foreign Affairs* 81, no. 5 (September–October 2002): 96–109.

[78] According to the calculation by Hu and Zou, *Shehui yu fazhan*, 7–9, based on United Nations Development Program (UNDP), *Human Development Report* (New York: Oxford University Press, 1999); UNDP, *The China Human Development Report* (New York: Oxford University Press, 1999), 58–62.

a time of rapid economic development and social and cultural change. It forms solid groupings and associations beyond family and employment relations. Ethically, however, institutional exclusion produces troubling questions about the equity and equality of the human and civil rights of citizens of the same nation. A slow urbanization naturally segregates the citizens and creates cultural biases against the excluded rural population.

Furthermore, institutional exclusion discourages and even hinders the development of creativity and ingenuity that often accompany people's horizontal and vertical mobility in a society. Chinese culture, social stratification, and social norms and values have all developed regional characteristics as well as a rural-versus-urban differentiation. As in other developing nations, naturally, a social stratification in both rural and urban communities has significantly developed vertically along the fault line of haves versus have nots very rapidly in China. The government estimates that an increasingly small group of upper-income earners are now controlling a staggeringly large portion of China's wealth: In 1990, about 10 percent of the Chinese owned 40 percent of the total bank deposits; by 2000, 1 percent of depositors (or 5 percent of the total population) owned 40 percent of the total bank deposits, and 20 percent of the depositors, mainly urban *hukou* holders, owned 80 percent of the total bank deposits, which is still the main form of savings and investment.[79] The aggregate national Gini index (a measurement of income equality) was a staggering 0.45 by 2001 (0.397 in 1999).[80]

In contrast to many other countries, the increasingly serious inequality of income distribution appears in China not only vertically but also horizontally or geographically. Social stratification in the PRC, therefore, is not only vertical, as in all other nations, but also rigidly spatial and horizontal, based on the administratively defined geographical location of the people under the *hukou* system.

---

[79] *Zhongguo minhang bao* [*Chinese Civil Aviation Daily,* Beijing], July 17, 2000; Ni Jianmin, Deputy Director of China Institute of Policy Studies, a front organization of the CCP's Central Policy Study Office, speech in Singapore, September 27, 2001.

[80] SSB, *Cong gini xishu kan pingfu chaju*, 30.

In the early 2000s, the PRC has about 1.3 billion people living in 23 provinces, four province-level regions, and four province-level metropolises. These 31 administrative units have a total of 675 cities, with about 350 million urban residents or nonagricultural *hukou* holders, 26.1 percent of the total population. These cities are administratively ranked at four levels: municipal or provincial (4), deputy provincial (SEZs or separately planning cities, 15), prefectural (229), and county (427).[81]

Generally, a city at or above the deputy-provincial level is considered to be among the elite metropolises, subject to the tightest migration control. Cities that have over a million urban residents are considered to be large cities; those with five hundred thousand, medium-sized cities. Together, these three types of cities constitute China's cultural and socioeconomic centers, the most desirable places to live. The remaining small cities and towns are urban areas of a lower social rank, but these clearly are still ranked higher socially and culturally by the people than the rural areas. The reform era has somewhat blurred the boundaries between some urban areas (especially the small cities and towns in remote regions) and prosperous villages in suburban regions like the Pearl River Delta and the Lower Yangtze River Delta. Table 1 presents this peculiar, horizontal social stratification in the PRC in the early 2000s.

Such a social division is a result and, in turn, a cause of the grossly uneven distribution of political power and economic resources and opportunities based on the people's *hukou* type and location. For a socialist PRC, the existence of such a complicated, comprehensive, rigid, highly entrenched social stratification, created and maintained by the people's government, is indeed one of the great ironies in human history. The findings of a study on the regional demographic features and the direction and volume of internal migration in China nicely fit

[81] Ministry of Public Security, *2000 Niandu quanguo fengxianshi renkou tongji ziliao* [*Statistical Information on the Population by Cities and Counties in the PRC, 2000*] (Beijing: Qunzhong Press, 2001), 302; Liu Junde and Wang Yuming, *Zhidu yu chuangxin: Zhongguo chengshi zhidu de fazhan yu gaige xinlun* [*Institution and Innovation: A New View on the Development and Reform of China's City System*] (Nanjing: Dongnan University Press, 2000), 6–8.

Table 1: China's Horizontal Stratification

1. Elite Chinese — urban *hukou* holders living in the metropolises, provincial capitals, and large cities — 6.3 percent of the total population.
2. High Class — urban *hukou* holders living in the medium cities — 10.4 percent of the total population.
3. Middle Class — urban *hukou* holders living in the small cities and towns (18.2 percent) and rural *hukou* holders living in the suburban areas of the metropolises and provincial capital cities (3.4 percent) — 21.6 percent of the total population.
4. Low Class — rural *hukou* holders living in the rural areas — 70.5 percent of the total population.

the pattern of such a horizontal stratification. Even the newly emerging "class relations and class consciousness" in China now "center upon place, power, and particularism."[82]

Even Chinese genes and the Chinese psyche are believed by some to have been adversely affected by the *hukou* system. One study believes that the dual society in China is producing a "reverse elimination" effect on national "population quality," decreasing the physical and mental quality of the Chinese nation and "even threatening the survival of our nation," since the excluded "low-quality" and poorly educated rural population grows faster: In the late 1980s, the rural population, excluded and poorer, had a 2.4 percent birth rate and 1.7 percent annual growth rate, whereas the supposedly higher-quality urban population had only a 1.4 percent birth rate and 0.9 percent annual growth rate.[83] Similarly, others believe that the *hukou* system has spoiled the supposedly lazy, arrogant urbanites,

[82] Wang Guixin, *Zhongguo renkou fenbu yu quyu jingji fazhan* [*Population Distribution and Regional Economic Development in China*] (Shanghai: Huadong Normal University Press, 1997), 308–352; Sally Sargeson, *Reworking China's Proletariat* (New York: Macmillan/St. Martin's Press, 1999), 17.

[83] Xia Jizhi and Dang Xiaoji, ed., *Zhongguo de jiuye yu shiye* [*Employment and Unemployment in China*] (Beijing: Zhongguo Laodong Press, 1991), 110, and Tian Bingxin. *Zhongguo diyi zhengjian: Zhongguo huji zhidu diaocha shougao* [*The First ID of China: Manuscript of Investigation of China's* Hukou *System*] (Guangzhou: Guangdong Renmin Press, 2003), 127–149.

created inferiority complexes, helplessness, and blind prejudice and hatred among the ruralites, and encouraged inbreeding that has lowered the population quality in the rural areas.[84]

The excluded Chinese peasants still by and large accept their fate under the PRC *hukou* system as it is. The extent to which those who are excluded in the rural and backward areas, three-quarters of the total Chinese population, will continue in their role as the reservoir to hold the unskilled millions, hence to make a multigenerational sacrifice for rapid modernization of the Chinese urban economy, remains increasingly uncertain. Unemployment pressure alone, likely to be significantly worsened by China's new WTO membership, may make the *hukou*-based institutional exclusion even less bearable. The 100-million-strong migrant (*liudong*) population — registered holders of temporary *hukou* and unregistered *mangliu* (blind floaters) — clearly a second-class citizenry outside their home towns in their own country, has already become a major source of the rising crime rate and even of organized crime in the PRC.[85] How much and how quickly trickle-down and spillover effects of prosperous, glamorous urban centers will be felt in rural areas will be key to the continuation of China's sociopolitical stability and economic growth under the *hukou* system.

CONCLUSION: HARD QUESTIONS AND TOUGH CHOICES

With reforms and improvements, the *hukou* system now still allows Beijing to rule and organize the Chinese people by dividing them into segments, bounded and controlled by the individual's *hukou* type and location. This omnipresent and powerful, albeit adapted and adjusted, system is alive and well, and performs important functions in China's sociopolitical control, economic development, and social and spatial stratification.

---

[84] Cheng Tiejun, "*Zhongguo hukou zhidu de xianzhuang yu weilai*" [The Current Status and Future of China's *Hukou* System], in *Zhongguo dalu de shehui, zhengzhi, jingji* [*Society, Politics, and Economy of the China Mainland*], Li Shaomin, ed. (Princeton, NJ: Center for Modern China, 1992), 408.

[85] Li Zhongxin, *Zhongguo shequ jingwu yanjiu*, 11–13, 23–24.

A leading function of the *hukou* system remains the control of internal migration. Adaptations and reforms have led to considerable decentralization of this operation. New measures have been devised to allow for a varied degree of de facto mobility for the powerful, the rich, the educated and talented, and for the needed manual laborers. Since 2001, the legal distinction between agricultural and nonagricultural *hukou* and the migration quota in the small cities and towns have started to be replaced by locally set "entry conditions" that still nonetheless function as effective tools for the government to regulate and restrict internal migration. Consequently, a classic case of dual economy and dual society has been developing in China for the past half century. In practice, not only does a legal rural–urban duality exist in China; but also there is the clear presence of a metropolitan-city-town multiplicity in China's unique sociopolitical, economic, and cultural stratification that is both vertical and horizontal.

The decades-old sociopolitical control through the tiered focal management of the targeted segments of the population continues. It has been only slightly relaxed, although its administration has been somewhat rationalized in the direction of crime fighting and more awareness of individuals' legal rights. The economic and cultural changes in the past decades have also weakened the effectiveness of the targeted-people scheme. Still largely operating in secrecy, the social control function of the *hukou* system is expected to continue as a pillar of the PRC's unparalleled organization of the largest nation on earth. It allows the police constantly to monitor and control those people selected as the most "threatening" individuals and groups in the society, thus consolidating the PRC's social order. In the summer of 2001, when the rural-to-urban migration quota was partially eliminated in the PRC, one MPS senior official called for further "reducing the undue burden on the *hukou* system by getting rid of its economic and education functions" so as to "enhance the *hukou* system" and "restore its original" main mission of population management and social control.[86] Indeed, the police

[86] Interviews reported by China Net's News Center, August 20, 2001, www.newsw.china.com (accessed March 23, 2002).

has been internally calling for a further enhancement of the targeted-people management in its battle against Muslim terrorist cells in the remote regions of western China, where many non-Han ethnic groups live.[87]

As "the central institutional mechanism defining the city–countryside relationship and shaping important elements of state–society relations in the People's Republic," the *hukou* system "not only provided the principal basis for establishing identity, citizenship, and proof of official status, it was essential for every aspect of daily life."[88] The *hukou* system fundamentally touches and determines the life of every Chinese since it comprehensively collects data on every citizen, identifies and stratifies individuals and regions, controls population movement, and allocates resources and opportunities.[89] A Chinese scholar concluded that the *hukou* system has been "affixing people's social career, role, personal identity, production and living space; restricting the free migration of people and labor; maintaining and strengthening the dual economic and social structure between the urban and the rural areas."[90]

A majority of the Chinese population, the rural residents, have been "peacefully" excluded under the PRC *hukou* system. The much smaller urban population (only 14–26 percent of the total population) has had qualitatively much better access to economic and social opportunities, and activities and benefits. It has also dominated Chinese politics. To a lesser extent, urban residents in smaller cities and in less developed regions have also been the excluded

---

[87] Cheng Zhiyong and Bo Xiao, ed., *Qiangzhan yu qiangan. [Gun-battles and Gun-cases]*, internal publication (Beijing: Qunzhong Press, 2000), 129–130, 164, 253–254.

[88] Cheng Tiejun and Mark Selden, "The Origins and Social Consequences of China's *Hukou* System," p. 644.

[89] Yu Depeng, *Chengxiang shehui: cong geli zouxiang kaifang — Zhongguo huji zhidu yu hujifa yanjiu (Urban and Rural Societies: From Separation to Openness — A Study of China's Hukou System and Hukou Laws)* (Jinan: Shangdong Renmin Press, 2002), 1–2.

[90] Peng Yiyong, "Shehui zhuyi shichang jingji yu hukou tizhi gaige" [Socialist Market Economy and the Reform of the *Hukou* System], *Xuehai* [*Sea of Learning*], Nanjing, no. 5 (1994): 39.

compared to those living in major urban centers or regions more favored by the government in terms of investment, subsidies, or policy flexibilities.

The Chinese reforms since 1978 have led to some changes of the *hukou* system. Money has eroded some of the old edges of the system, while creating new divisions and exclusions in China between the haves and the have nots. The rich, the powerful, and the talented (the Chinese "meritocracy")[91] have now achieved de facto national mobility granted to them by the adaptive measures of the *hukou* system. Controlled, limited, but practical labor mobility has also been developed for low-skilled or even unskilled laborers.[92] At the same time, the PRC *hukou* system has facilitated both regionalism and communitarianism in Chinese political economy.

A Chinese scholar concluded recently that China's "political elite, economic elite, and intellectual elite have all reached a consensus and joined an alliance" to rule China as an institutionally protected urban minority through the CCP's one-party monopoly of political power.[93] When the ruling elite is viewed as encountering serious problems of governance, the *hukou* system has become an even more crucial tool of repression and control. It has directly enabled the seemingly puzzling coexistence of a rapidly developing, fairly diverse, dynamic market economy and a stable communist one-party authoritarian regime in an era of revolutionary information technology.

By circumventing the Lewis Transition, China has so far achieved rapid economic growth and technological sophistication in a stable dual economy with relatively small and slow urbanization. Urban slums have so far remained insignificant in the PRC. Yet the *hukou*

---

[91] For how the meritocracy works in China in the 1990s, see Borge Bakken, *The Exemplary Society: Human Improvement, Social Control, and the Dangers of Modernity in China* (Oxford: Oxford University Press, 2000), 254–276.

[92] For the status and prospects of China's labor allocation, see Fei-Ling Wang, *From Family to Market: Labor Allocation in Contemporary China* (Lanham, MD: Rowman & Littlefield, 1998).

[93] Kang Xiaoguang, "Weilai 3–5 nian Zhongguo dalu zhengzhi wendingxing fenxi" [Analysis of the Political Stability Issue on the China Mainland in the Next 3–5 Years], *Zhanlue yu guanli* [*Strategy and Management*], Beijing no. 3 (2003): 1–2, 10.

system directly perpetuates a duality in the Chinese economy and a market segmentation that together lead to inefficiency and waste. In the long run, the currently significant benefits of the *hukou* system may fade, as there is no guarantee of a real and speedy spillover or trickle-down effect of the "in," prosperous urban sector in coastal China upon the excluded rural and inland regions.

How long a *hukou*-based rapid but uneven economic growth can last, at the expense of excluding the majority of the population, remains a legitimate and profound question. Another leading concern is the runaway vertical and horizontal social stratification of the Chinese society. The combination of these two stratifications not only has affected the allocation of resources, opportunities, and life chances in general for every Chinese, but also has largely shaped Chinese values, behavioral norms, and culture that are not conducive to rule of law, equity of human rights, or individual freedom. A small elite of urban *hukou* holders living in major urban centers are masters of this people's republic at the expense of excluding and discriminating against the majority of the people who are growing in discontent and rightfully angry.[94] This is indeed a very peculiar and precarious class structure and social stratification in our time — a "socialist feudalism," as the sociologist Martin Whyte calls it.

Clearly, the PRC *hukou* system right now poses serious ethical and legal questions that demand creative and effective solutions. The system has systematically created barriers against labor mobility, thus limiting the rationalization of a young market economy and perpetuating poverty for the majority of the population living in the rural areas as "surplus" and excluded labor. The lack of genuine vertical and horizontal mobility, in addition to the lack of freedom of speech and individual and property rights, has seriously impeded creativity and innovation in China. The *hukou* system has legitimized unfair treatment and naked exploitation of the excluded

[94] Incidentally, among my interviewees, privileged urban dwellers tend to take the PRC *hukou* system for granted and assert that the *hukou* system "really does not make much difference in life," while the excluded "outsiders," especially the ruralites, insist that the *hukou* system affects their lives personally, persistently, and profoundly. Author's interviews, 1999–2005.

population (mainly the rural residents). It contributes to the growing regionalization of the Chinese political economy with profound consequences for China's economic development, the capacity of the central government, and even the unity of the Chinese nation. Yet, to Chinese leaders, the *hukou* system still appears to be important, reliable, and effective. Currently, much of this system is still largely internalized as a part of the Chinese culture and enjoys a high degree of legitimacy, even among the excluded. Obviously, the *hukou* system relies heavily on the political power of the CCP to continue; yet the functions of the system have also become highly critical to the stability and continuation of the CCP political system. Mounting tensions in the system and the resultant scrutiny and criticisms are likely to force more changes as the PRC state may have to retreat further. Ultimately, the fate of the *hukou* system will reflect and determine the fate of the current PRC sociopolitical order and China's chance of realizing its enormous economic potential.

Chapter

3

Resources and Strategies: Conflicts and Their Consequences in the Chinese Real Estate Market

Tianfu Wang and Bobai Li

INTRODUCTION

Walking on the city streets of China nowadays, one may easily find that the skylines are crowded with stylish new high-rises and numerous cranes. All this reminds people that the Chinese cities are experiencing an era of (re)construction. Old courthouses and low-story buildings are being torn down, and replacing them are new ones in newly planned communities. In this round of urbanization, construction of residential housing plays a big role. After living in a small area with the whole family for a long time and two decades of increase in household income since the middle of 1980s, ordinary Chinese urbanites now not only desire for a larger and better-designed apartment but also can afford to purchase one.

In recent years, purchasing an apartment has become one of the most popular topics in casual talks among friends, neighbors, and colleagues, in radio and TV call-in programs, in newspaper write-in columns, in discussion boards on the Internet, and even in formal discussions among the National People's Congress representatives during their annual meetings. Without exaggeration, home buying touches every corner of the society and has sweeping influences on the daily lives of ordinary people. In addition to the overwhelming enthusiasm that comes with moving to new homes after years of suppressed desire for better living conditions, one of the other primary reasons for such heated discussions is that the process of purchasing an apartment is filled with traps, conflicts, and tactical moves on all sides of those who are bargaining. It is common that the purchase process results in home buyers' complaints to the administration, class law suits against developers, collective demonstrations on the streets, and, in extreme cases, bloodshed.

HOUSING DISTRIBUTION AND COMMERCIALIZATION

During the planned-economy era in China, housing in the cities was constructed and distributed by the state (in effect, the work unit or *danwei*). Land belonged to the state, and selling and buying of land were essentially not possible. A housing market basically did not exist.[1] Transfers of the right of use of land had to be approved by the government. Individual work organizations often started the construction of residential housing with applications to the government for a land lot. Once applications were approved, the organization would locate funds, either through financial allocation from the government or through approved withholding of profits. Next, the construction of the housing had to strictly follow the government regulations in building design and size of apartment units. Finally, distribution of apartments also followed the government regulations.[2] In addition, some urban residents applied to rent an apartment from the city bureau of housing management.

---

[1] Liu Lin, "Historical Retrospect: Development of the Chinese Real Estate," in *The Development Report of China's Real Estate*, vol. 1, ed. Niu Fengrui (Beijing: Social Sciences Documentation Publishing House, 2004), 11–18.

[2] Li Qiang, *Shehui fenceng he pingfu chaju* [*Social Stratification and Fortune Difference*] (Fuzhou: Lujiang Press, 1993).

Thus, all housing properties belonged to the state, and urban residents rented housing from the state. Consistent with low salaries during the state socialist period, urban residents only paid nominal rent. Take the example of Beijing. From the 1950s to the mid-1980s, household rent expenditure only accounted for 6–9 percent of the average income.[3] The rent covered only the maintenance costs. In short, there was no commercial housing before the middle of the 1980s in the Chinese cities. The primary housing source was the state-owned housing system. While enjoying the state-distributed and nearly free housing, residents and their families had to live in a small apartment. At the same time, they had no freedom in choosing where and how large their apartments should be.

Inevitably, housing distribution under the planned economy experienced a series of conflicts and problems. Due to the emphasis on heavy industry in economic policies and plans, consumer products had always occupied a secondary place. Housing was one example. At the beginning of the People's Republic of China in 1949, the average living area in the cities was about 4.5 square meters per person.[4] After more than 10 years of neglect, that figure decreased to 3.2 square meters in 1963. During the next 20 years, there was no change in the average living area. Before the launching of urban reforms in 1985, the figure recovered to 4.8 square meters, only about the level in 1949.[5] In other words, urban residents did not see any significant changes in living conditions even after three-and-a-half decades of "liberation." Obviously, this situation was not consistent with the expectations of the masses who looked forward to better living conditions. Compared with the former East European countries, the Chinese average living area was much lower.[6]

---

[3] Xie Zhiqiang, *Breaking Through: The Chinese Housing Reform* (Beijing: Social Sciences Documentation Publishing House, 1999).

[4] 1 square meter = 10.8 square feet.

[5] Xie Zhiqiang, *Breaking Through*.

[6] Ibid.

Another problem in this process was the unequal distribution of housing. Applications for housing construction went through the administrative hierarchy from the bottom to the top, and the distribution of housing (and resources for building apartments) came down from the top. This formed a typical redistribution process, in which the distance of a *danwei* from the center reflected its bargaining power in the redistribution.[7] Therefore, the higher the administrative rank of the city and *danwei* was, the better housing conditions the employees were able to enjoy. Within each *danwei*, distribution of housing also followed the same logic: Individuals with higher ranks chose better and larger apartments. Not surprisingly, those officials who were critical in the distribution process had convenience and incentives to occupy and hoard better and larger housing than they deserved,[8] which made the living conditions of ordinary workers more miserable.

Starting from the early 1980s, housing policies in the city began to change. After a series of experiments of raising rent, the government started to sell state-owned housing to individuals. At the same time, the government also increased rent subsidies and established public funds for purchasing residence. After about 10 years of experimentation and preparation, the transition of the housing policy was completed around the mid-1990s. In 1998, the housing distribution as in-kind welfare finally ended, and the government started to pay employees extra money instead.[9] *Danwei* stopped distributing housing that essentially cost workers nothing, and workers could no longer rent public housing with nominal rent. From then on, housing became a commodity.

As a result of the housing reform, urban residents have fundamentally changed their housing consumption. Instead of waiting for distribution of housing from the government, they now have to

---

[7] Andrew G. Walder, "Property Rights and Stratification in Socialist Redistributive Economies," *American Sociological Review* 57 (1992): 524–539.

[8] George S. Tolley, "Urban Housing Reform in China: An Economic Analysis," *World Bank Discussion Papers* no. 123 (1991).

[9] Liu Lin, "Historical Retrospect."

obtain an apartment from the market. They purchase their residence according to their household income and buying power. Meanwhile, they now have the freedom of choosing the location and quality of their own residence.

FAST GROWTH OF THE REAL ESTATE MARKET

Ever since the initiation of the marketization of housing, the real estate sector has been on a fast track. Indexes that show the spectacular growth include investment in construction, annual sales, and unit price of housing.

Increased investment in the real estate sector has surpassed investment in fixed assets in each year since 1998, as Fig. 1 shows. Between 2000 and 2004, the annual increase of investment in real estate across the whole country was well above 20 percent.[10] Take

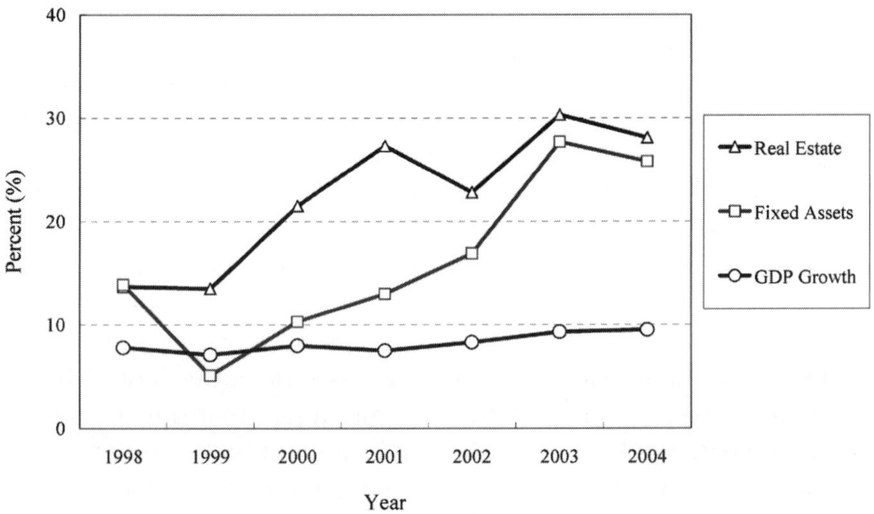

Fig. 1: Annual Increase Rates of Real Estate, Fixed Assets, and GDP in China, 1998–2004

[10] Niu Fengrui, ed., *The Development Report of China's Real Estate*, vol. 2 (Beijing: Social Sciences Academic Press, 2005).

the extreme case of Beijing. That figure was 50 percent in 2003, and reached 60 percent in 2004.[11] In accordance with the increase in investment, similar patterns of fast increases have also occurred in areas of transferred land, areas under construction, areas completed, and areas newly started in each of those years.

The sharp rise in supply has been paralleled by the greatly increased demand for new apartments. Part of the reason is the small living area per person before the housing commercialization. As household income rises and the desire for better living conditions goes up, demand for new housing grows quickly. Improvement in urbanites' living conditions only contributes to part of the expanding demand. Other factors include the reconstruction of the old city centers and population growth due to migration during the process of urbanization. The figure of sold commercial apartments is indicative. In 1997, areas of sold apartments were 90 million square meters, and this figure quadrupled to 380 million square meters in 2004. Consistently, total sales also increased by four times. The increase in sales has been accompanied by an increase in the proportion of apartments sold to individuals rather than to organizations, from 80 percent in 1998 to above 93 percent in 2004.[12]

Along with the fast-growing supply and demand is the astonishing rise of housing price. Based on different measures, the annual percentage increase of the housing price varies. However, the increasing trend is obvious even with the price now being at an unprecedented high level. Take the example of Beijing again. An average apartment in a decent location costs the equivalent of 10–12 years of an average household's income, a fact that directly stimulated the heated debate over "the real estate bubble" during the second half of 2004. High housing prices have different effects on the two sides of supply and demand. On the one hand, they encourage developers to build as much as possible in a short time span in

[11] Liu Lin and Du Changman, "Analysis on Beijing Real Estate Market in 2004 and the Forecast of 2005," ibid., 203–215.

[12] Xie Zhiqiang, *Breaking Through*.

order to achieve high profits; on the other hand, they remind home buyers to be cautious in making a decision that may cost them their lifetime savings. When the market mechanism does not succeed in regulating these two sides, the effects are often difficult to balance.

Pursuit of high profits by developers also has a big impact on the supply structure of the housing market. Because the government sets limits for the price of subsidized and cheap public housing, developers are reluctant to undertake such projects due to low profits. The percentage of total investment in cheap public housing dropped from 11 percent in 1999 to under 5 percent in 2004. Such an unbalanced supply structure further facilitates price hikes. Without a better public housing system, a large proportion of low-income families now are unable to afford to improve their cramped living conditions.

CONFLICTS BETWEEN HOME BUYERS AND DEVELOPERS

In the transaction to purchase an apartment, home buyers and developers have different interests. They attempt to achieve different goals — use value and exchange value, respectively.[13] To home buyers (excluding opportunistic investors), an apartment is used as a necessary shelter. Its use value includes its structure, size, design, location, and other qualities that satisfy home buyers' living requirements and preferences. But to developers, an apartment is a commodity that can potentially bring profits. In other words, developers want to sell their apartments at a price as high as possible. In pursuit of their own interests — improving living conditions for home buyers and making profits for developers — conflicts often arise between them.

Together with fast growth in the real estate sector, conflicts between home buyers and developers also have surged. The China Consumer's Association received more than 20,000 reports of

---

[13] John R. Logan and Harvey L. Molotch, *Urban Fortune: The Political Economy of Place* (Berkeley: University of California Press, 1987).

complaints related to the housing market in 2004.[14] These complaints covered a wide range of problems, including bad construction quality, overpricing, cheating in area measuring, false advertising, fraudulent contracts, and unilateral changes of community space design. Take Beijing as an example. In recent years, the number of complaints in the housing transaction has increased at an annual rate of above 20 percent. Money involved in complaints varies from hundreds of thousands to millions of yuan. The time involved in dealing with unresolved problems lengthens. Among all conflicts related to these complaints, only 10 percent get settled each year.

Unequal Resources

As a result of commercializing the residential housing, the market now takes control over the process of distribution. The setup of the real estate market supplies different endowments for home buyers and developers. These differences include informational, economic, organizational, discursive, and supportive resources from their allies (Table 1). It is quite obvious that developers command more resources than home buyers.

Buying a home in current China is filled with uncertainty and risk for buyers because of the intrinsic information asymmetry in the real estate market. This is because the quality of a real estate property is generically difficult to evaluate for most home buyers. In addition to getting educated and making wise decisions in terms of what and where to buy, home buyers also have to worry about the construction quality and legal conditions of the properties they are buying. To make things worse, developers take full advantage in exploiting this information asymmetry. In a primary market (i.e., a new real estate market), such information asymmetry would often motivate developers to construct low-quality buildings because high-quality properties cannot be fully appreciated in the market.[15]

[14] "Fewest Complaints in Beijing Housing Market Settled," *New Beijing News*, March 13, 2005.

[15] George A. Akerlof, "The Market for 'Lemons': Quality Uncertainty and the Market Mechanism," *Quarterly Journal of Economics* 84 (1970): 488–500.

Table 1: Comparison of Resources of Developers and Home Buyers

Resource Type	Developers (With More Resources)	Home Buyers (With Fewer Resources)
Informational	Familiar with law and regulations; knowing construction quality and cost; knowing apartment size	Unfamiliar with law and regulations; not knowing construction quality and cost; unfamiliar with the method of area measuring; Internet as an important platform
Economic	Capital intensive sector; high profit; super-rich stratum; able to hire lawyers and other professionals	Relatively well-off, but usually not able to hire professionals; individually, not comparable to developers
Organizational	Relatively small number; homogeneity; easy to organize; high return (incentives) in acting together; easy to monitor; often interacting in the form of club	A large number; heterogeneity; hard to organize; high cost and high return in acting together; hard to monitor; prone to "free-riding" and defection
Discursive	In control through paying media and academic figures for favorable reports and arguments; paying Internet writers for posting favoring articles and rumors	Basically absent in traditional media reports (except a small number of articles on "the real estate bubble" from economists and sociologists who are not bought out); mostly dependent upon free Internet
Alliance	In alliance with media and mainstream economists; also allied with local government for mutual economic interests	On their own; central government helps

Therefore, buyers are at a greater risk of overpaying for properties of unknown quality or legal status. In addition, a real estate transaction is a long and complicated process, and developers and buyers have to rely on binding contracts to complete a transaction.

However, few buyers have the knowledge to understand the complicated contract items, not to mention detecting contract problems or foreseeing contract violations.[16] Once contracts are signed, down payments are paid, and bank loans are arranged, the buyers are often at the mercy of the developers. This is especially true in China because new apartment units are frequently marketed and sold well before any of them are actually built.

Initial entry into the real estate sector requires a big investment. Thus, developers usually control a large amount of capital. Although there is no generally acknowledged profit rate in the real estate market, it is widely known that building houses make fast money and that developers try hard to cover up how much they earn from each project. The only published report, by the Fuzhou Bureau of Pricing, shows that the profit rate of real estate projects in Fuzhou varies from 50 percent to 90 percent. Some estimates in private hint of a much higher profit margin. Through one or two projects, developers usually are able to accumulate a good fortune. According to the most recent list of the top one hundred richest people in China by *Forbes China*,[17] 35 of them come from the real estate sector, far more than from any other sector. In addition, these developers have climbed into this super-rich stratum in a short time. Their immense financial ability enables them to hire top lawyers and other professionals if they and/or their firm get into any trouble. On the other hand, home buyers may come from better-off households than others, but in no way are their financial situations in the same class with developers.

Organizing developers is much easier than organizing home buyers. In certain geographic areas, there is only a limited number of developers — a group of homogeneous business persons. Developers also have high incentives to organize. Once they realize that they can obtain high profits by manipulating the housing price together, they certainly will do so. Meanwhile, organizational monitoring does not require extra effort due to their small number and rich resources.

---

[16] Oliver Williamson, *Markets and Hierarchies: Analysis and Antitrust Implications* (New York: Free Press, 1975).

[17] "China's Digital Riches in the Information Era," *Forbes China* 1, no. 1 (2003).

Developers often interact with each other on formal (e.g., sector conferences) and informal (e.g., club parties) occasions. Right after the recent regulating policy (mainly aiming to lower the housing price issued by the central government), Zhongcheng League and the housing section of the All China Industrial and Commercial Federation, two famous associations of real estate developers, called a conference in Shenzhen in order to discuss strategies in dealing with the situation.

Home buyers come from various strata with high heterogeneity. Their large number also makes it difficult for them to organize. Although their potential return is high, the cost of organizing usually runs above the individual home buyer's financial ability. Therefore, "free-riding" becomes a common problem in organizing home buyers. In addition, developers often pay close attention to the development of home buyers' mobilization, and they find that buying out the organizer often dissolves the whole movement.

By spending a large amount of money on advertising, developers also endeavor to control the discursive lead in the society. Not only do they control traditional media and public economic discussions by sponsoring "academic" conferences and subsequent reports, but also they pay Internet writers to post favorable articles and even spread rumors of rising prices on bulletin boards. Through controlling various channels of communication, both formal and informal, developers attempt to produce expectations of rising housing prices and cover up unfavorable information. Home buyers' opinions are almost absent in the mainstream media except for a small number of reports from journalists and scholars who are not bought out. The home buyers' perspective has never reached a status that rivals that of developers. However, the free Internet provides a convenient place for home buyers to exchange information. Countless discussion boards on the Internet cover almost every issue in the real estate market. To some extent, information on the Internet is more trustworthy than the mainstream media reports.

As mentioned above, developers form alliances with mass media and mainstream economists. The real estate sector pays a large proportion of the advertising income of the traditional media. In their economic self-interest, some mainstream scholars also join with developers. From time to time, high-profile economists talk up higher future housing prices. The local government often stands on the developers' side because local financial income depends on land sales and taxation flows related to the real estate market. To some extent, the powerful alliance in the real estate market consists of economic, political, knowledge, and media elites.

Home buyers do not have outside allies. Often they have to rely on themselves. The central government may help home buyers because it wants to keep conflicts in the real estate market under control. In this sense, some policies of the central government help home buyers in their uphill combat with developers.

Strategic Moves

Based on their different resources in the market as well as in the society at large, home buyers and developers apply different strategic moves that serve best in pursuing their own interests.

Because of their advantageous positions with more resources, developers have every incentive to exploit buyers' vulnerability. Market fraud, contract violations, and even open predation are easily found in the Chinese real estate market. For example, contracts are often broken unilaterally without compensation to home buyers by developers; handover of the apartment is often delayed; buildings with outstanding liens are sold frequently by developers without disclosure; apartment units are built smaller in space or inferior in construction quality than contractually specified; property deeds are routinely held by developers to use as collateral for loans[18]; and provision of amenities such as roads, gardens, parking lots, and other community utilities are indefinitely delayed long after sales are completed. In some cases, when market price goes up before the home buyers move in, some developers even demand extra payment or threaten to cancel the buying contracts.

---

[18] Benjamin L. Read, "Democratizing the Neighborhood? New Private Housing and Home-Owner Self-Organization in Urban China," *The China Journal* 11 (2003): 31–59.

The above pessimistic picture does not mean that home buyers have no leverage to protect their own interests. For most home buyers, buying an apartment may be the biggest purchase in their life, and they have every reason to guard themselves against fraudulent transactions. If the market and the formal institutions do not supply an adequate tool kit for them in dealing with developers, they have to be creative in finding new ones.

Individually, home buyers do not have equal resources in bargaining with developers. The effective and perhaps the only way for home buyers to gain leverage is to organize themselves and transform individual grievances into a collective action.[19] For home buyers, the collective action offers several advantages. First, by pooling together individual resources and efforts, home buyers are better equipped to pursue contract disputes against developers. Second, by combining individual grievances into a collective dispute against developers, home buyers can open themselves to a broader repertoire of actions, such as protests, class lawsuits, demonstrations, and even riots. They can expose their grievances to the media and the general public in a much more powerful way. Third, and most importantly, the Chinese political structure provides great opportunities for potentially successful non-state-targeted collective actions. Through organized collective actions, home buyers can appeal to the higher-level government and officials who are more concerned with political stability and thus are more likely to favor home buyers by exerting pressure on local officials and real estate developers. Overall, organized collective actions greatly increase home buyers' leverage in their conflicts with developers.

Given these conditions, it is not surprising that organized collective actions have become a routine in home buyers' strategic moves to protect themselves. This routine strategy has led to an institutional innovation: the spontaneous creation of home owners' associations (HOAs, *yezhu weiyuanhui*) in most new urban neighborhoods. Geographic closeness and the Internet provide low-cost and vital conveniences for HOAs to mobilize neighborhood residents.

---

[19] Michael Lipsky, "Protest as a Political Resource," *American Political Science Review* 62 (1968): 1144–1158.

In the early 1990s when the housing market had just emerged, newly constructed residential communities had no grassroots administrative organizations such as neighborhood committees to assume the functions of community governance and social control. This provided a political niche for some home owners to form spontaneous home owners' groups to handle problems related to their homes and neighborhoods.[20] With the increasing prevalence of market fraud, spontaneous HOAs became a universal phenomenon in the late 1990s and the early 2000s. These HOAs, usually led by a small number of activists, have served as a platform for an organized collective action against developers, such as by holding meetings, organizing protests, preparing lawsuits, and maintaining community websites. While the effectiveness of these HOAs varies, some have been very successful in winning contract disputes against developers. As these successful stories have been circulated, mainly through discussion boards on the Internet, forming HOAs has become a taken-for-granted notion and a necessary part of the home buying experience. Home hunters nowadays often form informal groups on the Internet that can easily be transformed into HOAs.

The Role of the Local Government

In order to curb developers' fraudulent behavior, the market needs formal institutions. In advanced market economies, the real estate market has always been heavily regulated by multiple organizational entities (e.g., the central and local government, real estate associations, broker agencies, financial institutions, and the legal system) and by well-established regulations (zoning codes, building codes, and real estate as well as financial laws).[21] However, the Chinese real estate market is ill regulated for various reasons.

First, the market lacks well-specified regulations that govern market transactions. When the first and the only real estate law was introduced in 1994, most of its contents were devoted to general

[20] Read, "Democratizing the Neighborhood?"

[21] Pearl Janet Davies, *Real Estate in American History* (Washington, DC: Public Affairs Press, 1958).

issues such as land use and property rights. There was virtually no mention of real estate transactions between developers and home buyers.[22] As a result, government agencies are often confused in offering the public assistance during property transactions, and home buyers experience extreme difficulties in seeking help, guidance, or arbitration from these agencies.

Second, the market also suffers from the absence of a well-established legal system to sanction market frauds and to resolve contract disputes.[23] There have been few reforms in the legal system to adapt to the new situation, which is characterized by more complex market transactions than before. Meanwhile, the legal profession is not yet fully developed so as to make legal services easily accessible to ordinary citizens. As a result, the legal implementation and enforcement of real estate contracts become highly problematic. This gives developers tremendous legal leverage in their building, marketing, and sale practices, while making it difficult and costly for home buyers to pursue legal protection. Most people sign their purchase contracts without the help of an attorney, and when disputes occur, they tend to seek informal instead of legal settlements.

Finally, corruption among the local government officials has also greatly undermined the effectiveness of formal institutions.[24] Due to the unique political and economic environment, local officials in China have pro-business incentives. For most local jurisdictions, real estate development is the most ostensible signal of economic development and the most lucrative source of government revenue. In the meanwhile, connection to private entrepreneurs is the most effective way of extracting political rents. As a result, most real estate developers are closely connected to senior local officials. Not only are they given the green light in acquiring land, capital, and building permits; but also they receive government assistance and protection during the entire process of their projects. In some cases,

---

[22] Cao Pei, *Real Estate Law in China* (Hong Kong: Sweet and Maxwell Asia, 1998); Patrick A. Randolph Jr. and Lou Jianbo, *Chinese Real Estate Law* (The Hague, Netherlands: Kluwer Law International, 2000).

[23] Read, "Democratizing the Neighborhood?"

[24] Ibid.

local officials even help to produce false reports of building inspection, or to suppress public complaints through unlawful administrative orders.

CONSEQUENCES OF CONFLICTS

Conflicts between home buyers and developers have a series of consequences that not only influence the behavior of the two sides involved, but also affect the changing social structure at large. Below, we outline some direct and indirect consequences that originate from conflicts in the real estate market.

For home buyers, one of the direct consequences is the high search cost. Because of developers' false advertising, contract fraud, and home buyers' inability to penalize developers after transactions, home buyers are very cautious in choosing a developer and/or an apartment unit. They have to invest lots of energy, time, and even money in a search — well above the costs in a market with relatively good trust between sellers and buyers. After a long and tiring purchase process, home buyers often have a level of sophistication usually achieved only by professionals in order not to be cheated by developers.

In addition to maintaining their advantageous position in information, developers also form powerful alliances with other elites. To some extent, this real estate interest group manipulates pricing and exploits home buyers' vulnerability in order to pursue high profits. On the other hand, obstacles and hardships home buyers experience reflect their disadvantages and even helplessness. In this sense, the negotiation process in the real estate market leads to the delineation of two opposing social groups. When home buyers' grievances cannot be channeled, they naturally resort to other strategies and tactics. In many communities, HOAs become the organization through which home buyers act collectively. In moderate cases, HOAs lead home buyers in administrative arbitration and class law suits; but in extreme cases, HOAs protest and even riot. Violent conflicts are not rare. These events reflect the hostility of the two camps.

One reason for the rampancy of developers' fraud is that the implementation of laws and regulations does not have actual consequences in deterrence and penalties. We mentioned above that the alliance of the local government and developers often downplays home buyers' grievances. However, home buyers' collective action attracts attention from the public and higher levels of government, which usually builds up pressures for the local government to change. In China today, these types of public pressures and attention from the higher ups are the effective ways to push for a better legal environment. The recently published and much discussed draft of The Property Law was the direct response of the central government to the heated conflicts between property owners and other related parties, including the local government and developers.

It is obvious that home buyers do not have faith in developers. In this situation, the market mechanism cannot function properly. Incentives for high profits drive developers to various strategies of cheating, and caution makes home buyers pay higher costs for extra information. However, disbelief in developers does not necessarily mean loss of faith in the real estate market as a whole. In addition to protecting home buyers' interests, conflicts during and after transaction also sustain basic trust in the housing market. This is because conflicts do not let cheating developers get away easily, and successful collective actions set the examples for compensation and for channeling home buyers' grievances. Through the cycle of conflict, compromise, conflict again, and compromise again, home buyers gradually build up their trust in the market — though not necessarily trust in developers. Therefore, in the event that both trust and legal mechanisms are inadequate, conflicts play an important role in the evolution of the newly emerging market.

Home buyers start their collective action in order to guard their own property. Their spontaneous organization shows their determination to protect their property rights. Sometimes, they fight not only against developers but also against obstacles set up by the local government. To a certain degree, home buyers act and participate to claim their rights. Some scholars have argued that market activities in China bring wealth for some who will inevitably acquire new collective interests — and sometimes even political interests — along with their economic leverage.[25] However, others caution that political participation in current China is largely determined by the extent to which the state allows (or does not allow) a certain degree of political expression.[26] Home buyers often meticulously avoid offending the government and are willing to cooperate with the local officials most times.[27] In fact, in their combat with developers and the local government, home buyers strategically exploit a political opportunity in which the central government frequently calls for social stability and requires the local government to pay more attention to public opinion. It remains to be seen whether the organization and collective action of home buyers will lead the well-off strata to be politically active. Nevertheless, the spontaneous organization of this group points to a new direction for individuals. Property owners now stand firmly and move strategically to protect their own interests, which is already a huge departure from the past.

DISCUSSION

As we have mentioned above, the current real estate market in China emerged as the product of the further economic reform as recently as the 1990s. In this structural transition process, the contour of social interests will inevitably be re-drawn. We clearly see this transformation in the sociological discussions on the social stratification and distribution of fortune in China. In a series of papers that propose "the market transition theory," Victor Nee asserts that the important role of political power gives its place to human capital in the emerging market in post-socialist societies.[28] His theory predicts

[25] Thomas Gold, "Bases for Civil Society in Reform China," in *Reconstructing Twentieth-Century China: State Control, Civil Society, and National Identity*, ed. Kjeld Erik Brodsgaard and David Strand (Oxford: Clarendon Press, 1998), 163–188.

[26] Tianjian Shi, *Political Participation in Beijing* (Cambridge, MA: Harvard University Press, 1997).

[27] Read, "Democratizing the Neighborhood?"

[28] See, for example, Victor Nee, "A Theory of Market Transition: From Redistribution to Markets in State Socialism," *American Sociological Review* 54 (1989): 663–681.

that in a redistributive era, the political mechanism that stratified people according to their distance to the political center will die out.[29] Another view refutes this transition idea, however, and argues for the continuation of the important role of political capital in the transition period.[30] Political elites from the redistributive era continue to benefit from their strategic positions, either by directly utilizing political power or by exchanging power for economic gains. In discussion of this line, the distribution of social resources in a transition period is not simply one way or the other, but is rather diversified.

The above debates help us in understanding the structural change in China at the macro-level. However, they are inadequate in describing the actual details of changes, which is why some scholars have long called for research on "specificity" in transition.[31] We know that economic reform produces new groups of winners and losers. However, the grouping of winners and losers may not be either the same in the old era or entirely new. Usually, this involves a re-grouping of social groups. In pursuing their interests, old beneficiaries maintain their advantageous position, and new rising groups make the best of new rules. More complicated is that the interests of some groups may overlap with each other, and they form strategic alliances under such conditions. Such alliances include various combinations: between old groups, between new groups, and more likely between old and new groups. Sun noted the coming of an era of interest bargaining between social groups in current China.[32]

In the transition era, the distribution of social resources becomes complicated. In pursuit of their interests, groups often go against each other. Interesting research questions include these: How do

[29] Li Qiang, *Shehui fenceng he pingfu chaju*.

[30] See, for example, William L. Parish and Ethan Michelson, "Politics and Market: Dual Transformations," *American Journal of Sociology* 101 (1996): 1042–1059.

[31] Andrew G. Walder, "Markets and Inequality in Transitional Economies: Toward Testable Theories," *American Journal of Sociology* 101 (1996): 1060–1073.

[32] Sun Liping, "Conflict and Harmony in the Era of Interests," *Nanfang zhoumo* [*Southern Weekend*], Guangzhou, 2004.

these groups interact with each other? How does their conflict start and evolve? What are the potential consequences of their conflicts for the whole social structure? While identifying the interest groups helps us in understanding the division and organization in the society, detailed study on the conflicts between these groups at the micro-level directly records the changing process in the emerging social structure. Conflicts in the real estate market described above have shown strategic moves that revolved around private properties. A similar case is the heated public debate in 2004 among economists on the loss of state assets during the process of selling state-owned firms.

The emergence of the real estate market was a direct product of the policy change — the decision to stop distribution of housing in kind and instead to commercialize residential housing. Once started, the real estate market follows its own logic, and conflicts between groups in this market exert impact on the reform process as a whole. This feedback effect is most clearly seen when conflicts in the real estate market directly change government policies. Conflicts and home buyers' strategic collective action communicate their interests to the government. One direct response is a series of policy changes that attempts to curb the sky-rocketing housing price. The issue of the draft property law also shows that the government aims to tame heated conflicts between home buyers and developers.

CONCLUSION

After living in the government-distributed small homes for decades, urban Chinese may now fully realize their desire for better living conditions. Commercialization of the housing sector has stimulated a sharp increase in the supply of apartment units, and rising household income has also created a booming demand. Purchasing a new home and moving into a new community have become the daily talks of ordinary urbanites across the country. Since the late 1990s, the average annual increase in the investment in the real estate sector has been higher than 20 percent. As total sales in the same time span have increased four times, housing prices have soared.

The two sides of the housing market pursue different interests: improvement in living conditions for home buyers and high profits for developers. Thus, they have intrinsic conflicts of interest during the transaction of an apartment unit. For various reasons, the malfunctioning market mechanism gives developers convenient opportunities to cheat. Home buyers often find themselves pinned in developers' traps. The failure of regulating institutions also leaves few solutions within the system for home buyers. Instead, home buyers resort to spontaneous self-organized collective actions to offset developers' resourceful strategic moves, though buyers face tough challenges of mobilization (free-riding) and defection. Buyers also skillfully utilize the political opportunity to seek help from the higher-level government.

The strategies of home buyers and developers are rooted in the resources that they are able to manipulate during the bargaining process. Economically powerful developers occupy a position with overwhelmingly asymmetric advantages in information, organizational mobilization, and discourse. They even form alliances with the media, some mainstream economists, and the local government. Compared with developers, homer buyers' resources are quite limited. They have no way to challenge developers. However, by putting resources together, home buyers may act as a group. The repertoire of home buyers' strategic moves includes group negotiation, class law suits, requests for administrative arbitration, and even public demonstrations.

The government splits into two parts on this issue. Starting from its own interests, the local government often provides conveniences to developers but sets up obstacles to home buyers. On the other hand, in order to channel home buyers' grievances, the central government from time to time issues policies to curb developers' ruthless predation.

Conflicts between home buyers and developers indicate the formation of two new social groups that were not seen in the past. Conflicts in the real estate market buttress home buyers' trust in the market and sustain its evolution. Meanwhile, conflicts also help in improving conditions in legal implementation. As home buyers often keep their distance from the political red line, their collective action does not immediately portend a new type of political participation. Nevertheless, they stand firm in protecting their own interests.

The recent history of the real estate sector is short, and where the ongoing conflicts will lead remains to be seen. However, the dynamic scene of conflicts in this market at least shows some clues to one aspect of social (re)grouping in the transition period. Research on this issue will certainly help us understand how the society restructures. For example, how do developers form alliances with the media, mainstream economists, and the local government? How will home buyers overcome the problem of mobilization (free-riding) during their collective action? And how will home buyers, developers, and the government negotiate with each other and reach compromises? Answers to all these and other questions will better our understanding of specific structural changes that are occurring in the transition era.

Chapter

4

Multifaceted State and Fragmented Society: Dynamics of Environmental Movement in China

Yanfei Sun and Dingxin Zhao

This study tries to understand the nature of China's environmental movement by examining three well-known environmental campaigns — the campaign to save the snub-nosed monkey in Yunnan in 1995–1997, the campaign to save the Tibetan antelope in Qinghai in 1996–2000, and the campaign against the Nu River (*Nujiang*) dam project since 2003. The paper aims at elucidating the complex political context under which China's environmental movement operates, the major allies and foes that the movement has, and the opportunities and problems that the movement is facing. It also intends to explain the results and dynamics of the three environmental campaigns, particularly why the first two campaigns were more successful than the last one in achieving the intended goals, as well as to provide insights into the possible future of the environmental movement in China.

Shortly after the emergence of the environmental NGOs (ENGOs) in China in the mid-1990s, they have attracted much scholarly attention.[1] They have been in the spotlight for two reasons. First, alongside China's economic success is the aggravation of environmental problems, ranging from pollution, deforestation, desertification, extinction of endangered species, to various forms of ecological disasters. Scholars who are concerned about China's environmental problems are eager to see the rise of a robust environmental movement that can counterbalance the environment-unfriendly economic forces. Second, the 1989 Tiananmen Pro-Democracy Movement and the collapse of the communist regimes in Eastern Europe kindled academic interests in civil society in China.[2] Scholars were searching

---

[1] Examples include Elizabeth Knup, "ENGOs in China: An Overview," *China Environment Series* no. 4 (1997): 9–15; Anna Brettell, "Environmental Non-governmental Organizations in the People's Republic of China: Innocents in a Co-opted Environmental Movement?" *The Journal of Pacific Asia* no. 6 (2000): 27–56; Peter Ho, "Greening without Conflict? Environmentalism, NGOs and Civil Society in China," *Development and Change* no. 32 (2001): 893–921; Fenshi Wu, "New Partners or Old Brothers? GONGOs in International Environmental Advocacy in China," *China Environmental Series* no. 5 (2002): 45–58; Fengshi Wu, "Environmental GONGO Autonomy: Unintended Consequences of State Strategies in China," *The Good Society* no. 12 (2003): 35–45; Elizabeth C. Economy, *The River Runs Black: The Environmental Challenge to China's Future* (Ithaca, NY: Cornell University Press, 2004); Guobin Yang, "Weaving a Green Web: The Internet and Environmental Activism in China," *China Environment Series* no. 6 (2003): 89–93; Guobin Yang, "ENGOs and Institutional Dynamics in China," *The China Quarterly* no. 181 (2005): 46–66; Jonathan Schwartz, "ENGOs in China: Roles and Limits," *Pacific Affairs* no. 77 (2004): 28–50; Jiang Ru, "ENGOs in China: The Interplay of State Controls, Agency Interests and NGO Strategies," unpublished Ph.D. diss., Stanford University, 2004. Phillip Stalley and Dongning Yang, "An Emerging Environmental Movement in China?" *The China Quarterly* no. 186 (2006): 333–356.

[2] For works of civil society in China, see *Modern China* no. 19 Special Issue (1993); Richard Madsen, "The Public Sphere, Civil Society, and Moral Community: A Research Agenda for Contemporary Chinese Studies," *Modern China* 19 no. 2 (1993): 183–198; Gordon White, Jude Howell, and Shang Xiaoyuan, *In Search of Civil Society: Market Reform and Social Change in Contemporary China* (Oxford: Oxford University Press, 1996); Timothy Brook, "Auto-organization in Chinese Society," in *Civil Society in China*, ed. Timothy Brook and B. Michael Frolic (Armonk, NY: M.E. Sharpe, 1997); Kjeld Erik Brodsgaard and David Strand, ed., *Reconstructing Twentieth-Century China: State Control, Civil Society, and National*

for some autonomous forces in the society that could curtail the reach of the authoritarian state.[3] They wished to see civic forces assert and expand their autonomy, and when time was ripe, challenge the state and push forward a democratic transition. As the ENGOs grow to be the most organized civic association in China, draw in a large number of participants, expand their trans-regional networks, and demonstrate their capacity of resource mobilization,[4] they naturally capture the attention of the scholars.

The literature on the ENGOs concerns with the state–society relationship and debates on how much autonomy they actually have from the state control. Saich argues that although the state control is visible, the newly rising ENGOs are able to employ strategies of negotiation, evasion, or feigned compliance to carve out a space for themselves.[5] Others tend to emphasize more the existence of clear limits imposed by the state upon the ENGOs, with the state setting both the terms of their existence and the permissible limits of

---

Identity (Oxford: Clarendon Press, 1998); Thomas Gold, "Bases for Civil Society in Reform China," in *Reconstructing Twentieth-Century China: State Control, Civil Society, and National Identity*, ed. Kjeld Erik Brodsgaard and David Strand (Oxford: Clarendon Press, 1998); *Civic Discourse, Civil Society, and Chinese Communities*, ed. Randy Kluver and John H. Powers (Stamford, CT: Ablex Publishing Corporation, 1999); Martin K. Whyte, "Urban China: A Civil Society in the Making?" in *State and Society in China: The Consequences of the Reform*, ed. Arthur Lewis Rosenbaum (Boulder, CO: Westview, 1999); Xin Gu, "A Civil Society and Public Sphere in Post-Mao China? An Overview of Western Publications," *China Information* no. 8 (1993–1994): 38–52; for an overview of the works on civil society in China, see Guobing Yang, "Civil Society in China: A Dynamic Field of Study," *China Review International* no. 9 (2002): 1–16.

[3] In this article, civil society is defined as a society in which membership in social organizations is "both voluntary and overlapping" and individuals join those social organizations only out of their own interests. For this definition of civil society, refer to Ernest Gellner, *Conditions of Liberty: Civil Society and Its Rivals* (London: Penguin Books, 1994); John A. Hall, *Civil Society: Theory, History, Comparison* (Cambridge, UK: Polity Press, 1995), 15.

[4] Elizabeth C. Economy, "ENGOs in China: Encouraging Action and Addressing Public Grievances." Statement presented at the Congressional-Executive Commission on China (2005), available at http://www.cecc.gov/pages/roundtables/020705/economy.php (accessed February 1, 2006).

[5] Tony Saich, "Negotiating the State: The Development of Social Organizations in China," *The China Quarterly* no. 163 (2000): 124–141.

member activities.[6] Moreover, even within the limits imposed by the state, the majority of the Chinese ENGOs do not openly confront the government.[7] They impose self-censorship to circumvent the state censure[8] and avoid contentious issues by only engaging in safe issue areas such as environmental education and tree planting.[9] In short, this debate is a continuation of the debate on whether the autonomous and semi-autonomous intermediate associations and social forces that emerged in the post-Tiananmen China are corporatist in nature or elements of civil society.[10]

Another thread of inquiry in the studies of the Chinese ENGOs concerns how the structures of the Chinese state and its patterned political processes have facilitated the rise of the ENGOs. Here, Saich argues that as the government was streamlining itself and divesting some of its functions, it needed the assistance of third-sector organizations to handle some of the social problems and this in turn opened up opportunities for the rise of the ENGOs in China.[11] Ho points out that it was China's grave environmental problems that prompted the government to promulgate environmental laws and

[6] Brettell, "ENGOs in the PRC," 27–56; Ho, "Greening without Conflict?" 893–921.

[7] Ibid.

[8] Ru, "ENGOs in China."

[9] Brettell, "ENGOs in the PRC," 27–56.

[10] For those who tend to conceptualize in the term of civil society, see, for example: Whyte, "Urban China," 77–141; for those who prefer corporatism, see, for example: Jonathan Unger and Anita Chan, "Corporatism in China: A Developmental State in an East Asian Context," in *China After Socialism*, ed. Barrett L. McCormick and Jonathan Unger (Armonk, NY: M.E. Sharpe, 1996). Dorothy J. Solinger, "Urban Entrepreneurs and the State: The Merger of State and Society," in *State and Society in China: The Consequences of the Reform*, ed. Arthur Lewis Rosenbaum (Boulder, CO: Westview, 1999): 121–141; Jonathan Unger, "Bridge: Private Business, the Chinese Government and the Rise of New Association," *The China Quarterly* no. 47 (1996): 795–819; for reviews of this debate, see Yijing Ding, "Corporatism and Civil Society in China: An Overview of the Debate in Recent Years," *China Information* no. 12 (1998): 44–67; Richard Baum and Alexei Shevchenko, "The 'State of the State'," in *The Paradox of China's Post Mao Reforms*, ed. Merle Goldman and Roderick MacFarquhar (Cambridge, MA: Harvard University Press, 1999): 333–447.

[11] Saich, "Negotiating the State," 142.

policies and to build state environmental protection institutions, all of which endowed legitimacy to the activities of the ENGOs.[12,13]

While these studies provide us with insights into the political context against which the ENGOs could rise, they have generally treated the state and society in fairly undifferentiated terms. Although from time to time there were voices to remind us of the fissures between different state agencies at the same level and between the central and regional governments,[14] discussions did not go further to explore how the frictions came into being and what ramification they have produced. After the death of Mao, the Chinese state structure has become increasingly complicated. Since the 1980s, the Chinese government has undergone several waves of major restructurings. During these processes, new government agencies were created, some governmental branches were strengthened, while some others lost their power or were even eliminated. The newly created agencies tend to act aggressively to expand their jurisdiction, while the segments that are losing their grounds do not want to give up. The whole development has contributed to a state structure featured with contestation and conflict. Therefore, we must disaggregate the state and pay attention to the political opportunities created by the tensions between the government's top leadership and the local governments and between different agencies of the central government as a result of the differentiation of their interests and functions, an issue that gets increasingly emphasized by the students of the state.[15]

---

[12] Ho, "Greening without Conflict?" 893–921.

[13] Some other scholars emphasize the crucial roles that international politics, international NGOs, and international media have played in the rise of the ENGOs in China. For example, Brettell, "ENGOs in the PRC," 46; Yang, "Weaving a Green Web," 89–93; Yang, "ENGOs and Institutional Dynamics," 46–66; Ru, "ENGOs in China," 146.

[14] Such as Tony Saich, *Governance and Politics of China* (New York: Palgrave, 2002).

[15] Joel S. Migdal, *State in Society: Studying How States and Societies Transform and Constitute One Another* (Cambridge: Cambridge University Press, 2001); Joel S. Migdal, Atul Kohli, and Vivienne Shue, *State Power and Social Forces: Domination and Transformation in the Third World* (Cambridge: Cambridge University Press, 1994); Michael Palmer, "Environmental Regulation in the People's Republic of China," *The China Quarterly*, no. 156 (1998): 788–808.

Not only the Chinese state, but the Chinese society has also become more complicated and fractured in the meantime. After the state loosened its control, more and more organizations and ideas started to appear in the society. However, those who expected the increasingly stronger society to pose a serious challenge to the authoritarian rule might be disappointed. In fact, when the societal forces just leashed out during the 1980s, they were indeed highly rebellious, as attested by the 1989 Pro-Democracy Movement which almost toppled the regime.[16] However, when the Chinese civil society passed the initial rebellious stage in the 1990s, it differentiated into groups with varying interests and ideas. These societal forces started to mutually cancel out, which enhanced the political stability of the regime, a mechanism that has been widely recognized in the sociological literature.[17]

The cleavages within the Chinese state and the society are clearly visible in China's environmental politics. In the three environmental campaigns we have studied, we found that the major rivals of the ENGOs are the investors, the local government, and the opposing forces in the civil society. While the top leadership of the government does exercise its control over the emergent ENGOs, it also recognizes the ENGOs' right to exist and is often attentive to the suggestions and protests of the ENGOs. What is more, the government-controlled media and some important agencies of the central government are actually the hardcore allies of the ENGOs. Environmental politics in today's China thus involves seven major actors, namely the top leaders of the central government, the environmental agencies of the central government, the local government, the media, the business groups, the environmental

[16] Dingxin Zhao, *The Power of Tiananmen: State-Society Relations and the 1989 Beijing Student Movement* (Chicago: The University of Chicago Press, 2001).

[17] Lewis A. Coser, *The Functions of Social Conflict* (Glencoe, IL: Free Press, 1956); William Kornhauser, *The Politics of Mass Society* (New York: Free Press, 1959); Zhao, *The Power of Tiananmen*; Dingxin Zhao, *Shehui yu zhengzhi yundong jiangyi* [*Social and Political Movement*] (Beijing: Shehui kexue wenxian chubanshe, 2006).

activists, and finally the societal forces that opposed the environmentalists. The first three are more on the side of the state, and the last four more on the side of society. Yet they are not related in a way in which the societal forces form an alliance to counterpoise the state actors. Instead, the relationship among them is a tangled one that blurs the traditional state versus society dichotomy. The central argument of this chapter is that the interests and actions of the seven actors are shaping the political context, creating opportunities and constraints, and defining the nature and dynamics of the environmental movement. In other words, to understand the nature and dynamics of China's environmental movement, we must move beyond the old state–society binary by properly disaggregating the major state and societal actors involved in the environmental struggle.

This chapter proceeds as follows. First, we provide a historical overview of the development of the environmental movement in China. Second, we look into two successful environmental campaigns that happened in the late 1990s. Third, we examine a less successful environmental movement centering on the issue of the Nujiang dam project. Finally, we discuss what we can learn from the empirical stories, in particular with regard to the nature of the major actors involved in the environmental politics and the effectiveness and limit of China's environmental movement.[18]

[18] Field research for this study was conducted in Beijing, Heilongjiang, Yunnan, and Jiangsu Provinces from April to August 2004. During this period, the first author interviewed ENGO members and participated in their activities. Follow-up interviews were conducted in December 2005 and January 2006. The study is based on an analysis of these interviews and ethnographic data, as well as newspaper reports, data collected from the web sites, newsletters, annual reports, and other documents produced by ENGOs. Sources of information about the three cases will be specified respectively. We thank the 2003 Starr Collaborative Research Grant from the International Research and Exchanges Board for the financial support for this research at its first stage.

THE DEVELOPMENT OF CHINA'S ENVIRONMENTAL MOVEMENT[19]

Environmentalist thoughts began to take roots in China in the late 1980s and early 1990s. It started with individual-based activities. Xu Fengxiang, Xu Gang and Tang Xiyang, among others, are pioneers in this regard. Through their writings and activities, they inspired love of nature or tolled the alarm bell for the deteriorating environment. In 1983, Huang Zongying published a widely popular reportage *Xiao muwu* [*The Little Cabin*] based on Xu Fengxiang's 18 years of life in Tibet dedicated to research on the local ecology. Xu has since become a symbol of devotion to science and love of nature. When Xu retired in 1995, she built a cabin on Lingshan Mountain in the outskirts of Beijing to introduce Tibetan culture and life, to disseminate environmental knowledge, and to raise awareness of environmental protection. Xu Gang is arguably the most prolific and influential environmental literary writer. His 1988 work *Famuzhe xinglai* [*Loggers Wake Up*] warns against the destructive logging practice in

[19] The focus of this paper is the Chinese grassroots ENGOs. Grassroots ENGOs can still be classified into non-student grassroots green NGOs and student green groups. They represent the most autonomous and active organized forms of that sprang from the Chinese society. There are still two other types of organizations active on the environmental scene in China, namely government-organized NGOs (GONGOs) and international NGOs, which have different relationship with the Chinese state. Neither of these two types will be discussed in this paper. See Wu, "New Partners" and Wu, "Environmental GONGO Autonomy" for environmental GONGOs in China. We do not profess to address the entire picture of environmental movement, which should also include the "not-in-my-backyard" movements. In today's China, pollution protests are numerous. See Jun Jing, "Environmental Protests in Rural China," in *Chinese Society: Change, Conflict and Resistance*, ed. Elizabeth J. Perry and Mark Selden (London: Routledge, 2003). Tong (Yanqi Tong, "Environmental Movements in Transitional Societies: A Comparative Study of Taiwan and China," *Comparative Politics* no. 37 (2005): 167–188) categorizes the environmental movement in China into two big types: ideology-driven and pollution-incised. This paper will not address the latter type. Therefore, what we will discuss in this paper is only a part of the gamut. Nevertheless, they comprise the most independent environmental organizations germinating from the Chinese society and the most active force in the Chinese environmental movement.

the forestry industry and urges a shift from logging to reforestation and protection. In the following years, Xu published more books describing the beauty of nature and raising alarms about the human-caused ecological woes. Tang Xiyang had been an editor of *Daziran* [*The Nature*] magazine from 1980 to 1990. The book *Huanqiu lüse xing* [*A Green World Tour*], which he coauthored with his wife Marcia Marks and published in 1993, reports on their visits to nature reserves in China, Europe, and the United States, and reflects on the human–nature relationship. It is a rallying cry for China's conservationist movement.[20]

In the early 1990s, against the backdrop of rapid environment deterioration and the fermentation of environmentalist thoughts, the ENGOs emerged in the Chinese society. Although Friends of Nature (FON) is not the very first ENGO in China, no one can dispute that its establishment in 1994 was a landmark event in the history of the Chinese environmental movement.[21] FON's fast growing membership spread across China and mainly comprised journalists, teachers, other professionals, and students. The organization takes environmental education and nature conservation as its prime activities, but it also steps into other more contentious environmental campaigns when issues arise. It is the most important ENGO in China.

Liang Congjie, Wang Lixiong, Yang Dongping, and Liang Xiaoyan were the four founders of the organization. They were all celebrity intellectuals. The background of Liang Conjie, FON's founding president, is especially impressive.[22] His grandfather Liang Qichao

---

[20] For information about Tang Xiyang, see Economy, *The River Runs Black*, 138–141.

[21] Peter Ho (Ho, "Greening without Conflict?" 893–921) mentions that one green group was founded in 1991 but was shortly suspended by the government.

[22] Of the other three founding members, Wang was a freelance writer. His fiction *Huanghuo* [*Yellow Peril*] is a very influential political allegory published in 1990 (under the pseudonym "Baomi," which literally means "keep secret"). In the following years, he wrote on the topics of the Chinese political reform and on Tibetan issues. Yang was a university professor in Beijing and author of the best-seller *Chengshi jifeng* [*City Monsoon*] published in 1994. At the time, Liang was an editor of the journal *Dongfang* [*The Orient*], one of the most important forums for intellectual debate in China. Both Yang and Wang were contributors of *The Orient*.

was a most renowned reformer and scholar in late Qing and early Republican China, and his parents, Liang Sicheng and Lin Huiyin, were leading intellectuals of their own time. Liang himself was a member of the National Committee of the Chinese People's Political Consultative Conference (CPPCC).[23] For over a decade, Liang's unique social capital has been a great asset of FON, and he has used it well to push the environmental movement forward and to benefit the growth of the organization. As a member of the CPPCC, Liang has utilized this venue to submit proposals on environmental issues every year. His letters to top leaders carried considerable weight and has at times facilitated solutions to the issues in question. Liang's social prestige and his position enabled him and his organization to act more audaciously and with less political risks than most of the ENGOs. However, it does not mean the state would not sanction FON when it was considered to have gone beyond the limits. In 2003, the Ministry of Civil Affairs, through the organization that sponsored FON's registration, threatened that FON would not be able to pass its annual evaluation and thus would face closure if it did not oust Wang Lixiong, a founder and then Secretary of FON. Wang had frequently criticized the government's Tibetan policy and openly confronted the government on many other grounds, and therefore was regarded as "dangerous" by the government. For the survival of the organization, Liang, with much poignancy, had to make the painful decision of dismissing Wang from the organization.

Liang may be seen by some of us as a very cautious person. He imposed organizational self-censorship by circumventing what he

---

[23] The CPPCC is a political advisory body in China. The members are chosen by the Chinese Communist Party (CCP), but are relatively broad based. They are from the CCP, the satellite parties of the government, and mass organizations. The CPPCC also contains public personages from all walks of life, representatives of compatriots of Taiwan, Hong Kong, and Macao as well as of returned overseas Chinese and other specially invited people. The CPPCC typically holds a yearly meeting at the same time as plenary sessions of the National People's Congress. It participates in political consultations with regard to major state policies and important issues concerning the people's life and it makes suggestions to the CCP and administrative agencies. However, the suggestions are not legally binding.

deemed as too sensitive issue areas, such as pollution, and by restricting the expansion of membership, which otherwise would have easily soared to over tens of thousands. When Wang Yongchen, who was in charge of the tree-planting group for FON at the time, organized more than 700 Beijing citizens to participate in one of its activities, Liang expressed his uneasiness over the scale, which Wang did not share. Wang thereupon left FON and embarked on setting up her own organization, Green Earth Volunteers (GEV). However, under Liang's leadership, FON has not shrunk from standing at the forefront of most of the advocacy actions. For instance, it led the campaigns to save the snub-nosed monkeys in Yunnan Province and Tibetan antelopes in Qinghai Province, and was deeply involved in the campaigns against dam project on the Nujiang, the three rather contentious environmental campaigns that we will soon turn to.[24]

Around 1995, student green organizations started to appear in Chinese universities. By now, almost every university or college has at least one environmental group, and these groups have started to form regional networks or alliance.[25] Two figures have played pivotal roles in the rise of the student environmental organizations. In the summer of 1996, Tang Xiyang launched a college student green camp expedition to the habitat of the snub-nosed monkeys in Yunnan. Since then, the National College Students' Green Camp has been organized every summer. The Camp provides a training ground for young environmentalists and links geographically dispersed student green groups together. Many student green groups have emulated the model of the Green Camp and organized similar

[24] FON's reliance on Liang's personal charisma and authority has caused some concerns about the succession of leadership and the future of the organization after the aging Liang. In 2004, some board members of FON pushed for organizational reforms, which received Liang's consent. The first important step that FON took was to install an executive director under the President. It announced the job application to the public. In the end, Xue Ye, a bookstore owner in Guizhou Province, was chosen for this position out of more than 80 applicants.

[25] Hongyan Lu, "Bamboo Sprouts After the Rain: The History of University Student Environmental Associations in China," *China Environment Series* no. 6 (2003): 55–66.

events. Another important figure is Wen Bo, who co-founded the China Green Student Forum and facilitated the Green Camp when he was a college student. Later in the capacity of the China Adviser of Global Greengrants Fund, he has supported and guided the growth of student green groups through distributing small grants.

Student organizations engage in a range of activities. They stage a variety of routine activities including but not limited to celebrating the Earth Day and the World Environment Day, organizing lectures or exhibitions to promote environmental awareness on campus, providing environmental education to nearby kindergartens and elementary schools, and organizing tree planting and recycling (especially of used batteries). Student environmental groups are affiliated with the Communist Youth Leagues of their schools but enjoy varying degrees of autonomy. A few student green groups, such as the Scientific Exploration and Outdoor Life Society of Beijing Forestry University and Green Union of Harbin Institute of Technology, stand out in having demonstrated considerable organizational capacity comparable to non-student ENGOs. In many provinces where there are no metropolitan cities and where international NGOs are largely absent, the student green groups are often the most powerful and established local environmental organizations. In recent years, through establishing regional alliance and various Internet forums, the student green groups have been growing faster and are more regionally connected than other types of ENGOs.

In 1996, Global Village of Beijing (GVB), another bellwether of the ENGO community, was founded by the enterprising Liao Xiaoyi. GVB locates itself in a different niche than FON, concentrating its efforts in recycling, sustainable energy, environmental education, and other areas. Compared to FON, whose conservation focus draws its attention to remote nature reserves, GVB is generally more urban centered. Even in the same field of environmental education, while FON's environmental education van goes to the vast rural hinterland to disseminate environmental knowledge to elementary school students, GVB's efforts mostly focus on making TV programs, composing pamphlets and textbooks, and building green communities. GVB is less likely than FON to get involved in environmental issues that might result in confrontation with the government, partly because of the difference in their areas of specialization. FON's conservation actions are likely to collide with the interests of the local government or interest groups, while GVB's urban renewal projects are much appreciated by the government at all levels. In fact, GVB has always been aggressively seeking to involve government agencies in its projects. There is a tendency for the grassroot ENGOs to cluster around the more established ENGOs working in similar fields, particularly in Beijing, which command resources and act sometimes as intermediary grant distributors. For example, FON is at the center of the concentric network of conservation groups, while groups working on recycling and sustainable energy gather around GVB.

In the same year of 1996, Wang Yongchen started GEV. It is a very loose organization with no formal membership. Its tree-planting and bird-watching activities sometimes attracted thousands of volunteers, who dispersed when the activities came to an end. As an organization, GEV has much less influence than FON and GVB. However, Wang's job as a reporter for the China National Radio and her role as an organizer of the Environmental Journalist Salon not only made her more ready to take up thorny issues but lent much power to her voice.[26] Wang was a central figure in a series of anti-dam campaigns since 2003.

Since the late 1990s, the development of environmental movement has revealed two trends. First is the proliferation of the ENGOs all over China. There are now more than 2000 environmental groups officially registered as NGOs, with perhaps as many registered as for-profit business enterprises or not registered at all.[27] They can be found not only in metropolitan cities but also in the small cities and countryside. Second is the expansion and diversification

---

[26] The Environmental Journalist Salon was started in 2000 by Wang Yongchen. Since 2002, the *China Youth Daily* has co-hosted the salon. The monthly gatherings have brought together mainstream journalists to listen to presentations by government officials or experts on environmental protection.

[27] Economy, "ENGOs in China."

of their concerns and activities. Web-based ENGOs, such as Green Web and Greener Beijing, have emerged.[28] Some ENGOs also started to tackle politically sensitive issue areas. For example, the Center for Legal Assistance to Pollution Victims, founded in 1998, helps pollution victims to sue polluters. Huo Daishan's Huai River Guardian (*Huaibe weishi*), founded in 2003, carries out citizen monitoring on the illegal discharging of wastewater to the heavily polluted Huai River. Yu Xiaogang's Yunnan-based Green Watershed calls for implementing participatory social impact assessment in evaluating big dam project as well as protecting the rights and interests of dam-affected indigenous people. Concepts such as citizens' rights to know, participatory rights, and environmental justice have appeared more and more frequently in the rhetoric of environmentalists and increasingly shaped the framings of China's environmental movements.

The proliferation of the ENGOs since the late 1990s is a direct result of the loosening of the state's grip over social organizations in the bleak early post-Tiananmen years. To accommodate the new situation, the state published the Regulations on the Registration and Management of Social Organizations in 1998. Even though it is a set of rather restrictive regulations by the Western standard, it grants legitimacy to organizations that are not under direct control of the government. Under the Regulations, a newly established social organization must find a sponsoring institution (*zhuguan bumen*) before going through the registration procedure with the Ministry of Civil Affairs. Such a requirement does create barriers for NGOs to acquire legitimate status, but it is not a formidable task in practice, for the NGOs are able to find loopholes to bypass those regulations. Many ENGOs in China now either are registered as for-profit business entities with the Administration of Industry and Commerce[29] or chose

[28] Yang, "Weaving a Green Web," 89–93.

[29] GVB is the first organization that registered as a for-profit business entity. Other NGOs soon followed suit. It was not until April 2004 that GVB was able to register as a People-run Non-Enterprise Entity [*minban feiqiye danwei*] under the Bureau of Civil Affairs.

to remain unregistered.[30] These circumventive practices have been acquiesced by the state. The controlling agency — the Ministry of Civil Affairs — simply does not have enough staff and has no capacity to monitor the NGOs.[31] Even if they have the manpower, they may not do anything about it because repressive measures on the mushrooming ENGOs are likely to induce domestic resistance and international outcry, which the government wants to avoid. Moreover, while the Chinese government worries that the newly developed NGOs could be used for anti-government purposes, it holds positive views about the role that NGOs can play in society. With the expansion of the market economy, most economic decisions in China, especially the local investments, are no longer made by the central government. Since the central government is no longer directly responsible for most of the environmentally detrimental economic activities, it is not the direct target of the ENGOs.

The Chinese society has also become increasingly complicated under the reform. The state is no longer able to take care of everything as it used to. Therefore, the government has tried to promote a "big society, small government" model of governance to unload the state's burdens to the society.[32] The environmental protests staged by the ENGOs could alert the government to some otherwise neglected environment issues and create agendas that the government could deal with. Therefore, as long as an ENGO remains apolitical, its evasion and violation of the Regulations have been tolerated.[33]

The state's tolerance, however, has a clear limit: When the state suspects the involvement of an NGO in some forbidden political activities (such as promoting an immediate adoption of a Western style multi-party democracy or challenging the state policies on the

---

[30] Saich, "Negotiating the State," 124–141; Nick Young, "Introduction: Searching for Civil Society," in *250 Chinese NGOs: Civil Society in the Making*, ed. China Development Brief (Hong Kong: China Development Brief, 2001); Ho, "Greening without Conflict?" 893–921.

[31] Ru, "ENGOs in China."

[32] Saich, "Negotiating the State," 124–141; Ho, "Greening without Conflict?" 893–921.

[33] Ru, "ENGOs in China," 87–89.

issues of Tibet, Taiwan, or Falungong), it moves quickly to strike down, as the FON's forced dismissal of Wang Lixiong illustrates. Also, in 2005, in the aftermath of violent mass protests over polluting industries in Zhejiang, Tan Kai and five other individuals, all of whom were the members of the China Democratic Party banned by the government, established an organization called the Green Watch and declared its mission to be monitoring pollution independently. The government very quickly banned the organization, detained the six founding members for a period of time, and arrested its leader Tan Kai. This said, we must add that because most of the ENGOs at this stage are not motivated to challenge the communist rule directly, the above kind of heavy-handed repression is rare.

Two conclusions can be drawn from the above discussion: First, the Chinese government has been generally supportive of the ENGOs' development since their emergence. After a few years of its interaction with the ENGOs, it is also gaining experiences on how to deal with them. Besides a few major state policies and issues that are not allowed to be touched, the state has grown tolerant to the ENGOs' challenges to the environmentally adverse governmental decisions (especially when they are made by the local government). Yet, the state has no hesitation to repress an ENGO when it is seen as a dissident organization in disguise.

Second, as the social space for the NGOs gradually opens up, more and more ENGOs with different goals and functions start to appear. The relationship of these ENGOs with the state shows a spectrum, from resolutely apolitical, to cautiously taking up advocacy actions, to more boldly pushing the boundaries. Recently, a few ENGOs started to tread new issue areas and adopt new framings and tactics. Some of them even take advocacy actions as part of their regular programs.

After this overview of the movement's history, we now turn to three most celebrated and influential environmental campaigns staged by the ENGOs — the campaign to save the snub-nosed monkey in Yunnan in 1995–1997, the campaign to save Tibetan antelopes in Qinghai in 1996–2000, and the campaign against the Nujiang dam project since 2003 — to see how an environmental movement actually operates in China, what kind of roles the state actors have played in those campaigns, who are the allies and foes of the ENGOs in those campaigns, why some campaigns are more successful than the others, and what challenges the environmental movement in China is facing. We will be brief on the first two cases since they have been much reported and studied,[34] and pay more attention to the more recent and indeed more complicated and interesting case of the Nujiang campaign.[35]

SAVING THE SNUB-NOSED MONKEY AND THE TIBETAN ANTELOPE

The campaign to save snub-nosed monkey started in 1995 when wildlife photographer Xi Zhinong based in Yunnan learned that the local Deqin County was going to log over 100 square miles of pristine

[34] For a more detailed account about the campaign for the snub-nosed monkey, please see Ru, "ENGOs in China," 186–209; Economy, *The River Runs Black*, 149–156; and Shen Xiaohui, *Xueshan Xunmeng* [*Seeking Dreams in the Snowcapped Mountains*] (Shenyang, China: Shenyang Chubanshe, 1998). Shen was an official of the State Forestry Administration but was also a core member of FON. At Tang Xiyang's invitation, he participated in the Green Camp expedition to Yunnan in summer 1996 and wrote a book on the campaign to save the snub-nosed monkey. It is the best book so far to learn the details about the campaign. About the campaign to conserve the Tibetan antelopes, please see Ru, "ENGOs in China," 210–247; "Economy," *The River Runs Black*, 153–156. Information about the Chinese NGOs' conservation efforts for the Tibetan antelopes was also from interviews conducted in 2003, supplemented by media reports, newsletters of FON, the website of Shanhai tongmei which provides the most comprehensive information in Chinese: http://www.green2008.com/zjzl/index.asp (accessed December 12, 2003), Tibetan Antelope Information Center's website: www.taic.org (accessed December 12, 2003).

[35] Sources of Nujiang are from interviews conducted in December 2005–January 2006, media reports, and a great number of websites, which include http://www.chinariver.org/gb/articles/index_nujiang.html (accessed February 1, 2006), http://www.nujiang.ngo.cn/ (accessed February 1, 2006), http://www.chinarivers.ngo.cn (accessed February 1, 2006), and http://www.xys.org/dajia/nujiang.html (accessed February 1, 2006).

forest, which constituted about one-fifth of the endangered monkey's habitat. Xi sought help from Tang Xiyang, a pioneer environmentalist. Under Tang's advice and help, Xi wrote a petition to Song Jian, the State Councilor and the head of the State Environmental Protection Commission.

FON's involvement was crucial to the campaign from the very beginning. Because FON has active members in many mainstream media outlets, the media also play a crucial role here.[36] With extensive coverage from the media, this issue captured public attention. Meanwhile, Liang Congjie, the President of FON, through his political venue, had this issue reach the notice of Vice Premier Jiang Chunyun. At the same time, student green groups were also mobilized. Lectures about the monkey were arranged, Xi's film was shown and a candlelight vigil was held for the endangered species. In the summer of 1996, Tang Xiyang launched the first Green Camp (partially funded by FON), leading over 30 college students to Deqin. The expedition attracted enormous spotlight and sustained lasting public attention to the issue.

The top officials from the central government quickly responded to the petition letters. They ordered the Yunnan provincial government

[36] Although the Chinese media are controlled by the state, environment-related news is in a grey zone on which the media do sometimes have the freedom to report. In fact, the Chinese media have been a powerhouse of the environmental movement. For relationship between media and environmental movement, see Bo Wen, "Greening the Chinese Media," *China Environment Series* no. 2 (1998): 39–44; Kanping Hu, "Harmony and Diversity: The Relationship Between Environmental Journalists and Green NGOs in China," in *Green NGO and Environmental Journalist Forum*, ed. Jennifer Tuner and Fengshi Wu (Washington: Woodrow Wilson Center, 2002), http://www.wilsoncenter.org/cef; Kanping Hu and Xiaogang Yu, "Bridge Over Troubled Waters: The Role of the News Media in Promoting Public Participation in River Basin Managements and Environmental Protection in China," in *Promoting Sustainable River Basin Governance: Crafting Japan-US Water Partnership in China*, ed. Jennifer L. Turner and Kenji Otsuka (Japan: Institute for Developing Economies, 2005); Craig Calhoun and Guobin Yang, "Media, Civil Society, and the Rise of a Green Public Sphere in China," *China Information*, forthcoming.

to intervene, and the logging was banned summarily. The central government also dispatched a work team to Yunnan in January 1996 to investigate the issue. To compensate the poverty-stricken county for the financial losses as a result of the logging ban, the Yunnan provincial government allocated 8 million yuan annually. In addition, Deqin County also benefited from an annual allotment of 3 million yuan from the State Council during a five-year period and some financial assistance from the Ministry of Forestry. The fledging environmentalist community congratulated each other that the habitat of the snub-nosed monkey was saved.

However, in 1998, Xi Zhinong was tipped off that logging in Deqin County continued secretly. With his leads, the Central Chinese Television (CCTV) sent reporters undercover to investigate at the logging site. The ensuing media exposure sparked a national outcry. The outraged Premier Zhu Rongji intervened personally. The responsible county leadership was reprimanded and punished: The head of Deqin county had to "confess his mistakes" at a meeting held by Yunnan Forestry Department, and the deputy head of the county was fired.

The campaign for saving the Tibetan antelope is another major event that galvanized the burgeoning environmental movement in China. Tibetan antelopes roam on the vast inhabitable border areas of Tibet, Qinghai, and Xinjiang.[37] Because of the high demand in the Western market for shahtoosh shawl, made from the animal's fine down wool, Tibetan antelopes were poached to near extinction, despite the trade bans and extensive legal protection. International NGOs were also involved in the campaign, but our attention here will mainly be on China's indigenous ENGOs.

FON learned the story of the Tibetan antelopes from Yang Xin, a river explorer and photographer, in the end of 1995. Yang Xin in turn was inspired by the martyrdom of Sonam Dorje, who was the head

[37] Roughly the area of three present-day nature reserves — the Jiangtang Nature Reserve of Tibet, the Arjin Nature Reserve of Xinjiang, and the Kekexili Nature Reserve of Qinghai.

of the West Working Committee (*xibu gongwei*) of Zhiduo County, Qinghai Province.[38] Led by Sonam Dorje, the Committee fought against the rampageous poaching in the part of the Kekexili region under the jurisdiction of Zhiduo County. Sonam Dorje, however, was killed in a gunfight with the poachers in 1994. Deeply moved by his heroic death, Yang Xin vowed to build a nature preservation station in Kekexili as a base to combat poachers. He founded the Green River in 1999, a Sichuan-based ENGO dedicated to the conservation of the headwater areas of the Yangtze River.

FON's early efforts from 1996 to 1998 took the form of supporting Yang Xin to build the station. It became more directly and actively involved in the campaign after Zhawa Dorje, brother-in-law of Sonam Dorje, came to Beijing at the invitation of FON and the magazine *Green Weekend* in October 1998. The charismatic Zhawa Dorje reassembled the West Working Committee after Sonam Dorje's death and turned it into an armed anti-poaching team, better known for its nickname the Wild Yak Brigade (hereafter referred to as the Brigade). FON arranged several media events and university lectures for Zhawa Dorje. It also introduced Zhawa Dorje to other ENGOs in Beijing. Zhawa Dorje's presentations inspired the Chinese environmentalists and college students alike. The ensuing spate of sympathetic media reports portrayed the Brigade as an altruistic lone hero, which persisted in regular patrols in the desolate Kekexili to protect the endangered species despite forbidding natural conditions and extreme financial straits. The Brigade emerged from media coverage with a halo. Perhaps it is due to their thirst for romanticism, idealism, and heroism in a highly materialistic urban world that the media transformed the Brigade into a legend and the ENGOs turned it into an icon. Efforts to save the Tibetan antelopes were quickly mobilized and donation was flooding in to the Brigade consequently.

[38] The West Working Committee was established in 1992 by Zhiduo County. Its original mission was to explore and manage the mineral resources in the county in order to develop the local economy. Yet Sonam Dorje shifted its focus to fighting poaching of Tibetan antelopes.

The ENGOs also tried to win the support of the central government. For instance, Yang Xin's project to protect the headwater areas of the Yangtze River and to build the Sonam Dorje Nature Preservation Station was applauded by the heads of the State Environment Protection Administration (SEPA). Liang Congjie's proposal to SEPA and the State Forestry Administration on coordinated anti-poaching efforts between the three provinces of Tibet, Qinghai, and Xinjiang was partly adopted by the authority, catapulting the widely publicized Kekexili No. 1 Action in April 1999. Some new ENGOs also joined the cause in 1999. Among them were the Tibetan Antelope Information Center and Greener Beijing, both of which were well-versed in using Internet to disseminate information and mobilize support. Together, they organized exhibitions and concerts to raise fund for the Brigade. The Chinese ENGO's campaign to conserve the antelope was centering on supporting the Brigade, which they believed was the only team that could effectively fight poaching activities.

However, the ENGOs, due to their high-profile endorsement of the Brigade, unintentionally waddled into the muddy water of local politics. When the establishment of the Kekexili National Natural Reserve and Management Bureau (hereafter referred to as the Kekexili Bureau) was approved in 1997 by the State Council, several local forces, including the Brigade, were contending for a few state-sponsored positions. The Beijing ENGOs took this into their own hands to see the Brigade members to be incorporated into the Kekexili Bureau. Their forceful promotion of the Brigade, however, infringed upon the authority of and was resented by the Yushu prefectural government. It also invoked animosity from other local forces that had interests in the Kekexili Bureau. In the end, Yushu Prefecture moved on to disband the Brigade in August 1999.

When the news of the disbanding reached Beijing, FON, together with 17 journalists who had reported on the Brigade, wrote a petition to Vice Premier Wen Jiabao, appealing for a revocation of this decision. Yet, even the intervention directly from Wen Jiabao could not completely override the local politics. The intervention only temporarily halted the dissolution scheme. At the end of 2000, when things quieted down, the Yushu government disbanded the Brigade again; only this time they admitted the majority of the Brigade members to the Kekexili Bureau as a gesture of compromise.[39] Afterwards, the disheartened FON and other ENGOs gradually withdrew their attention and support from Qinghai. Yet, despite the demise of the Brigade, the endangered species is now much better protected, thanks to the campaign fought by the ENGOs and their media allies.

CAMPAIGN AGAINST THE NUJIANG DAM PROJECT

Since 2003, the ENGOs in China have plunged into a series of anti-dam campaigns. Important battles have been fought against dam projects on Yangliuping, Mugecuo, Nujiang, and Jinshajiang. Among them, the campaign against the Nujiang dam project is the most influential and contentious one to date.

The high-growth Chinese economy created huge demands for electric power, which in recent years gave rise to a hydropower development craze. This craze, however, is also closely related to the structural reform of China's energy sector in the past two decades. The sector has undergone deepening corporatization and marketization since the early 1980s.[40] In 1997, the Ministry of Electric Power was dismantled and replaced by the State Power Grid Development Company and the State Power Corporation (SPC). The government increasingly kept itself from interfering in enterprise management so as to push the state-owned enterprises to become more independent market entities. At the end of 2002, the SPC was split into 11 smaller companies.[41] Thus monopoly over

[39] The four officials of the Brigade were asked to return to Zhiduo County. Ru ("ENGOs in China," 210–247) provides a more rich account of the Brigade and the convoluted local politics.

[40] See Chen Lifen and Yang Xiaoli, "Reform and Development of China's Electric Power Industry," *Energy for Sustainable Development* no. 3 (1997): 62–66.

[41] They are five power generation companies, namely China Huaneng, China Datang, China Huadian, China National Power, and China Power Investment; two power grid companies, namely National Power Grid and China Southern Power Grip Co. Ltd.; and four auxiliary companies.

the energy sector was broken down and competition greatly intensified, which in turn facilitated a massive wave of hydropower development.

Yunnan Province, which by some accounts holds a quarter of China's hydropower potential, has become the center of attention after the Three Gorges Dam. The government planners and hydropower companies hoped to construct at least 30 large dams and hundreds of smaller projects in northwest Yunnan where Nujiang, Mekong, and Jinshajiang cascade off the Tibetan Plateau.

Originating from the Tibetan Plateau, Nujiang is one of China's major international rivers. It stretches over 2,000 km through Tibet and Yunnan and winds its way through Thailand and Burma, where it is called Salween, before emptying into the Indian Ocean. Its untapped hydroelectric power is among the highest of all rivers in China. The river passes through a mountainous region with more than 7,000 species of plants and 80 rare or endangered animals or fish. In 2003, the region's impressive geology and biological diversity prompted the UNESCO to designate it as a World Natural Heritage Site.

In March 2003, the Huaneng Power International, Inc. and the Yunnan provincial government signed an agreement on the joint development of hydroelectric power in Yunnan. On June 14, Yunnan Huadian Nujiang Hydropower Company Ltd. was established. July 18 saw the official inauguration of Yunan Nujiang Liuku Electric Power Plant. Its parent company Huaneng Power International is one of China's largest independent power producers. Li Xiaopeng, the son of former Premier Li Peng, serves as Chairman of the Huaneng Group.

In August, Nujiang Lisu Autonomous Prefecture of Yunnan Province submitted "The Report on the Hydropower Project on the Middle and Lower Reaches of Nujiang" to the National Development and Reform Commission (NDRC) for review.[42] The report proposed

---

[42] The NDRC is a macro-economic regulatory department of the State Council. Its mandate is to develop national economic strategies, long-term as well as annual economic plans, and to report on the national economy and social development to the National People's Congress.

to build two reservoirs and 13-cascade dams that would have a total generating capacity of 21.32 million kw. The NDRC approved the project proposal, and was going to submit it to the State Council for final approval.

However, a SEPA official who attended the NDRC meeting refused to give his endorsement to the Report, citing the reason that this project had not gone through an environmental impact assessment, as mandated by the Environmental Impact Assessment Law, which had been passed on November 29, 2002, by the Standing Committee of National People's Congress and would take effect on September 1, 2003. But his dissenting voice was too weak to resound at the meeting. During the meeting interval, the official phoned Wang Yongchen and broke the news. Wang Yongchen had played an important role in preventing the construction of the Yangliuping dam, which if built would effectively destroy the 2,250-year-old Dujiangyan Irrigation Project, one of the world's most extraordinary premodern marvels of construction and a World Heritage Site designated by the UNESCO.[43] She was also very actively involved in stopping the dam construction on Mugecuo Lake, a Tibetan sacred lake in Sichuan Province.[44] The phone call from the SEPA official sparked Wang's another consequential battle in her personal biography and an

[43] See Yiyi Lu, "Environmental Civil Society and Governance in China," Chatham House Asia Program Briefing Paper (2005), August 1–8; Andrew C. Mertha and William R. Lowry, "Unbuilt Dams: Seminal Events and Policy Change in China, Australia, and the United States," *Comparative Politics*, forthcoming.

[44] In the campaign against dam building on Mugecuo, environmentalists organized media coverage of the issue as usual. In addition, they petitioned to Prime Minister Wen Jiabao, who responded timely by ordering more investigation on the dam site. Thereafter, SEPA sent an investigation team to Mugecuo, and the long report after the three-day investigation assured the government that a dam on the lake would not cause environmental or other problems. Although the campaign did not halt the dam, it represented an important learning experience for the NGO and media environmental activists (Hu et al., "Bridge over Troubled Waters," 125–141).

unprecedented anti-dam campaign in the history of China's environmental movement.

On the phone, Wang recommended He Daming, a Yunnan-based river expert, to the SEPA official. He Daming was the director of the Asian International River Center affiliated to Yunnan University. SEPA gathered scientists and experts like He and moved quickly to prepare the first offence, which took the form of a symposium held on September 3, 2003. At the symposium, most of the experts they had invited voiced their strident objection to the Nujiang dam project. He Daming especially delivered a pounding criticism on the project, which was later often cited by environmentalists and media. Wang Yongchen and her journalist friends of the Environmental Journalist Salon were also present. Their reporting of the symposium made the voice of opposition reach the public at large. The meeting thus launched the campaign to preserve Nujiang and heralded a growing coalition of environmental activists, journalists, scientists, and SEPA officials.

The Yunnan provincial government, one of the biggest beneficiaries of the Nujiang dam project, wasted no time in retaliating. As a tit-for-tat response to SEPA's move, it ordered the Environmental Protection Bureau (EPB) of Yunnan Province to organize two expert meetings immediately following the SEPA-organized symposium, and the local experts presented at the two meetings predominantly rooted for the Nujiang dam project. In response, SEPA sponsored another two-day expert meeting in Yunnan in October. Debates between the adamant anti-dam Beijing experts and equally resolute pro-dam Yunnan experts were so contentious that at some moments it verged on personal attacks.

Several days after this meeting, at a conference of China Environmental Culture Promotion Association (CECPA),[45] Wang

[45] CECPA is a national GONGO set up by SEPA in 1992. It tried to incorporate social elites from all walks of life into its support network. Its board is comprised of nationally renowned figures in fields encompassing academia, media, arts, literature, sports, entertainment, industry and the ENGOs.

Yongchen collected altogether 62 signatures of the attendees, who are also the board members of CECPA, for a petition that voiced concerns about the Nujiang dam project. Among the signers were some well-known scientists, writers, entertainers, and the ENGO leaders. Media coverage of their appeal and the celebrity effect kindled national discussion on the issue.

At the same time, Wang and other activists were mobilizing the ENGO community into the anti-dam cause. Conferences such as the Third China International ENGOs Forum convened in Beijing in November 2003 and attended by more than 400 ENGO representatives from all over China and other countries provided them with good opportunities to draw the ENGOs' attention to Nujiang.[46] In Beijing, GEV and FON organized or sponsored various public talks and seminars on Nujiang and more generally on dams and world heritage preservation.

In Yunnan, the most consistent vocal critic of the Nujiang dam project was from Green Watershed, founded in 2002 by Yu Xiaogang, who earned his PhD in watershed management in Thailand. In November 2003, he organized a "Voice of Water" forum on Nujiang with the theme "Let me flow freely." In addition to advocating preserving Nujiang for its ecological value, Green Watershed also raised the issue of protecting the interests of dam-affected indigenous people. Goaded by a sense of righteousness for the underprivileged and indignation toward what they saw as predatory development, Green Watershed insisted that the indigenous people should be included in the decision-making process of hydroelectric projects and integrated into the river basin management system. It worked hard to inform and thus empower the local communities by organizing workshops for them to discuss the social impacts of the damming and to study *A Citizen's Guide to the World*

[46] The Third Forum was organized by GVB, People's University, and International Fund for China's Environment. This bi-annual NGO forum launched by International Fund for China's Environment in 1999 has become a key platform for the Chinese ENGOs to communicate with international communities.

Commission on Dams.[47] In May 2004, Green Watershed took a group of Nujiang villagers to the Manwan dam site, where Yu had previously conducted a social impact assessment in 2001. Having witnessed the dismal living conditions of the relocated Manwan residents, the participants felt the urge to fight for their own rights. In its anti-dam activities, Green Watershed has touched the sensitive issues of human rights, social justice, and good governance and inevitably brought itself into confrontation with local authorities head-on. These intrepid moves greatly irked the Yunnan government, which viewed Yu as a rabble-rouser and tried to silence Green Watershed. It ordered a thorough investigation of the organization, pressured partner agencies to dissociate themselves from Green Watershed, and barred Yu from leaving China by confiscating his passport.[48]

Yet even in Yunnan, where the provincial government and the prefectural government of Nujiang so adamantly favored dam construction and resented any dissension, the state apparatus was not entirely in unison. At a plenary session of the CPPCC in February 2004, a leader of the Yunnan Provincial China Democratic League,

---

[47] The Guide was produced by the International Rivers Network to provide people with guidance on how to use the World Commission on Dams (WCD) report in their struggles for justice and human rights. This 59-page booklet provides background on the formation of the WCD, a detailed summary of the WCD report, and suggestions for how activists can use the report to stop destructive development projects and promote better alternatives. The WCD was established by the World Bank and IUCN (The World Conservation Union) in response to the growing opposition to large dams. On November 16, 2000, the WCD published its groundbreaking report, *Dams and Development: A New Framework for Decision-Making*. It concludes that dams' contributions to human development have come at a grave social and environmental cost. Deciding the past model of dam building as no longer acceptable, the report recommends a new approach to decision-making based on the principles of equity, efficiency, participatory decision-making, sustainability, and accountability. It emphasizes that the rights of the indigenous people who are affected by dam projects should be respected. While the Guide provides movement framework for the anti-dam activists in China, it is the target of ire of the pro-dam side.

[48] Fu Tao, "Respite for Yunnan Anti-Dam NGO as Movement Mourns Loss of Key Activist," *China Development Brief* (January 20, 2005), http://www.chinadevelopmentbrief.com/node/104 (accessed February 1, 2006).

one of the eight satellite parties that the Chinese government allows to exist, questioned the Nujiang dam project and submitted a proposal which suggested that any hydropower project on Nujiang should take into account the sustainable development of the entire river basin. This move of the Yunnan China Democratic League was influenced by the Green Watershed. Yu Xiaogang was overjoyed at the submission, which meant that the voice of the grassroots ENGOs about the Nujiang dam now finally reached the Yunnan provincial leaders.

Meanwhile the ENGOs in Beijing and across China were also acting. In January 2004, Li Xiaoxi, an environmental activist and a representative of People's Congress from a district of Beijing, wrote a letter to Premier Wen Jiabao to express her opinion on the Nujiang issue. In February 2004 at the annual CPPCC conference, Liang Congjie submitted two proposals written by Shen Xiaohui, a SFA official and a board member of FON, calling on the State Council to annul the proposal of the Nujiang dam plan submitted by the NDRC. Outside Beijing, the Chongqing Green Volunteer Union, led by Wu Dengming, went to 10 universities in Chongqing to appeal for students' attention to the "last pristine river" in China. They collected more than 15,000 petition signatures of college students.

Unlike the earlier environmental campaigns, the campaign against the Nujiang dam project was perceived to have higher political risks. After all, this is a project supported by a provincial government and backed up by the powerful hydropower interest group and some branches of the central government. In comparison with the other environmental campaigns, relatively few ENGOs have been actively involved in the campaign. The majority of them showed their moral support but opted out from participation. Still, the anti-dam voices are sonorous. The activists were doubtless resourceful and energetic and they also had supports from high-profile scientists, and were backed up by SEPA. But most importantly, their voices were greatly amplified by the media. As in the campaigns to conserve the snub-nose monkey and the Tibetan antelopes, media's role was again crucial. Reporter-activists like Wang Yongchen were at the forefront of the anti-dam campaigns and played the role of movers and shakers, and the journalists from the influential media such as the *China Youth Daily*, *Southern Weekend*, CCTV, Phoenix TV, *Waitan Pictorial*, and *Science Times* all have showed their strong support or sympathy to the cause.

The campaigners even tried to bring international pressure to bear on the Chinese government. In November 2003, some Chinese ENGOs, including GEV, FON, and Green Watershed, participated in the Second International Meeting of Dam-Affected People and their Allies in Thailand. The Chinese NGOs asked for support on the Nujiang case, and the conference issued a joint appeal against the Nujiang dam project, signed by representatives from more than 60 countries. The petition was also sent to the UNESCO World Heritage Committee, since nine out of the 13 proposed dams would fall into the "Three River Parallel" World Heritage Site. In response, the UNESCO World Heritage Committee expressed its "grave concern" to the Chinese authority. Since the lower reaches of the Nujiang River are in Thailand, after the conference over 80 Thai ENGOs also sent a joint letter, endorsed by the Thai Prime Minister, to the Chinese Embassy, urging China not to develop the river in a way that may harm the downstream residents.

In early February 2004, Premier Wen Jiabao, in an unexpected move, ordered the "suspension" of the Nujiang plan. It is reported that Premier Wen stated his opinion on the project: "Large hydro-electric dam plans like this that have aroused a high level of societal concern and disagreement from the environmental protection side should be carefully reviewed and decided scientifically." Environmentalists were exhilarated by the news, hailing this as a victory of their side. The news reached Wang Yongchen when she was on a fieldtrip with a group of journalists and environmentalists in the Nujiang valley. After they were back to Beijing, they held a photo exhibition on Nujiang and set up a website dedicated to the protection of Nujiang.

Yet, at the time when the environmentalists assumed their victory and shifted their attention, the pro-dam side was preparing a counterattack. The Primer's kind of vague statement that "Large hydro-electric dam plans like this ... should be carefully reviewed and decided scientifically" led to different interpretations. Since the statement did not altogether reject the idea of the dam project, the hydropower interest group was able to read it as an urge to modifying and resubmitting the dam proposal. The new version addressed some of the most serious criticisms raised by the environmentalists and emphasized the project's benefits to poverty alleviation and environmental protection. In their coming-back, the pro-dam side also adopted other tactics: they invited domestic and international experts, officials, and some renowned individuals in the society to Nujiang with the purpose of swaying them, and they mobilized supporting forces to attack the conservationists.

The environmentalists received their first blow in October 2004 at an international symposium on the hydropower and sustainable development sponsored by the UNDP, the World Bank, and the NDRC in Beijing. Although members of Green Watershed presented their papers at the conference and five Yunnan villagers were able to register as conference participants with the help of Yu Xiaogang and others, the ENGOs were by and large marginalized at the conference. The invited speakers, from foreign delegates to the local officials from the Nujiang region, spoke predominantly in favor of dams. Furthermore, Zhang Boting, the Vice Secretary-General of Chinese Society for Hydro-electric Engineering, delivered his tirade on the ENGOs, charging them for deterring China's development and depriving the local people of their opportunities to get better off.

Strikingly, the pro-dam side emulated several important tactics that the anti-dam forces had used. Above all, they forged a strong alliance with forces in the society. In April 2005, they arranged a high-profile 12-member group to visit Nujiang on an investigative tour. In the group were Lu Youmei, He Zuoxiu, and Fang Shimin (better known by his pseudonym Fang Zhouzi). Lu Youmei, a member of the Chinese Academy of Engineering, recently retired as the General Manager of Three Georges Project Corporation. He Zuoxiu is a physicist and a member of the prestigious Chinese Academy of Sciences. He is also known as a crusader against supernatural and unscientific thinking. On this count, there is much similitude between He and Fang Zhouzi. Fang, a U.S. educated biologist by training, founded and still controls a California-based website *Xinyusi* [the *New Threads*].[49] It was one of the first Chinese-language electronic magazines that appeared in the early 1990s and is still among the most influential. Fang made his reputation by exposing pseudoscience, plagiarism, and corruption in China's academia as well as his critical attitude toward Christianity and Falungong on his website. Since the beginning of 2005, Fang Zhouzi and He Zuoxiu had sparred with the environmentalists in a big debate on "whether humankind should be in awe of nature" and the rancor lingered.[50] In the three-month long debate, Fang and He's camp slung a string of labels at their opponents such as hypocritical, irrational, benighted, superstitious, anti-science, anti-human, inflammatory, radical environmentalists, and bogus environmentalists, while their disputants also accused them of scientism and anthrocentrism. The debate thus bipolarized the forces within the civil society. Fang and He's Yunnan trip facilitated the alliance between two majors foes of the ENGOs.

After their four-day tour on Nujiang, Fang, He, and other members of the team delivered speeches at Yunnan University. There, Fang Zhouzi gave a scathing speech on anti-dam activists, lampooning their opposition to the Nujiang dam project for lack of scientific validity, condemning them for feeding the public with groundless

[49] Website can be found at http://www.xys.org.

[50] In January 2005, a great debate on human–nature relationship swept over China in the wake of the Asian tsunami. The debate was sparked by He Zuoxiu's pointed criticism of the view that humans should revere nature, expressed in an interview with *Huanqiu* [*The Globe*] magazine. Among the environmentalists, Wang Yongchen was the first to respond with an article "Revering Nature is Not Anti-Science" on *Beijing News* on the next day. Fang Zhouzi's acerbic refutation to Wang entitled "Revering Nature IS Anti-Science" incurred many rejoinders from environmentalists and their league, followed by another round of rebuttals from the "No-reverence" camp. In addition to *Beijing News*, which organized the debate and carried altogether 31 contributed articles, other newspapers also published various articles in relation to the topic. The controversy also spread to the Internet when the chat room of the popular website sina.com.cn invited representatives from both sides to engage them in a point-to-point debate. Like many other debates, this debate reflects the pluralization of the civil society in China.

messages, and calling them bogus environmentalists. When Fang Zhouzi posted his speech transcript on the website of *Xinyusi*, it quickly spread to other websites and caused a fracas on the Internet. After the Yunnan trip, Fang and his followers continued to discredit and ridicule the environmentalists on *Xinyusi*.[51] For instance, the anti-dam side's war cry was to preserve "the last pristine river" (sometimes they would say "one of the two last pristine rivers") in the campaign. However, it was pointed out by their opponents that there were already hydropower stations built on Nujiang and thus the river could not be called pristine. Some environmentalists' representation of the Nujiang valley is imbalanced: while they sang about the pristine and idyllic Nujiang, they failed to mention the already damaged ecology of the Nujiang valley. These and some other weaknesses and mistakes of the environmentalists made them vulnerable to the attacks of Fang Zouzi and the like. Perhaps for the first time in their history, the ENGO's creditability was subject to serious questioning.[52] Fang Zhouzi's relative analytical rigor, aggressiveness, pungent rhetoric, reputation as an independent intellectual, and leverage over the public opinion via *Xinyusi* have made him an invaluable ally to the pro-dam forces. The pro-dam side's alliance with Fang Zhouzi not only strengthened its artillery to attack the environmentalists but also secured a powerful medium for them to counterpoise the mainstream media in China, which were overwhelmingly sympathetic to the environmentalists. Under the vehement barrage of Fang and his band, environmentalists appeared outmaneuvered on the Internet.

---

[51] See http://www.xys.org/dajia/nujiang.html (accessed February 1, 2006).

[52] In their debate, Fang also claimed that he himself, rather than the members of the ENGOs, was the real environmentalist. He also argued that he had no presumed stance on the Nujiang dam project but he has not yet found *any* good reason to oppose the dam project (the emphasis is ours). See especially his speech entitled "Controversy on the Nujiang Dam Project: Environmentalism and Bogus Environmentalism" given at the Tongji University on November 25, 2005; and his article "An Appraisal of the Views Opposing the Hydropower Development on Nujiang." Both texts are available at http://www.xys.org/dajia/nujiang.html (accessed February 1, 2006).

Petition to high officials, a method employed effectively by the environmentalists, was adopted by the pro-dam side as well. In May 2005, He Zuoxiu and Lu Youmei coauthored and submitted a report to the top state leaders, endorsing the Nujiang project and denouncing the ENGOs.[53]

In August 2005, when word came out that the central government agencies had reviewed the EIA of the revised Nujiang hydropower development plan and were planning to approve it in the coming months, the anxious environmentalists sent a public letter to the central government, urging the public disclosure of the EIA report on the Nujiang dams before making a final decision. Signed by 92 organizations and 459 individuals, the letter cited extant Chinese laws to call for a democratic decision-making process about hydropower development to keep all stakeholders fully informed and to allow their participation. To the chagrin of the environmentalists, the central government did not respond this time.

In October 2005, *China Investment*, a journal affiliated with the NDRC, sponsored the Symposium on China's Hydropower Development and Environmental Protection. The hydroelectric interest group and its allies such as Fang Zhouzi and He Zuoxiu dominated the meeting. Most of the SEPA officials and environmentalists who were invited felt this was a trap and found excuses to be absent. A handful of the ENGO representatives who did attend kept silent

---

[53] In their report, they wrote: "At present, an issue demands our serious concern and caution: an abnormal trend has distorted the truth and misled the public. Some 'trendy' NGOs, under the name of 'environmental protection,' oppose building dams and hydro-electric projects. Through telling lies that the present time has already entered the phase of dismantling dams, and disingenuously attributing water pollution and environmental deterioration to dams, and so on, they have created extremely absurd public opinion. Banded together with quite a number of journalists, they have spun [their lies] and dangerously misled the public and the society, negatively influenced the normal development of our country. They run counter to the principle of scientific development and the notion of the human-oriented sustainable development." (He Xianghong, "Liang Yuanshi shangshu Hu Wen cu Nujiang gongcheng fugong" [Two Academicians Petition Hu Jintao and Wen Jiabao about Resuming the Nujiang Project], *Wenhui Po*, September 11, 2005).

when bombarded by attacks from all fronts. Both the ENGOs and SEPA were the targets of denunciation.

Entering 2006, the number of Chinese media reports on Nujiang evidently dropped, so did oppositional voices on the part of SEPA and the ENGOs. The environmentalists felt the issue was hopelessly slipping away and beyond their reach. According to a Hong Kong newspaper *Wenwei Po*, the EIA for the Nujiang hydropower planning was completed and would go to the NDRC for approval.[54] The result looks like a compromise. The review panel concluded that four out of the 13 proposed dam projects could go ahead. The newspaper also quoted a close source to say that since Nujiang was an international river, the EIA was classified and thus could not be disclosed. This certainly disappointed the anti-dam environmentalists.

DISCUSSION

An immediate lesson we learn from the above empirical cases is that the nature and dynamics of the environmental movement in China is far more complicated than most published works on this subject have portrayed. While the ENGOs are not motivated to challenge the regime, under some circumstances they can confront the local government or the powerful corporate interest groups. Both within the state apparatus and within the civil society, the ENGOs have alliances and face oppositions. For instance, in the Nujiang case, we have observed the alliance between the SEPA and ENGOs catalyzed the campaign and won the first round of the battle. In response, the hydropower interest group sought coalition in the civil society and staged a forceful counterattack. The trajectory of the Nujiang campaign was shaped by the alignment between the state actors and the actors in the civil society. Therefore, in order to understand the nature and dynamics of China's environmental movement we should

[54] Wang Kou, "Nujiang shuidian wancheng huanping chencha" [Nujiang Hydropower Completed the Review of the Environmental Impact Assessment]," *Wenhui Po*, January 11, 2006.

view neither the state nor the society as a single entity with fixed interests and mode of action. Instead, we must disaggregate both the state and the society to the level appropriate to the issues we want to address and look at the opportunity structure that gave rise to the alliances and oppositions that shape the dynamics of the movement.

As the three environmental campaigns show, generally seven major actors have been involved in China's environmental politics. To understand the nature and patterns of the development of the environmental movement in China, we must understand the interests, resources, and power of each of the seven actors. In the following we will examine the roles of four of the seven actors to see how the characteristics of each of them have shaped the environmental politics in China. The four actors we will discuss are the top leaders of the central government, the environmental agencies of the government, the local government, and the sectors of the societal forces opposing the ENGOs. We omit the discussion of the business interest groups, the mainstream media, and the ENGOs because the positions of these three are much more clear at this stage. We start with the top leaders of the central government.

The Central Government. For the last three decades, the Chinese central government has increasingly attached greater importance to environmental protection, even though economic development has always enjoyed priority. The 1978 Constitution declared the state's commitment to "protect the environment and natural resources." Environmental protection has been integrated into the long-term planning of the state and the concept of "sustainable development" has been embraced since the early 1990s. This general drift toward safeguarding the environment is also reflected in the creation of laws and regulations and the establishment and strengthening of supportive institutions.[55] This "greening of the state" (Peter Ho's phrase) was a direct response to both the deepening environmental

---

[55] Palmer, "Environmental Regulation in the PRC," 788–808; Ma Xiaoying and Leonard Ortolano, *Environmental Regulation in China: Institutions, Enforcement, and Compliance* (Lanham, MD: Rowman and Littlefield, 2000).

degradation as well as diplomatic pressure to adapt to international norms.[56]

With environmental protection incorporated into the state agenda, legitimacy has been extended to social organizations in the field. The government also needs the ENGOs since the size of the environmental problems that China is facing is far beyond what the state could handle alone. The various activities of the financially independent ENGOs not only greatly lower the financial burden of the government,[57] but also supplement those of the state environmental agencies. Except for worrying that the ENGOs may escape from the state control and engage in dissident activities, the central government has many reasons to welcome and support the ENGOs' activities.

State environmental laws and regulations provide political opportunities for various actors to act, which in turn shape the contours of the environmental movement. The 1989 Environmental Protection Law stipulates that all units and individuals have a duty to protect the environment. The Environmental Impact Assessment Law, which was passed on November 29, 2002, by the Standing Committee of Chinese National Congress and came into effect on September 1, 2003, was hailed as another landmark in the history of the making

---

[56] Lester Ross, "China: Environmental Protection, Domestic Policy Trends, Patterns of Participation in Regimes and Compliance with International Norms," *The China Quarterly* no. 156 (1998): 809–835.

[57] For a majority of the non-student grassroots NGOs, most of the funding is from foreign foundations, foreign embassies, and multinational corporations in China. Sometimes, a few large Chinese NGOs act as small grant distributors of foreign funds for smaller Chinese NGOs. There is some variation within the NGO community on this issue. For example, for those which are more established and more adept at grant application, an overwhelmingly high percentage of the funds are foreign grants. For those starters and who have not learned how to apply for grants yet, the very limited funds are from membership fees and sporadic donations. As a result, lack of funding is a big problem that constrains the stable growth of many NGOs. For student NGOs, sometimes for a special activity, they get money from the Communist Youth Committee of the school. They also carry out fund raising among local companies and sometimes manage to get some hundred yuan for a special activity such as summer camp.

of a legal system of environmental protection. The Environmental Impact Law demands obligatory environmental assessment studies by construction companies for all construction projects and encourages public participation in the EIA process. Since its publication, it has empowered SEPA and the ENGOs to take actions against some environmentally detrimental projects and directly engendered the Nujiang campaign and later the EIA public hearing on the plastic covering of the lake bed of Yuanmingyuan in April 2005.[58] The new law also shapes the framings of the environmentalist movement, which has come to accentuate citizens' rights to know and to participate in decision-making processes as granted by the law.

Due to routinization of state rule and fiscal decentralization in Reform China, the top leadership of the state finds their power no longer without circumscription. In today's China, when the local governments or some branches of the central government make decisions, as long as they act within their jurisdictions and follow legitimate procedures, the top state leaders will find it hard to overturn their decisions, especially those made by the powerful provincial governments. In reality, as has been shown by the cases of the three environmental campaigns, China's top leaders have more or less acted beyond the interests of various social groups and the local governments. They adopted no fixed positions in their decision making with regard to environmental campaigns. They were very

[58] Since November 2004, the Yuanmingyuan Park officials carried out a 30-million-yuan project to cover the park's lake beds with plastic sheets, which were supposed to prevent water seeping away. However, the project never underwent required EIA, and experts and environmentalists blasted the scheme for its damage to the ecosystem. The dispute reached a climax in April 2005 when SEPA held a public hearing on the environmental impact of the project. It was the first public hearing sponsored by SEPA and was lauded to have historical significance. More than 120 people, including some from the Yuanmingyuan Administration Bureau, ENGOs representatives, and experts from research institutes, attended the hearing. The hearing ended with SEPA ordering most of the plastic membrane covering to be removed. The Yuanmingyuan case was widely covered by the media. Two influential websites, i.e., people.com.cn and news.xinhuanet.com, live broadcast the public hearing held on April 13, 2005.

likely to give support to the ENGOs if there was no or little opposition to the environmental movement. However, when the ENGOs faced strong oppositions, the central government might withdraw their support totally or partially, and let the social conflicts and bureaucratic routines play themselves out. Therefore, in the Nujiang case, we observe that the top leaders supported the environmental movement when the SEPA–ENGOs alliance took the offensive, but when the hydropower interest group sought coalition in the civil society and staged a forceful counterattack, the central government adopted a compromising stance.

To say that the central administration increasingly acts as a transcendental political force is not to deny the immense power it still wields and the enormous weight its decisions carry. Hence different social groups and branches of the governments are contending for the endorsement of the top leadership. Petition to the top leadership is always a major part of the collective action repertoire of the Chinese ENGOs, and in the Nujiang case, the oppositional force of the environmental movement adopted this strategy as well.

SEPA. Several entities within the Chinese administrative system have jurisdictions over environmental issues. Here, however, we will mainly focus on SEPA since it has played the single most important role in China's environmental politics. The predecessor of SEPA was the Environmental Protection Office created by the Chinese government in the 1970s. Despite a few setbacks, the power of this national-level environmental protection administration has continued to ascend since its creation.[59] In the early 1980s, the Office was promoted to the status of a bureau. In 1984, it was renamed as the National Environmental Protection Bureau (NEPB). In 1988, as part of the administrative reform, NEPB was separated from the Ministry of Urban and Rural Construction and Environmental Protection and renamed as the National Environmental Protection Agency (NEPA), and its bureaucratic rank was raised to a level that is half-notch

[59] Abigail Jahiel, "The Organization of Environmental Protection in China," *The China Quarterly* no. 156 (1998): 757–787; Economy, *The River Runs Black*.

below a ministry. In the 1998 radical reform of government administration, when the number of ministry-level government bodies was significantly reduced from 40 to 29, NEPA was upgraded to the ministerial status and changed to its current name SEPA. In concomitant with the institutional upgrading, the promulgation of environmental protection laws has also greatly empowered SEPA. The Environmental Impact Assessment Law in particular provided an important legal framework under which SEPA could assert and shore up its authority.

SEPA's power further expanded after Pan Yue joined SEPA as one of its Vice Ministers in March 2003. Pan has been known as a young enterprising political reformer within the CCP and the vicissitudes of his political life have been viewed by some as a barometer of the political reforms in China. Ambitious, outspoken, and resolute, Pan was always able to cause a stir at every post he held, from the Vice Chief Editor of the *China Youth Daily* to the Vice Director of Office for Economic Restructuring of the State Council. Urging the CCP to adopt political reforms as it shifted from a revolutionary party to a ruling party, and advocating more tolerant religious policies, Pan stood out as an anomaly in the ruling elite. Not long after Pan assumed his post in SEPA, he delivered a keynote address entitled "Environmental Culture and National Renaissance" at a CECPA conference in 2003. In this widely circulated speech, he criticized the traditional mode of industrial production and argued that the establishment of an eco-friendly sustainable economy should be a crucial part of China's revitalization.[60] Pan was the main facilitator in establishing a new economy index dubbed the "Green GDP," which would deduce environmental costs from the traditional GDP. He pushed for the Green GDP to be integrated in the appraisal system of local officials, who were used to be evaluated solely by their performance in advancing the local economy. In January 2005, on behalf of SEPA, Pan ordered to suspend the construction of 30 large-scale projects across the country, including a

[60] Pan Yue, "Huanjing wenhua yu minzu fuxin" [Environmental Culture and National Revitalization], Speech at the Chinese Association of Environmental Culture Promotion (2003).

new hydropower plant in Yunnan being built by the Three Gorges Project Corporation, citing their failure to comply with the new Environmental Impact Assessment Law.

SEPA, in enforcing its authority, inevitably ran counter to the interests of other state actors. As the Nujiang case shows, SEPA's different stance on the hydropower development has pitted itself against the hydropower interest group and the local governments which are the chief beneficiaries from the dam project. In particular the large power companies are extremely well connected in the government, and they have the capacity to resist SEPA's injunctions.

SEPA, in its institutional building and power expansion, also impinged on the vested interests of other bureaucratic agencies. The tension between SEPA and the environmental department under NDRC because of their overlapping jurisdiction has long existed. The powerful NDRC used to retain the upper hand. For instance, NDRC became the lead agency for China's "Great Western Development" (*xibu da kaifa*) campaign in 2001,[61] while SEPA was excluded from the 22-agency leading group identified at the campaign's outset in 1999 despite the fact that "ecological construction" was one of the major tenets of the campaign.[62] Before the Environmental Impact Assessment Law became effective, NDRC usually took charge of the assessment of whether a large construction project met the environmental standards. The 2002 Law only stated that the environmental protection administrative agency under the State Council should be responsible for assessing the environmental impact reports but did not specify which agency. It thus opened a crack for intra-agency power contention, and SEPA has grasped this opportunity to stage repeated strikes on violators to establish its authority and tipped the power equilibrium.

[61] In 2000, China launched its plan to develop its poor and vast western region. The Great Western Development plan is a massive five-year program designed to steer state resources, outside expertise, foreign investment, and private capital into the region to develop its economy.

[62] Economy, *The River Runs Black*, 108.

Nevertheless, SEPA's authority building process is constrained by its new and hence weak position within in the bureaucratic system as well as its relatively poor resources. SEPA has only approximately 300 staff members. Its authority cannot even penetrate the local EPBs. In theory, the local EPBs are subordinate to both SEPA and the local governments. Yet, since the EPBs rely on the latter for virtually all their funding, they tend to be more compliant to the will of the local governments than to SEPA.[63] That is why on the issue of the Nujiang dam project, the Yunnan provincial EPB followed the Yunnan government, not SEPA.

Facing the constraints, SEPA are compelled to look outside of the polity for alliance or coalition, and the ENGOs become the natural ally of SEPA because of their similar goals and ideology. As our Nujiang case indicates, they become increasingly closer in recent years. The ENGOs are worthy allies for SEPA on several grounds. The ENGOs have an impressively large membership and a cross-country network that can be mobilized. They enjoy sizable moral capital — the ENGOs have the image as an independent group working for the public good and representing the voice of the grass-roots. The ENGOs' intimate relationship with the media enables them to have considerable sway on the society. SEPA was very impressed by the ENGOs and media's success in resisting the juggernaut of the hydropower interest group and stalling the Dujiangyan dam project. The ENGOs have more leeway than SEPA to adopt a critical stance toward state-sponsored economic projects. A few figures in the green community have political resources that can be valuable to SEPA too. For example, Liang Congjie, as a member of the CPPCC, once wrote a letter to the State Council appealing to include SEPA in the leading group of the "the Great Western Development" campaign.[64]

SEPA has always been very supportive of the ENGOs. It expresses its support through giving awards and honors to environmentalists, attending the ENGO initiated activities, and co-sponsoring

---

[63] Jahiel, "Organization of Environmental Protection," 757–787; Economy, *The River Runs Black*; Jonathan Schwartz, "ENGOs in China: Roles and Limits," *Pacific Affairs* no. 77 (2004): 28–50.

[64] Economy, *The River Runs Black*, 148.

events with the ENGOs. Some SEPA officials have also established personal friendships with leading figures of the green community. Pan Yue, after assuming his position in SEPA, has earnestly sought the coalition of the ENGOs and publicly addressed the ENGO community as a "government's ally." Under his orchestration, the 2003 CECPA incorporated all major ENGOs, including even the student ENGOs, as its board members. The CECPA organized training workshops for student green groups from 157 universities across China. We can see through the above three environmental campaigns that while the cooperation between SEPA and ENGOs were still incidental in the two earlier cases, the Nujiang campaign signaled the formation of a strong coalition, in which the environmentalists fought on the front stage, while SEPA maneuvered on the back. Although the Nujiang campaign faded away, the SEPA–ENGO coalition was still in place and solidified. In January 2005, three days after SEPA had announced to suspend the construction of 30 large-scale projects across the country which breached the Environmental Impact Assessment Law, 56 ENGOs issued a joint statement cited by more than 20 major media outlets, hailing the decision and showing their moral solidarity with SEPA.[65] In the much-publicized EIA hearing on the Yuanmingyuan project of plastic covering in April 2005, SEPA provided an institutionalized venue for the ENGO members to participate in the environmental decision making. Right after the first public hearing, the CECPA and GVB held a training workshop for the ENGOs to improve their presentation and debating skills in public hearings. Much of the training was delivered by SEPA departmental heads.[66]

SEPA's support of the ENGOs' activities has two seemingly paradoxical consequences. On the one hand, alliance with SEPA imparts a sense of legitimacy to the actions of the ENGOs and emboldens

[65] For the text of the letter, see http://www.fon.org.cn/index.php?id=4842 (accessed February 1, 2006).

[66] Nick Young, "Public Enquiries Draw SEPA and Green NGOs Closer Together," *China Development Brief* (April 22, 2005), http://www.chinadevelopmentbrief.com/node/72 (accessed February 1, 2006).

them to stage bold actions. SEPA's backup is the most important reason to explain why in the Nujiang campaign the ENGOs were able to challenge the powerful hydropower goliath head-on. Although environmentalists had previously engaged in anti-dam activities, the ones before the Nujiang campaign certainly did not entail the same level of political risks and involve the same level of mobilization. Furthermore, the tactics employed by the ENGOs in the Nujiang campaign went beyond the collective action repertoires in prior campaigns. In addition to submitting petitions and proposals to the central government, securing intensive media coverage, and involving students, the green NGOs in the Nujiang campaign also tried to reach foreign NGOs for support and appealed to international organizations to place pressure on the decision making of the Chinese government.[67] Such moves are indeed unprecedented. On the other hand, however, as long as the Chinese government is able to tolerate the above kind of bold actions, we expect that China's environmental movement will actually become more regulated in the eyes of the state authorities in the future. By cooperating with SEPA, the ENGOs have a higher chance to restrict their activities within the institutional-legal framework set by the state. Fighting together with a central government agency, the members of the ENGOs also feel the governmental support and their loyalty to the regime may increase. Even if an environmental campaign does not go successfully, it will be hard for the ENGOs to vent grievances against the central government because a central government agency has stood by them. Instead, such setback would give the activists a sense of reality on the complexities of the issues involved, and lower their expectation

[67] The ENGOs' seeking foreign NGOs' help to stop the Nujiang dam project has given the pro-dam side a good excuse to lambaste them. For example, Zhang Boting (penname Shuibo), in one of his many articles criticizing the ENGOs and defending the Nujiang project, cautioned that the anti-dam ENGOs had "malicious intent" and employed "shameless tricks" by linking the project with diplomatic issues to "sabotage the hydropower development of our country." The article entitled "Hydropower Development in China: Be Aware of the Anti-dam Organizations Creating Barriers by Raising Diplomatic Questions," is available at http://www.xys.org/dajia/nujiang.html (accessed February 1, 2006).

for any immediate radical change. In a nutshell, the cooperation between SEPA and ENGOs tends to institutionalize China's environmental movement.

The Local Government. In the above, we have discussed the need to analyze different branches of the highest level of the administration instead of treating them as an abstract murky whole. The disaggregation of the state also means that we should distinguish the differences between the central and local governments, which have different attitudes toward the environmental movement. The top leaders of the central government are more immune to various local pressures. In turn, they have a more holistic view of the Chinese society and are more positive toward the environmental protection and preservation. In contrast, the local government is closer to the society and more susceptible to the pressure of various business interest groups. While the central government in China is rich due to the huge amount of surplus generated in recent years, many local governments in China, especially those in the less developed hinterland regions, are run under financial constraints. Unfortunately, but understandably, they tend to value economic development more than environmental protection. In short, the central and local governments' relationships with the ENGOs vary significantly. While the central administration frequently supports the cause and activities of the ENGOs, the relationship between many local governments and the ENGOs can be antagonistic. In the snub-nose monkey case, the ENGOs' interests in preserving the forests collided with the economic interests of the local government of Deqin County, for which logging constituted a major source of revenue. In the Tibetan antelope case, the ENGOs were embroiled in the local politics willy-nilly and were resented by the Yushu prefectural government. Finally, in the Nujiang case, the coalition of the ENGOs and SEPA was partially defeated by a stronger alliance formed between the Yunan provincial government, the hydropower interest groups, and some forces in the society.

In all our three empirical cases, the ENGOs exploited the cleavage within the state apparatus, namely that between the central administration and the local government, with different levels of success. Two hypotheses may be drawn on the tendencies in China's environmental politics in relation to the local government. First, the ENGOs tend to fight more effectively in their environmental battle if they are not tangled in the local politics. However, when they become unintentionally involved in the local politics, they are snarled in something about which they have little knowledge, and they waste energy in barking up the wrong tree. The Brigade case has clearly showed this point. Second, the chance for the ENGOs to win an environmental battle is higher when the ENGOs face a lower-level local government (that is, the county or prefectural government). However, when the opponent of the ENGOs is the more powerful provincial government, the chances for them to win an environmental battle are significantly smaller. The provincial government is able to lobby in Beijing as effectively as the ENGOs do. It also has environmental and other institutions under its control and has the resources to mobilize support in the society. As the Nujiang dam case indicates, while the SEPA–ENGOs coalition won the first round of the battle, the Yunan provincial government together with the hydropower interest group successfully lobbied the top leadership, and allied with some segments of the civil society to stage a forceful counter mobilization.

The Society. In the 1980s, when the Chinese state just began its transformation from a totalitarian regime to an authoritarian regime, and when it started to loosen its control over the society, we saw a rebellious newly emerging but poorly organized society that repeatedly challenged the authoritarian rule, which culminated in the 1989 Movement.[68] Scholars who are interested in the development of civil society in China may have wished that similar events that happened in the 1980s should happen again in today's China. However, during the 1990s, when the Chinese state became more tolerant toward the existence of various forms of societal forces and civil society in its

[68] Zhou Xueguang, "Unorganized Interests and Collective Action in Communist China," *American Sociological Review* no. 58 (1993): 54–73; Zhao, *The Power of Tiananmen*.

real sense started to emerge in China, instead of rising to challenge the authoritarian rule, the society became fragmented and behaved more and more like its conservative Western counterpart. Several factors were behind this development. First, the Chinese economy has run extremely well in the last 15 years or so, and most sections of the Chinese population, especially the educated elite, have benefited from the process. It is hard to imagine that any population under this kind of economic situation will rise in unison against the state.

Yet, there is also a deeper mechanism at work. A strong civil society, while preventing the absolute domination of the state power over the society, tends to contribute to the political stability of the regime because once a state allows the civil society to develop, it will inevitably differentiate into groups with different interests and identities.[69] It started to happen in China in the early 1990s first among intellectual circles. In the 1980s most politically oriented intellectuals in China had a half-liberal half-Marxist anti-government political view. When the Chinese economy did not go well, they created a widespread crisis discourse that contributed to the rise of the 1989 Movement.[70] In the 1990s, however, the politically oriented intellectuals have differentiated into liberals, economic liberals, leftists, neo-leftists, nationalists, postmodernists, feminists, and so on.[71] These groups disagreed on many things ranging from China's economic policy and political development to social programs and foreign policies. Unless the state adopts a hard-line approach to suppress them all, Chinese intellectual elites are less likely to be unified to oppose the state as they did during the 1989 Movement. By the late 1990s, such pluralism further spread into other spheres of the Chinese society. For example, we can see in the Internet chat rooms and in the media people promoting diverse views and frequently engaging in debates. Now, as the

---

[69] Kornhauser, *The Politics of Mass Society*; Zhao, *The Power of Tiananmen*; Zhao, *Social and Political Movement.*

[70] Ruth Cherrington, *China's Students: The Struggle for Democracy* (London: Routledge, 1991); Orville Schell, *Mandate of Heaven*. (New York: Simon & Schuster, 1994); Zhao, *The Power of Tiananmen*.

[71] Wang Chaohua, ed., *One China, Many Paths* (London: Verso, 2003).

Nujiang dam case clearly shows, such pluralism has extended to the social movement sector.[72] We may well expect that, if the trend continues, every kind of social movement in China that breaks out will face some kind of anti-movement opposition, as it is common in the United States today.[73]

What kind of impact will this recent diversification of civil society have on the development of the environmental movement in China? Although it is still too early to provide a clear answer to this question, based on what happened during the three environmental campaigns we have studied and our understanding of the nature of civil society in the modern West, we could make three conjectures, which also serve to end this chapter. First, we expect that China's environmental movement will undergo a major change with the emergence of its critics in the civil society. Before the Nujiang dam case, the ENGOs enjoyed being portrayed as independent groups

---

[72] The rise of societal forces in China has fractured the civil society. Through the debate and conflict created by the fractured civil society, Chinese have also gradually acquired a sense of the complexity of reality, and what is possible and impossible. This tends to stabilize the regime. See Chap. 5 of Zhao's *Social and Political Movement* for a more detailed discussion on the issue.

[73] The recent China Blog Gate incident reveals how erroneous it can be to interpret the present-day China in simplistic society vs. state terms. On March 8, 2006, two very popular Chinese Web logs by two journalists, Wang Xiangfeng's "Massage Milk" and Yuan Lei's "Milk Pig," turned blank and only carried messages saying they had been temporarily closed "because of unavoidable reasons known to all." On the same day *Reuters* reported the closure of two of China's "most adventurous" Web logs under government orders and claimed this was "the latest in a wave of shutdowns as Chinese censors tighten controls in cyberspace, especially while the national parliament meets" ("China Shuts Two Popular Blogs in Latest Crackdown," *Reuters*, March 8, 2006, http://today.reuters.com/news/newsArticle.aspx?type=internetNews&storyID=2006-03-08T121716Z_01_PEK314460_RTRUKOC_0_US-CHINA-BLOG.xml). This news spread to at least 200 international news media. However, to everyone's surprise, it turned out to be a prank — the owners shut down their own blogs and a day later the two sites were back to normal operation. It was reported that Wang and Yuan have used this trick to express their dissatisfaction at the Western media's stereotypical reporting about China (Raymond Zhou, "Reports of Blogs' Death Exaggerated," *China Daily*, March 14, 2006, http://www.chinadaily.com.cn/english/doc/2006–03/14/content_534795.htm).

working for the public good and representing the voice of the people, and faced no rivals on the moral ground. As the result, some of their unprofessional behaviors and inaccurate claims were unchecked. However, in the Nujiang case, focusing on some of the baseless data and claims made by some ENGO members, Fang Zhouzi and his followers attacked the very legitimacy of the anti-dam cause. The environmentalists, never having encountered such barrages, seemed to be flustered. Yet, it is almost certain that the ENGO members will learn from the experience, and that the conflict will only benefit the development of a more robust environmental movement in the long run. In short, we expect an improvement in the quality of China's environmental movement with the existence of oppositional forces in the society.

Second, while the rise of a more pluralistic society will enhance the quality of China's environmental movement, if the current trend continues, the impact of the ENGOs on Chinese politics will decline. They may gradually lose their current sway over the Chinese media. Their influence on the Chinese government may also decline once they face increasing differentiation within and more rivalry from outside. Therefore, as time goes on, environmental protests will certainly become more numerous, and the impact they have on Chinese politics may not increase accordingly.

Finally, the nature of civil society in a country is shaped by the very culture of that society. Under the pressure of the Western imperialism, Chinese intellectuals during the May 4th Movement in 1919 saw "Mr. Science and Mr. Democracy" as the key to China's revitalization.[74] Over the course of the 20th century, science and technology have acquired almost a religious status in a country that is otherwise known as being weak in religiosity. We mentioned earlier that Fang Zhouzi and his followers were able to gain an edge over the ENGOs in their confrontation. Here, we would add that they gained an upper hand not just because the environmentalists had made some obvious mistakes in making their claims. Equally important, while

[74] Chow Tse-tsung, *The May Fourth Movement: Intellectual Revolution in Modern China* (Stanford, CA: Stanford University Press, 1967).

Fang's scientific reasoning had drawn many admirers in the society, the environmentalists found it hard to defend themselves in front of a set of science-based claims made by Fang and his follower. The science-as-sacred culture created by China's modernizers (the liberals, nationalists, and communists alike) has great implications for the environmental movement in China. At least in the near future, we expect that an environmental movement in China is more likely to succeed if its opponents are not able to justify their actions by certain claims based on science and technology. However, if a project brings an obvious economic benefit while its potential negative impact can be "solved" on the paper by some scientific calculation and designing efforts (such as in the hydropower and nuclear power cases), an environmental movement to oppose such a project is less likely to prevail. To place our argument in a comparative light, the anti-dam movement in today's China is like the anti-nuclear power movement in the United States before the 1970s. At that time, most Americans including the journalists had a progressive understanding of nuclear power, and believed that nuclear power was good for peaceful use but bad when used for wars. It was not until the Three-Mile Island and Chernobyl accidents that such a dualistic understanding of nuclear power was transformed in the American media and public opinion to a runaway and devil's bargain frame. It was only then that the anti-nuclear movement was able to win more support.[75] Will Chinese also need disasters of similar scale to learn the limitation of science and technology? We hope not.

ABBREVIATION LIST:

CECPA: China Environmental Culture Promotion Association
CCP: Chinese Communist Party
CPPCC: Chinese People's Political Consultation Conference

[75] William A. Gamson, *Talking Politics* (Cambridge: Cambridge University Press, 1992); William A. Gamson and Andre Modigliani, "Media Discourse and Public Opinion on Nuclear Owner: A Constructionist Approach," *American Journal of Sociology* no. 95 (1989): 1–37.

CCTV: Central Chinese Television
EIA: environmental impact assessment
ENGO: environmental non-governmental organization
EPB: Environmental Protection Bureau
FON: Friends of Nature
GONGO: government-organized non-governmental organization
GEV: Green Earth Volunteers
GVB: Global Village of Beijing
NDRC: National Development and Reform Commission
NEPA: National Environmental Protection Agency
NGO: non-governmental organization
SFA: State Forestry Administration
SEPA: State Environmental Protection Administration
WCD: World Commission on Dams

Chapter

5

Food Safety and the Development of Regulatory Institutions in China

Waikeung Tam and Dali L. Yang

Much of the American literature on regulatory politics has emphasized the principal–agent relationships between citizens and their elected representatives and between the representatives as legislators and the regulatory agencies. Particular attention has been given to the issue of bureaucratic autonomy and accountability in electoral democracies.[1]

Like the United States in the Progressive Era, regulatory issues have also come to the fore of public policy in China. Yet, unlike the United States then or now, the regulatory developments in China are occurring within an authoritarian context, where the executive branch has predominated in the formulation and implementation of regulatory laws and policies. Thus it stands to reason that the theories and approaches developed for democratic political settings

[1] See, for example, John D. Huber and Charles R. Shipan, *Deliberate Discretion?: The Institutional Foundations of Bureaucratic Autonomy* (Cambridge: Cambridge University Press, 2002).

cannot be easily transplanted to China without much adaptation. Moreover, China's status as a late developing economy also implies that regulatory developments there may share more features with other developing economies than with the economies that have well-established regulatory systems.

Though not elected via competitive elections, China's national leaders have not been oblivious to popular support and political legitimacy. Throughout the reform era, the Chinese leadership has made economic reform and development as the core of their mission in order to sustain communist party rule and improve the legitimacy of the CCP. Today, however, China's elites increasingly recognize that the single-minded focus on the GDP growth has occurred at the expense of other important measures of development. The SARS crisis of 2003 drove home the message to China's new generation of leaders — notably President Hu Jintao and Premier Wen Jiabao — that economic growth must be complemented by more attention to the broader measures of social development.[2] In this context, issues of public health and safety have gained prominence. In the age of market uncertainty, the state must not only promote growth but also provide support for the disadvantaged and protect the interests of consumers.

In this chapter, we draw on recent developments in food safety regulation, which has become an increasingly salient issue for China's rising middle class, to elucidate the patterns of Chinese regulatory development. We pay special attention to the scandal involving the sale of fake and substandard milk powder. We begin with a discussion of the food safety situation in post-Mao China and of how the regulatory regime operates. We then highlight some of the deficiencies of that regime. Next we address some salient issues concerning the building up of a regulatory state in China, including the regulatory chasm between urban and rural areas, the appropriate role of the state in socioeconomic regulation, and the conflict

---

[2] See, for example, Joseph Fewsmith, "Promoting the Scientific Concept," www.chinaleadershipmonitor.com, Issue 11 (Summer 2004); H. Lyman Miller, "The Hu-Wen Leadership at Six Months," www.chinaleadershipmonitor.com, Issue 8 (Fall 2003).

between food safety and employment. Finally, we review some of the institutional responses to the crises of food safety.

THE MILK POWDER SCANDAL AND THE GROWING CONCERN OVER FOOD SAFETY

In April 2004, a scandal involving fake infant milk powder in Anhui's Fuyang municipality brought China's food safety regulation into the international spotlight.[3] The scandal, which China Central Television (CCTV) revealed to the national audience on April 19, involved the deaths of at least 12 babies and hundreds of cases of serious infant malnutrition (e.g., big head and small body symptoms) arising from the consumption of fake and substandard milk powder. The day after the CCTV broadcast, Premier Wen dispatched a special investigation team to Fuyang. This local scam quickly evolved into a nationwide scandal. Authorities soon uncovered massive amounts of fake and substandard milk powder in at least 10 other provinces.[4]

The milk powder scandal has highlighted major weaknesses in China's food safety regulatory regime, especially in rural areas. The first big-headed baby was admitted to the Fuyang People's Hospital in January 2003. The Fuyang Administration for Industry and Commerce, the government regulator of retail markets, began to receive complaints about the quality of infant milk powder in May 2003. Yet for months the Fuyang authorities failed to take any action. They finally launched an initiative to rectify the problem in late December 2003 only after the media began to report on fake

---

[3] Jim Yardley, "Infants in Chinese City Starve on Protein-Short Formula," *New York Times*, May 5, 2004; Yardley, "Tainted Milk Scandal Grows: Chinese Infant Deaths Highlight Lack of Consumer Protection," *International Herald Tribune*, May 5, 2004; "China 'Fake Milk' Scandal Deepens," *BBC News: Asia-Pacific*, April 22, 2004, http://newsvote.bbc.co.uk/mpapps/pagetools/print/news.bbc.co.uk/2/hi/asia-pacific/3648583.stm.

[4] Major web news portals in Chinese have followed this development with dedicated channels. See, for example, http://news.sina.com.cn/z/milkpowder/index.shtml.

milk powder sales in Fuyang.[5] Even then the local initiative was at best ineffectual, and the number of babies suffering from serious malnourishment caused by the consumption of fake milk powder continued to rise.

By April 2004, the Fuyang milk powder scandal had become a national issue. Between April and August 2004, the State Administration of Quality Supervision, Inspection and Quarantine undertook a nationwide drive to inspect 496 milk powder producing firms. As a result of this drive, 54 firms were ordered to terminate production for having produced milk powder that failed to meet national standards on protein content and other trace elements. Of these cases, 30 were transferred to the police for further investigation, 10 people were detained for criminal violations, and five others were put on the police wanted list.[6]

The Fuyang milk powder scandal is not an isolated case, and the national attention it has received is indicative of how food safety has in recent years become a growing concern among ordinary Chinese. For 2003, the Ministry of Health received reports of 379 severe food poisoning cases; these cases affected 12,876 people, including 323 deaths. The 2003 numbers were up by 196 percent, 80 percent, and 134 percent, respectively, when compared to that of 2002.[7] In 2003, the General Administration of Quality Supervision, Inspection and Quarantine conducted a nationwide inspection of some 2,000 types of foodstuffs and found that almost one-fifth failed to meet government

---

[5] Fu Zimei and Hu Jian, "Liezhi naifen baolu chu shenme" [What Does Substandard Milk Powder Reveal], *Renmin ribao* [*People's Daily*, Beijing], May 17, 2004; Fan Lixiang, "Anhui Fuyang sharen naifen shijian zeren luoshengmen" [Shirking of Responsibility in the Fatal Milk Powder Incident in Anhui Fuyang], *Ershiyi shiji jingji baodao* [*21st Century Business Herald*], April 26, 2004.

[6] *Beijing yule xinbao* [*Beijing Star Daily*], August 13, 2004, http://news.sina.com.cn/c/2004-08-13/04274022884.shtml.

[7] "Babuwei lianshou shipin anquan jianguan fengbao" [Eight Ministries Join Hands To Unleash Storm of Food Safety Regulation], *Ershiyi shiji jingji baodao*, May 17, 2004; Elaine Kurtenbach, "Polluted, Fake, Unsafe Foods Alarming Food-Loving Chinese," *Associated Press*, May 20, 2002.

standards. Even in Beijing, almost a quarter of the pork in markets was found to be unfit for consumption.[8]

The popularity gained by the CCTV program "Weekly Quality Report" (*Meizhou Zhiliang Baogao*), which counts as its cosponsor the General Administration of Quality Supervision, Inspection and Quarantine, is indicative of the public concern over food safety. Shortly after its debut in 2003, Weekly Quality Report became one of the CCTV's most-watched programs.[9] The state's failure to protect the public from unsafe foodstuffs and its sluggish response to food poisoning cases have even provoked public demonstrations. In March 2003, more than 3,000 schoolchildren in Liaoning's Haicheng became sick from drinking a soy milk product in school. Some 1,000 angry parents blocked the railroad to protest the local government's response.[10]

THE EVOLVING ARCHITECTURE OF FOOD SAFETY REGULATION

The discussion above suggests that food safety regulation has emerged as a major governance issue in China. It also begs the question of what's wrong with China's food safety regulatory regime.

The most salient feature of China's food safety regulatory system is the fragmentation of regulatory authority among different government

---

[8] "Lianghui fangtan: yifa baozheng shipin anquan" [Interviews of the National People's Congress and the Chinese People's Political Consultative Conference: Using Law To Protect Food Safety], *Yangshi guoji wangluo* [*CCTV International Network*], March 7, 2004, www.southcn.com/news/community/shzt/consumer/core/200403180608.htm; Vivien Cui, "Quarter of Capital's Pork Is Unfit To Eat," *South China Morning Post* (Hong Kong), February 3, 2004; Liang Qiwen, "Expert Warns Food Safety Could Affect Nation's Birth Rate," *China Daily* (Beijing), April 26, 2004.

[9] Launched in 2003, the "Weekly Quality Report" focuses on muckraking counterfeit products, particularly foodstuffs. See *Singtao Daily* (Hong Kong), May 17, 2004.

[10] Ma Tao and Wu Peishuang, "Erqianwubai xuesheng dounai zhongdu konghuang" [Soy Milk Poisoning of 2,500 Schoolchildren Causes Panic], *Zhongguo xinwen zhoukan* [*China Newsweek*], April 14, 2003.

agencies.[11] Currently, the Ministry of Health (MoH), the Ministry of Agriculture (MoA), the General Administration of Quality Supervision, Inspection and Quarantine (GAQSIQ), the State Administration for Industry and Commerce (SAIC), the Ministry of Commerce (MoC), and the State Food and Drug Administration (SFDA) are actively involved in regulating food safety. This fragmentation of regulatory authority is in sharp contrast with the regulatory regime in the United States. Except for meat and poultry, which are regulated by the U.S. Department of Agriculture (USDA), the U.S. Food and Drug Administration regulates almost the entire food chain. Its principal duties include regulating drugs and feed given to animals to be used as food for humans, enforcing the limits on how much pesticide can remain on food crops, establishing standards of identity and quality for foodstuffs, developing food labeling laws, inspecting food processing plants to check for adulteration and mislabeling, determining the safety of food additives and food colors, and initiating court proceedings against lawbreaking entities.[12]

The fragmentation of the food safety regulatory regime in China is partly a legacy of stop-and-go changes in both legislation and institutional reforms. China's Food Hygiene Law (*Shipin weishengfa*), promulgated in 1995, puts the Ministry of Health in charge of supervision and management of food hygiene. The MoH's principal regulatory authorities include issuing hygiene license to businesses engaged in food production, marketing or sales; monitoring, inspecting, and providing technical guidance for food hygiene; appraising and publicizing the status of food hygiene; investigating and dealing with food poisoning or food contamination incidents; and imposing financial penalties or revoking the hygiene license of violators of the Food Hygiene Law.[13] The Ministry of Agriculture is responsible for

---

[11] For discussion of the fragmented structure of bureaucratic authority in China, see Kenneth Lieberthal and Michel Oksenberg, *Policy Making in China: Leaders, Structures, and Processes* (Princeton, NJ: Princeton University Press, 1988).

[12] William Patrick, *The Food and Drug Administration* (New York: Chelsea House, 1988), chap 5.

[13] The Food Hygiene Law of the People's Republic of China. Available on the Ministry of Health's website: www.moh.gov.cn.

formulating and enforcing quality and safety standards for agricultural inputs and farm products. For instance, the MoA sets the limits for pesticide residues in agricultural products and monitors compliance with such standards.[14]

The GAQSIQ and the SAIC are also influential players in food safety regulation. The Product Quality Law (*Chanpin zhiliangfa*), enacted in 1993 and amended in 2000, authorizes the GAQSIQ to take the lead in regulating product quality, including the quality of foodstuffs. The GAQSIQ issues production permits for food processors and producers, supervises licensed food enterprises for compliance with regulations concerning food manufacturing, packaging, labeling, and is empowered to crack down on unlicensed food processing and production. It can issue fines, confiscate products, and ban food manufacturers from continuing production if they have violated the relevant rules.[15] The SAIC oversees food safety in the "circulation" area: It issues business licenses and oversees food hygiene in urban and rural markets. Like the GAQSIQ, the SAIC is empowered to fine and revoke the business license of violators.[16] The Ministry of Commerce can enact and amend standards and rules regarding the procedures for food processing, packaging, storage, transportation, and sales.[17]

It should be noted that other bureaucratic agencies are sometimes involved in food safety regulation as well. For example, the China Petroleum and Chemical Industry Association (formerly the Ministry of Chemical Industry) and the Ministry of Public Security have the authority to oversee the production, storage, and sales of methanol and industrial alcohol.[18]

---

[14] See the Ministry of Agriculture's website: www.agri.gov.cn/MOA/zhize.htm.

[15] See the website of the General Administration of Quality Supervision, Inspection and Quarantine: www.adsiq.gov.cn.

[16] See the website of the State Administration for Industry and Commerce: www.saic.gov.cn.

[17] Dai Yan, "System to Safeguard Food Safety," *China Daily* (North American ed.), November 28, 2003.

[18] Cheng Gong, "Geji jianguan bumen ruhe jinjue dushi" [How Should the Regulatory Agencies Eradicate Poisonous Food], *Nanfang zhoumo* [*Southern Weekend*], May 20, 2004.

The Chinese leadership has recognized the fragmentation of the food safety regulatory regime. As part of the 2003 government streamlining program, food regulation was put into the State Food and Drug Administration (SFDA) — an apparent effort to emulate the U.S. FDA.[19] The SFDA is authorized to exercise comprehensive supervision over the safety of food, health products, and cosmetics. Its portfolio includes coordinating the relevant bureaucracies to draft laws and administrative regulations concerning food safety. Two of its six specialized departments are dedicated to food regulation: Food Safety Coordination and Food Safety Supervision. The Food Safety Coordination Department coordinates with other departments and agencies to devise and enforce the annual plan and other programs for food safety, to set unified food safety standards, to collect and analyze information on food safety, and to disseminate food safety information to the public. The Food Safety Supervision Department is empowered to design regulatory measures and means, investigate major food safety incidents, and coordinate campaigns to combat counterfeit foodstuffs.[20]

Continuing Fragmentation of Regulatory Authority

Despite the Chinese leadership's desire to remodel the SFDA after the U.S. FDA, this approach was stymied even before the SFDA's creation.[21] Resistance from other bureaucratic interests has limited the transfer of power and responsibility to the SFDA.

As noted earlier, the Food Hygiene Law authorizes the Ministry of Health and local health bureaus to supervise food hygiene and to impose fines on lawbreaking enterprises and collect the fines as a

---

[19] For various other initiatives to rationalize the government setup, see Dali Yang, *Remaking the Chinese Leviathan* (Stanford, CA: Stanford University Press, 2004), chap 2.

[20] See the website of the State Food and Drug Administration: www.sda.gov.cn.

[21] The discussion below is primarily based on Tang Yuankai, "Doctor's Orders: Medicine Regulation," *Beijing Review*, May 29, 2003, 23–24; Josephine Ma, "New Agency Set To Rein in Food and Drug Market," *South China Morning Post*, March 19, 2003, 8.

source of revenue. Not surprisingly, the MoH jealously guarded its power to oversee food safety and strongly resisted the creation of a U.S.-style FDA.[22] In the process of establishing the SFDA, the MoH argued that the FDA is an executive organ of the Department of Health and Human Services and lobbied national leaders to put the SFDA under its control. Other relevant agencies similarly feared that a powerful SFDA will take over their revenue-generating regulatory powers. Opposition from these bureaucratic interests helps to explain the SFDA's limited authority.

For its part, the SFDA leadership was keenly aware of these competing interests and was careful with its first steps. In an interview shortly after the SFDA's establishment, former SFDA Director General Zheng Xiaoyu stressed that the SFDA would not take over the food safety regulatory functions of agricultural, industrial and commercial, health, and technical agencies[23]; instead, it will concentrate its authorities on comprehensive oversight, coordination, and strengthening of law enforcement.[24] This was at best an ambiguous definition of the SFDA's mission, however, and indicated the challenges ahead for the SFDA. Although the SFDA was given ministerial rank to facilitate its interaction with other ministries, it has faced substantial obstacles in securing the cooperation of other agencies.

The milk powder scandal is an apt illustration of problems of coordination. In July 2003, the SFDA issued a directive "Notice on Implementing the Food and Drug Safety Project." The directive stipulated that relevant agencies should update the SFDA on a bi-monthly basis on the implementation of the project. Among the key products included in the Project were milk products.[25] The fake milk powder

---

[22] Some mainland academics also fear that the MoH would be the most formidable challenge to the SFDA's supervisory function. Josephine Ma, "Sweeping Food-Safety Law Needed," *South China Morning Post*, March 6, 2004.

[23] In June 2005, Shao Mingli replaced Zheng Xiaoyu as the Director General of the SFDA.

[24] Tang Yuankai, "Doctor's Orders."

[25] State Food and Drug Administration, "Guanyu yinfa shipin yaopin fangxin gongcheng shishi fangan de tongzhi" [Notice on the Implementation of Food and Drug Safety Project], July 21, 2003, www.sda.gov.cn/cmsweb/webportal/W945325/A33066084.html.

incident in Fuyang, however, revealed that the SFDA did not receive adequate cooperation from the health and industry and commerce departments or from the Quality Administration. Partly to help break down the walls among these government agencies, the SFDA has worked through Vice Premier Wu Yi and Secretary General of the State Council Hua Jianmin to coordinate policy making and implementation on food safety.[26] This is similar to developments in several other areas, such as the protection of intellectual property rights.

Although the Chinese leadership has sought to emulate the FDA in establishing the SFDA, the SFDA's resemblance to the U.S. FDA is skin-deep at best. The SFDA is far from being an agency with enough authority to exercise unified and comprehensive supervision over food safety. Instead, regulatory authority over food safety remains divided among different government departments. Meanwhile, the SFDA and local food and drug bureaus complain about inadequate resources. Sometimes, their quest for revenue conflicts with the optimal regulatory goals.

The fragmentation of regulatory authority and responsibility for food safety among at least six government ministries and administrations (MoH, MoA, GAOSIQ, SAIC, MoC, and SFDA) offers a daunting challenge for regulatory implementation. In certain aspects, there may be excessive enforcement; in others, shirking of responsibility and shifting of blame may be the outcome. Jin-Wook Choi, for example, has observed that blurred responsibilities and authorities of regulators and the resultant regulatory failure were among the most significant underlying causes of the financial crisis in South Korea in 1997.[27]

In important respects, the milk powder scandal provides a striking illustration of these bureaucratic symptoms. First, the fragmentation of regulatory power reduced the information flow on food safety issues and stymied cooperation among different regulatory agencies. While the Fuyang health bureau had compiled a list of

[26] "Badawei guanbuhao yitou zhu?" [Are Eight Ministries Unable To Regulate a Pig?], *Ershiyi shiji jingji baodao*, May 17, 2004.

[27] Jin-Wook Choi, "Regulatory Forbearance and Financial Crisis in South Korea," *Asian Survey* 42, no. 2 (March–April, 2002): 263–266.

unqualified milk powder for its anti-counterfeiting initiative, this list was not shared with the industry and commerce bureau. The latter missed various targets in its drive to root out fake milk powder. It was not until after the arrival of State Council's interdepartmental investigation team in Fuyang that information sharing among these bureaus truly improved.[28] If these bureaus were not sharing information well, they were truly mercenaries in sharing resources. A senior official of the Fuyang Administration for Industry and Commerce (AIC) complained that the local Administration of Quality Supervision, Inspection and Quarantine (AQSIQ) had asked his office to pay 382,000 yuan for tests that the AQSIQ had performed for the AIC during the fake milk powder investigation. The Fuyang AIC suffered from budget problems and found these charges quite burdensome.[29]

Second, the fragmentation of regulatory authority is reflected in incongruities among the regulations and standards adopted by the different agencies. When it comes to food, the diverse opinions of different government agencies can be downright confusing to the consumer. For instance, after CCTV exposed the use of cancer-causing chemicals in vermicelli (*longkou fensi*) production in Yantai, the GAQSIQ announced that about 30 brands of vermicelli were fit for consumption. But the Ministry of Health's list included only seven brands.[30]

Third, the poor delimitation of regulatory authority among government departments provides fertile ground for shirking and buck-passing. When asked by journalists why his office took almost a year to take action against fake milk powder, a bureaucrat at the Fuyang AQSIQ blamed the Fuyang AIC, claiming that "according to the Product Quality Law and State Council's regulations, the AIC should hand the case to the Quality Administration when it uncovered unqualified foodstuffs in the production sphere (*shengchan lingyu*).

---

[28] "Liezhi naifen baolu chu shenme."

[29] "Guanyuan shizhi haishi zhidu quehan, liezhi naifen dangwen shuize" [Official Negligence or Institutional Defects — Who Should Be Held Responsible for Unqualified Milk Powder?], *Dongfang wang* [*Eastern Net*], May 17, 2004, www.southcn.com/news/community/shzt/mp/view/200405190543.htm.

[30] "Babuwei lianshou shipin anquan jianguan fengbao."

The Fuyang AQSIQ did not act because the AIC had not transferred the case to it." The Industry and Commerce Administration, however, blamed its inaction on the Health Bureau. A deputy director of the Fuyang AIC denied that his office should be held accountable for the fake milk powder. He contended that although the Product Quality Law and State Council's regulations stipulate that the SAIC oversees product quality in the circulation arena, the Food Hygiene Law also assigns regulation of food hygiene to the Ministry of Health. In accordance with the principle that the specialized law (*zhuanmen fa*) should have precedence over the generalized law (*putong fa*), this deputy director contended, the supervision over milk powder quality should primarily be the responsibility of the MoH and local health bureaus. The SAIC, at most, plays a complementary role in the supervision of food safety.[31] Officials at the Health Bureau, however, also sought to evade the blame. Although the Food Hygiene Law puts the health department in charge of supervision and management of food hygiene, the Fuyang health bureau maintained that the severe malnutrition problems arising from the consumption of fake and substandard milk powder should be handled by the AIC.[32]

The overlapping and unclear delineation of regulatory authority and the subsequent shirking of responsibility explain why victims of the fake milk powder in Fuyang had to resort to the mass media. The intervention of CCTV helped capture the attention of national leaders and elicited a vigorous response from the national government.[33]

---

31 "Guyuan shizhi huanshi zhidu quehan, liezhi naifen dangwen shuize."

32 "Anhui Fuyang sharen naifen shijian zeren luoshengmen."

33 Frustrated by the inability and unwillingness of Fuyang officials to solve the problem of fake milk powder, Gao Zheng, whose infant niece was hospitalized, complained to the mass media. His complaints helped in the mass media's uncovering the severity of the problem. See "Shei diyige jiekailiao Fuyang liezhi naifen shijian de neimu?" [Who is the First Person To Uncover the Inside Story of the Fuyang Fake Milk Powder Incident?], *Xiandai jinbao* [*Contemporary Golden News*], April 28, 2004, www.southcn.com/news/community/shzt/mp/latest/200404280684.htm. The Fuyang People's Hospital informed Fuyang TV stations, rather than Fuyang health officials, of the fake baby formula and its widespread harm. *Xinxi Shibao* [*Information Times*], April 30, 2004, http://cn.news.yahoo.com/040430/250/2246v.html.

THE REVENUE IMPERATIVE

Money Over Safety

As counterfeiting activities can bring considerable economic benefits to localities, such as increased government revenue and employment opportunities, many local officials (especially those at or below county level) have tolerated them. In most cases, fake and substandard products are not sold around the places where they are made. Instead, they are transported to other localities. This further reduces the incentives for local authorities to crack down on counterfeiting businesses.[34]

Local governments may protect counterfeiting businesses by laxly enforcing regulations over food safety. As local governments vie for investment, some officials (particularly those in poorer areas) have even embraced investment that engaged in counterfeiting. It is reported that a large proportion of the fake milk powder uncovered in Fuyang was actually produced in parts of Zhejiang Province as well as Heilongjiang Province and Inner Mongolia. Pengxi Town in Zhejiang's Taishun County alone had eight businesses that produced counterfeit and substandard milk powder. These businesses were able to obtain hygiene licenses in spite of poor sanitation. The director of the Taishun Health Bureau maintained that, in issuing the hygiene licenses, the economic imperatives for attracting outside investment overrode other considerations. The deputy head of Pengxi Town also noted that these firms provided almost 100 jobs.[35]

Similar dynamics also appear to be at work within the regulatory institutions. A vice mayor of Fuyang suggested that regulatory forbearance (*zeren bu daowei*) led to the fake milk powder tragedy in

---

[34] Yang, *Remaking the Chinese Leviathan*, 96–97.

[35] "Jixing fazhanguan daozhi liezhi naifen beiju" [Distorted Concept of Development Led to the Tragedy of Fake Milk Powder], *Jiaodian fangtan* [*Focus*], China Central Television, June 16, 2004, www.people.com.cn/GB/shehui/8217/34282/34284/2577776.html. See also Dai Dunfeng and Liu Jianping, "Zhuicha liezhi naifen haisi yinger chanyelian" [Tracing the Production Chain of Fatal Fake Milk Powder], *Nanfang Zhoumo* [*Southern Weekend*], April 29, 2004, http://cn.news.yahoo.com/040429/119/221kd.html.

Fuyang.[36] This regulatory forbearance has at least two origins — the revenue imperative and corruption. The pursuit of revenue by regulatory bureaucracies is an important factor behind the lax enforcement of food safety regulation. As the fiscal situation of many county governments has deteriorated since the 1994 fiscal reforms, county-level regulatory agencies like the industry and commerce bureau have relied on the collection of fines and license fees to cope with inadequate budget support.[37] Many regulatory bureaucrats have assigned top priority to these activities, which affect their personal income and welfare benefits.[38] Since the late 1990s, as a result of government reforms and the divestiture of businesses affiliated with the armed forces and other government and state institutions, the central government has stipulated that funds for regulatory administrations be covered through government budgets rather than the collection of fees and fines. Yet in poorer areas such as Anhui Province, where the local government is likely to be cash-strapped, under-funding for the government bureaucracy remains a common phenomenon. In consequence, the local administrations in less developed areas tend to be eager to engage in revenue-generating regulatory activities.

This emphasis on revenue-generating regulatory activities has perverse effects on the regulation of food safety. First, regulators may put emphasis on imposing financial penalties on lawbreakers and be less willing to adopt more effective means of cracking down on counterfeit foodstuffs, such as closing down production lines or initiating criminal prosecution against violators. The substitution of fines for criminal prosecution (*yifa daixing*) is a common practice in Fuyang. In June 2003, the Fuyang AQSIQ found one milk powder producer whose fake milk powder had caused the death of at least

[36] Ibid. and "Ensuring Food Safety Must Be a Priority," *China Daily*, May 24, 2004.

[37] Yongnian Zheng, "State Rebuilding, Popular Protest and Collective Action in China," *Japanese Journal of Political Science* 3, no. 1 (2002): 59–62.

[38] Industry and Commerce Bureau of Loudi City, Hunan, "Gongshang xingzheng zhifa renyuan guanli tizhi xianzhuang pouxi" [An Analysis of the Current Management System of the Enforcement Personnel of the Industry and Commerce Bureau], January 21, 2004, www.saic.gov.cn/gshlt/gshlt_detail.asp?gshltid=420.

one infant. In spite of the severity of the incident, the Fuyang AQSIQ merely fined that producer a modest amount instead of closing his business down and initiating criminal proceedings against him.[39] That producer went on producing substandard milk powder until the following April when the State Council's investigation team arrived.[40] In effect, regulators depended on such wayward business illegalities to generate fines and levies; closing such businesses down would be akin to killing the goose that lays the golden egg.

Second, regulators also collected fees and charges by issuing business licenses. According to a member of the State Council's investigation team, the Fuyang investigation revealed that many unqualified enterprises had obtained all the necessary licenses — business license, hygiene license, hygiene quality report, and taxation registration certificate. An AIC official noted that the health and AQSIQ authorities issued hygiene certificates and quality approval to a famous baby formula enterprise even before it started trial production. It turned out that the quality of its products was far below government standards.[41] In short, it appears that regulators forgot that their chief mission was the supervision and guarantee of food safety rather than the generation of revenue or the facilitation of business malfeasance.

---

[39] Some wholesalers and retailers of fake milk powder in Fuyang point out that the amount of fines is generally small compared to the high profitability of selling the counterfeiting products. See "Zhuicha liezhi naifen haisi yinger chanyelian." A number of lawmakers and academics also remark that the financial penalties against counterfeiting are not sufficient enough to serve as an effective deterrence. "Shipin anquan li fa Guangdong yingxianxing yibu" [Guangdong Should Take the Lead in Making Legislation on Food Safety], *Nanfang Zhoumo* [*Southern Weekend*], May 26, 2004; "Lianghui fangtan: yifa baozheng shipin anquan."

[40] "Yige fuqin de zhuiwen: yuanhe zanhuan zhixing guowuyuan guiding" [Inquiry By a Father: Why Postpone Implementing State Council's Rule], *Nanfang Zhoumo* [*Southern Weekend*], April 29, 2004, http://cn.news.yahoo.com/040429/119/221ju.html. For a report on other instances of *yifa daixing* and their impact on the spread of fake milk powder, see "Liezhi naifen baolu chu shenme."

[41] "Badawei guanbuhao yitou zhu"; Zhou Limin, "Fuyang nongcun yinger datou guaibing zhuizong" [Tracking the Big-Headed Disease of Infants in Rural Fuyang], *Banyuetan* [*Fortnightly chat*], April 21, 2004, http://news.sina.com.cn/c/2004-04-19/08082343117s.shtml.

Bureaucratic Competition and Corruption

Third, regulatory agencies have from time to time vied against each other for revenue-generating regulatory activities. Such bureaucratic competition tends to distort central regulatory policies.[42] In 2001, the State Council issued Circular No. 57, which transfers the responsibility for regulating product quality in the circulation arena (markets) from the GAQSIQ to the SAIC. The GAQSIQ is to focus on supervising product quality in the production phase. The Fuyang government also published this circular in the *Fuyang Daily*. However, since Fuyang does not have many production enterprises on which the AQSIQ can levy administrative fines and fees, implementation of Circular No. 57 would substantially erode the revenue base of the Fuyang AQSIQ. To protect the AQSIQ's financial interest, the Fuyang government postponed the implementation of the circular. Both the AQSIQ and the AIC were allowed to regulate the circulation arena. Thus, revenue concerns stymied the central government's effort to clarify the responsibilities among regulatory organs. One grieving parent lamented, "If Circular No. 57 had been implemented so that there was a clear division of labor between the Fuyang AQSIQ and AIC, my daughter might not have died."[43]

Finally, the factors enumerated above are also compounded by bribery. According to Deputy Procurator General Sun Qian, state enforcement officials' involvement in corruption has become a major reason behind the proliferation of counterfeiters in recent years. Official corruption leads to regulatory forbearance as corrupt regulators neglect their tasks and refuse to hand over perpetrators to criminal investigation and prosecution.[44] Official corruption was an important factor in the Fuyang case as well and helps to explain the

---

[42] Information in this paragraph is based on "Yige fuqin de zhuiwen: yuanhe zanhuan zhixing guowuyuan guiding."

[43] Ibid.

[44] Cheng Jie, "Zuigaojian jiang duban zhijia shoujiaan" [Supreme People's Procuratorate Will Supervise Investigation of Production and Sales of Counterfeit Goods], *Beijing qingnianbao* [*Beijing Youth Daily*], April 30, 2004, www.peopledaily.com.cn/GB/shehui/1062/2477175.html.

widespread sale of the fake milk powder in Fuyang for more than a year after the initial cases of infant malnutrition had been reported to government offices. Two Fuyang AIC officials, for instance, were later prosecuted for taking bribes and failing to investigate a fake milk powder case.[45]

Our study of food safety regulation presents a view contrary to that of Andrew Mertha, who claims that the fragmentation of regulatory authority can contribute to successful policy enforcement (of trademarks).[46] Although inter-bureaucratic competition over overlapping jurisdictions and revenue imperative have occurred in both food safety and trademark regulation, anti-counterfeiting enforcement is more effective in the latter. The crux of this difference lies in the fact that the principal consumers of trademark enforcement (foreign firms) have provided enforcement bureaucracies with substantial side-payments, whereas the principal consumers of food safety enforcement (the public and food producers who abide by law) rarely or cannot offer many side-payments to bureaucracies.

The Rural vs. Urban Regulatory Divide

Besides the problems of regulatory fragmentation and organizational conflict-of-interest, the problem of food safety also highlights the regulatory chasm between urban and rural areas, the appropriate role of the state in socioeconomic regulation, and the conflict between different policy objectives.

Almost all fake milk powders were produced and sold in rural areas, and the victims tended to be villagers. As regulatory prowess in urban areas has improved and as urban consumers have become more savvy, villages have, in recent years, become the dumping

[45] "Shexian xunsi wubi, Fuyang liang gongshangsuo fusuozhang yin naifen shijian beixingju" [Two Deputy Directors of the Fuyang AIC Were Arrested for Alleged Corruption in Fake Milk Powder Incident], *Beijing yule xinbao* [*Beijing Star Daily*], May 18, 2004, www.southcn.com/news/community/shzt/mp/investigation/200405180386.htm.

[46] Andrew C. Mertha, "'Policy Enforcement Markets': How Bureaucratic Redundancy Contributes to Effective IPR Policy Implementation in China," *Comparative Politics* 38, no. 3 (April 2006): 295–316.

grounds of fake and substandard products. A 2003 survey by the China Consumers Association reports that villagers are most worried about product quality and substandard and fake products. Villagers identify seeds, pesticide, and food as having the greatest quality problems.[47] Some analyses attribute the prevalence of counterfeit products in rural China to the low purchasing power of many villagers (which creates a huge demand for cheap and substandard goods), weak rights consciousness, and the lower education level of rural residents. Although these analyses contain some elements of truth, they are only partial explanations.[48]

In the Mao era, a comprehensive network of supply and marketing cooperatives (*gongxiaoshe*), generally collectively owned, existed in rural areas. The state exercised close supervision over the *gongxiaoshe* as well as the producers. During the reform era, the *gongxiaoshe* have failed badly and most of them have been privatized, leased, or closed down after 1997.[49] They have been replaced by numerous small wholesale markets, household-based shops, and mobile peddlers. The state, however, has not instituted an effective regulatory framework in rural areas to catch up with the drastic

---

[47] The survey was based on face-to-face interviews with 13,948 village household heads. The sample covered Hubei, Jilin, Zhejiang, Anhui, Fujian, Jiangxi, Shandong, Chongqing, Guizhou, Shaanxi, Qingdao, Xiamen, and Chengdu. Hu Yongping, "Zhongzi nongyao he shipin yi chengwei nongmin xinzhong zhidatong" [The Quality of Seeds, Pesticide and Food Has Become an Agonizing Issue to Peasants], *Zhongguo wang* [*China Net*], December 26, 2003, www.southcn.com/news/community/shzt/mp/rural/200404210797.htm.

[48] The average market price of a bag of qualified milk powder is 15 yuan, and a new-born baby needs to consume about 120 bags in the first year. Thus, the cost of feeding a new-born baby amounts to 1,800 yuan, which is far above the average household income (1,600 yuan) in rural Fuyang. On the other hand, the average market price of a bag of substandard milk powder is a more affordable 10 yuan. See Zhou Renjie and Shi Shilun, "Nongcun repan wumei jialian naifen" [Villages Are Eager To Have Qualified Milk Powder at Low Price], *Yangshi guoji wangluo* [*CCTV International Network*], May 3, 2004, www.southcn.com/news/community/shzt/mp/rural/200405030053.htm.

[49] Tian Yi and Wang Fengjun, "Weilie naifen quanguo liutonglian" [The National Circulation Chain of Fake and Substandard Milk Powder], *Ershiyi shiji jingji baodao*, April 29, 2004; "Anhui Fuyang sharen naifen shijian zeren luoshengmen."

market transformation. The SFDA so far has only established its presence at the provincial level and in selected cities.

Thus, the SFDA was largely absent in the early stage of the Fuyang fake milk powder case until the scandal drew Beijing's attention. The GAQSIQ only reaches the county level. Only the SAIC has extended its reach down to the township and village levels in the form of the *gongshangsuo*, or industry and commerce offices; yet the *gongshangsuo* is limited in the number of personnel or resources relative to the huge regulatory needs in rural China. The rural areas in Ruyuan County (a poor locality in north Guangdong) have three *gongshangsuo* only, and each is responsible for about four towns or townships. Employees from these *gongshangsuo* have rarely visited several outlaying villages let alone conducted inspections on foodstuffs on sale there. A senior official at the Shaoguan AIC admitted that, given the relatively small number of staff and limited resources, his office was unable to handle complaints from villagers in a timely manner. This regulatory vacuum has led counterfeiters to believe that rural localities are beyond the reach of the SAIC and other regulatory agencies. As a retailer who had sold substandard milk powder in a Fuyang town noted, "the Fuyang AIG generally does not extend its regulatory arms to this remote town."[50] Consequently, it is more likely to find counterfeit and substandard foodstuffs and goods in rural markets than in metropolitan areas.[51] A sort of Gresham's Law has prevailed.

Whereas regulation of sales and production in rural areas is spotty, consumer-oriented regulatory actions in urban areas have improved. Regulatory agencies prioritize food safety issues in urban areas for the following reasons. First, given the better communication and higher population density in cities, the impact of severe food safety incidents tends to be more visible in urban vs. rural areas and may even dent a city's reputation and affect its ability to attract investments. Moreover, unlike in more remote rural areas, it

---

[50] "Zhuicha liezhi naifen haisi yinger chanyelian".

[51] Wang Haiyan, "Yige yuebei shancun de shangpin liutong muoshi jiedu" [An Analysis of the Mode of Commodity Circulation in a Rural Mountainous Village in North Guangdong], *Nanfang dushibao* [*Southern Metropolitan News*], April 24, 2004, www.southcn.com/news/community/shzt/mp/rural/200404240109.htm.

is also easier for urban residents to organize collective actions such as demonstrations against an inept official response. The demonstration and blocking of the railroad in Haicheng is a vivid illustration.[52]

The political salience of food safety has prompted municipal authorities to devote more and more resources to food safety regulation. Following the massive media exposure of problems with hot-pot condiments, the Chongqing municipal government immediately sprung into action. The Chongqing AQSIQ purchased new testing equipment and recruited a dozen experts to test whether hot-pot condiments were contaminated with paraffin wax.[53] In Guangzhou, the municipal government acquired 13 vehicles in early 2004 to monitor the quality and safety of foodstuffs in urban markets. These vehicles are installed with food-testing equipment capable of conducting 12 kinds of instant tests, such as measuring the presence of carcinogenic materials and formaldehyde levels. The vehicles are dispatched to markets to conduct inspection in response to calls to a telephone hotline.[54]

Second, the organization of the food retailing industry in cities makes it more amenable to regulatory action. In contrast with the countryside, where retail is generally scattered and populated by mom-and-pop stores, urban retail networks tend to be concentrated and increasingly dominated by supermarkets or chain stores. Jealous of their own reputation, the supermarkets and chain stores generally set up and implement detailed procedures and mechanisms to monitor food safety. Some supermarkets have their own quality controllers to scrutinize foodstuffs in the stores.[55] It is thus relatively easy for regulators of urban markets to monitor and regulate the urban retail network.

---

[52] "Erqianwubai xuesheng dounai zhongdu konghuang."

[53] Cheng Bizhong and Wu Xiangquan, "Chongqing zhijianju: huoguo zhong jia shila nan chachu" [Chongqing AQSIQ: Difficult To Combat the Addition of Paraffin Wax to Hot-pot Condiments], *Ershiyi shiji jingji baodao*, May 17, 2004.

[54] *Nanfang dushibao*, April 2, 2004; "Food-Testing Vehicles Arrive on Call," *China Daily*, March 18, 2004.

[55] "Wenti shipin pinfan chuxian, jidai chutai yiguan daodi de haofa" [The Frequent Recurrence of Problematic Foodstuffs Urgently Begs for a Comprehensive Law], *Xinhua wang* [*Xinhua Net*], May 12, 2004, www.agri.gov.cn/gndt/t20040512_203008.htm.

In contrast, the household-based shops in the countryside, unable to use scale to drive down the costs of their purchases, tend to be less attentive to quality. They rarely require wholesalers to present production permits or hygiene certificates, and often do not provide receipts to consumers.[56] Faced with intense competition, they are tempted to sell fake and substandard products for a quick profit. With the proliferation of rural stores and with limited resources, regulators settle for minimal regulation of the retail scene in the countryside.

THE ROLE OF THE STATE IN SOCIOECONOMIC REGULATION

'The Fuyang fake milk powder tragedy raises the question of the appropriate role of the state in socioeconomic regulation as well. As noted above, many villagers have very limited purchasing power; according to one estimate, villagers were willing to pay about 10 yuan for a bag of milk powder, whereas a bag of milk powder that meets government standards on nutrition cost 13 yuan.[57] The relatively low rural purchasing power discourages supermarkets from setting up their sales network in villages to meet the lower end of market demands.

The Chinese media has called on qualified businesses to enter the rural market and provide villagers with safe and affordable products.[58] The SFDA also emphasizes that a prerequisite for effective food safety regulation is to encourage large food enterprises to organize sales networks in the countryside and act as the dominant food suppliers there.[59] An important issue ensues, namely, the appropriate ways to

[56] "Yige yuebeishancun de shangpin liutong mushi jiedu."

[57] "Nongcun repan wumei jialian naifen."

[58] Wang Chao and Li Na, "Zao da chengshi fengsha, liezhi chanpin zai nongcun zhici jialian maidehuo" [Being Cracked Down in Large Cities, Unqualified Products Are Sold Cheaply in Villages], *Xi'an wanbao* [*Xi'an Evening News*], May 13, 2004, http://www.southcn.com/news/community/shzt/mp/rural/200405130482.htm. See also "Liezhi naifen baolu chu shenme"; "Nongcun repan wumei jialian naifen."

[59] Zhao Peng and Fu Zimei, "Naifen jiagongchang: Yumu zahui hunzhu" [Milk Powder Processing Plants: How Unqualified Ones Pretend To Be Qualified], *Renmin wang* [*People's Net*], June 7, 2004, http://www.peopledaily.com.cn/GB/guandian/183/6103/6104/2546592.

achieve the aforementioned goal. What role should the government play? Should it take up the responsibility to guide qualified enterprises to enter the rural markets and produce affordable goods for rural residents, as some analysts suggest?[60] If so, what types of policy instruments should the government adopt? Will not the presence of such stores further weaken the household stores and thus the government's objective of helping in creating employment in rural areas? The last question brings out another crucial issue in constructing an effective regulatory state — conflict between divergent policy objectives, in this case between food safety and employment.

Policy Conflict Between Food Safety and Employment Creation

China's food processing industry has been dominated by numerous and scattered family workshops (*jiating xiaozuofang*), which have fewer than 10 employees.[61] These workshops have become major sources of fake and substandard food because of their poor production conditions and quality control.[62] To eliminate these major sources of unsafe foodstuffs from markets, the Chinese government

[60] Zhang Tianwei, "Naifen xianxiang: shichang nengbuneng yu daoyi jianrong" [The phenomenon of Milk Powder: Can Market and Morality Co-exist], *Beijing qingnian bao* [*Beijing Youth Daily*], May 5, 2004, http://www.southcn.com/news/community/shzt/mp/view/200405050211.htm.

[61] Family workshops accounted for about 70 percent of China's food processing enterprises. See Xinhua, "Lawmakers Urge Food Safety from Cropland to Table," *China Daily*, March 2, 2004.

[62] In Henan Province, for instance, the vast majority of family workshops do not have production permits and the necessary quality test facilities. Their employees generally lack the sanitary knowledge or consciousness required for safe production. See "Henan: bacheng shipin qiye wu shengchan xukezheng" [Henan: 80 Percent of Food Production Enterprises Lack Production Permits], *Dahe bao* [*Great River News*], January 25, 2005, www.tech-food.com/news/2005-1-25/n0029413.htm. In Guangzhou, many cooking oil processing plants operate within residential buildings, and each only possesses one oil-squeezing machine. See "QS zhidu yuandan luoshi, Guangzhou yu qicheng shipin qiye tieding chuju" [The QS System Will Be Carried Out in the New Year, About 70 Percent of Food Enterprises in Guangzhou to be Closed Down], *Xinxi shibao* [*Information Times*], December 26, 2003, www.tech-food.com/news/2003-12-26/n0017468.htm.

initiated the market access system (*shipin shichang zhunru zhi*) in August 2002. Food producers would be issued production licenses only when they met the official standards concerning production conditions and facilities, and the quality of foodstuffs. The government divides foodstuffs into 28 categories with 555 varieties. The system was initially applied to five categories: rice, wheat flour, vinegar, sauce, and cooking oil. In 2003 it was extended to 10 new categories such as meat products, milk, and instant noodles.[63]

With the outbreak of the Fuyang fake milk powder scandal and the subsequent calls for greater state efforts to rectify the food market, some local authorities have hastened the implementation of the market access system.[64] In late 2004, the Guangzhou AQSIQ declared that it would place all categories of foodstuffs under the system within two to three years.[65]

The market access system has nonetheless undermined another important government policy objective — employment generation. Most of the family workshops have neither the necessary capital nor the expertise to upgrade themselves to meet the requirements of the market access system.[66] By substantially raising the threshold for

---

[63] See "Lawmakers Urge Food Safety from Cropland to Table"; "Market Access Set for Food Producers," *China Daily*, March 3, 2005; "Zhongguo ershiba lei shipin niandi quanbu naru zhiliang anquan shichang zhunru zhidu" [28 Categories of Food in China Will Be Placed Under the Market Access System Next Year], *Zhongguo xinwen wang* [*China's News Network*], December 19, 2004, http://finance.sina.com.cn/roll/20041219/04501235380.shtml.

[64] See for example, "Lawmakers Urge Food Safety from Cropland to Table."

[65] "Zhongguo ershiba lei shipin niandi quanbu naru zhiliang anquan shichang zhunru zhidu."

[66] As an owner of an alcohol-producing workshop in rural Guangxi complained, "it was prohibitive for my small business to bear the 100,000 yuan upgrading fee, which was several times higher than my workshop's fixed assets." See "Xiao shipin qiye ruhe maiguo shichang zhunru guan?" [How Can Small-Scale Food Enterprises Step Over the Hurdle of the Market Access System?], *Zhongguo shipin xinxi wang* [*China's Food Information Net*], September 22, 2004, www.tech-food.com/news/2004-9-22/n0025372.htm. Moreover, fierce market competition and the resultant small profit margins in some categories of foodstuffs like cooking oil and sauce also discourage many family workshops from making further investment to comply with the market access system. See "QS zhidu yuandan luoshi, Guangzhou yu qicheng shipin qiye tieding chuju."

entering the food processing industry, the market access system has forced many family workshops to close down. In Chongqing, among the 12,000 food enterprises whose products were placed under the market access system, only 345 had obtained production licenses by late 2004.[67] In Guangxi, 90 percent of the alcohol-producing enterprises were denied market access and this raised serious employment concerns.[68] By the end of 2003, the market access system in Guangzhou had eliminated nearly 70 percent of the family workshops that produced rice, wheat flour, vinegar, sauce, and cooking oil.[69]

The above examples show that to a certain extent, a more effective food safety regulatory system (the market access system) has been constructed at the expense of employment opportunities. If, as the Guangzhou AQSIQ declared, the market access system is applied to all categories of foodstuffs for the next few years, the unemployment problem is likely to worsen. Local authorities may need to choose between the promotion of food safety, and generation of employment. Indeed, this dilemma is not confined to food safety regulation. Fubing Su and Tim Wright have demonstrated that local governments are also facing a dilemma in choosing between the advancement of coal mine safety (closing down small, unsafe coal mines) and job creation and a healthy local economy.[70]

CRISIS AND INSTITUTIONAL DEVELOPMENT

The spate of severe food safety cases in recent years and the failure of the government to stem them demonstrate an urgent need to

[67] "Chongqing: Shipin zhunru qixiao?" [Chongqing: The Market Access System Is Unfavorable to Small-scale Enterprises?], *Chongqing qingnian bao* [*Chongqing Youth News*], November 12, 2004, www.tech-food.com/news/2004-11-12/n0026726.htm.

[68] "Xiao shipin qiye ruhe maiguo shichang zhunru guan?"

[69] "QS zhidu yuandan luoshi, Guangzhou yu qicheng shipin qiye tieding chuju."

[70] Fubing Su, "The Political Economy of Industrial Restructuring in China's Coal Industry, 1992–1999," in *Holding China Together: Diversity and National Integration in the Post-Deng Era*, ed. Barry Naughton and Dali Yang (Cambridge: Cambridge University Press, 2004); Tim Wright, "The Political Economy of Coal Mine Disasters in China," *The China Quarterly* no. 179 (September 2004), 644.

strengthen the food safety regulatory regime. The recurrence of serious food safety incidents and the exposure of many food safety scandals by muckraking journalists in the late 19th and early 20th centuries in America helped prompt the United States government to pass the Federal Food and Drug Act of 1906 and establish the FDA.[71] The situation with respect to food safety in today's China bears some similarity to that episode in the U.S. history. Caught between political censorship and intense competition in the media marketplace, editors and journalists have eagerly reported on consumer-related stories such as food safety incidents. Aside from the widely acclaimed CCTV's Weekly Quality Report program, investigative reports related to food safety have proliferated in the Chinese media, and Chinese news portals, have set up dedicated areas or channels devoted to this topic. These reports both reflect and contribute to the growing public concern with food safety and other public safety issues.

Partly in response to a growing public concern, the Chinese central government announced that it would hold local leaders and the heads of relevant departments accountable for serious food safety incidents.[72] In Fuyang, three senior officials were ordered to resign (*zeling cizhi*) for their roles in the milk powder scandal.[73] Many subprovincial governments have started to adopt the food safety jurisdictional responsibility system (*shipin anquan shudi zerenzhi*) to drive local leaders to expend more effort to maintain food safety

---

[71] James Harvey Young, *Pure Food: Securing the Federal Food and Drugs Act of 1906* (Princeton, NJ: Princeton University Press, 1989).

[72] "Wu Yi tan naifen shijian" [Wu Yi Discusses Milk Powder Incident], *Zhongguo xinwenshe* [*China News Agency*], May 13, 2004, http://cn.news.yahoo.com/040513/72/22e9e.html.

[73] The three Fuyang officials are the deputy mayor in charge of industry and commerce affairs, the AIC director, and the deputy health bureau director responsible for food safety regulation. Xia Changyong, "Jianchabu yansu chachu Fuyang liezhi yinger naifen shijian youguan zerenren" [The Ministry of Supervision Seriously Investigates and Punishes Responsible Officials in the Fuyang Fake Milk Powder Case], *Renmin Ribao*, June 9, 2004, www.peopledaily.com.cn/GB/shizheng/1027/2558651.html.

within their jurisdictions. In January 2005, for example, the Guangzhou municipal government implemented this system, under which the leadership of county and district governments and of the relevant departments are held accountable for serious food safety incidents and the operation of unlicensed food enterprises within their jurisdictions.[74] Meanwhile, authorities also began to bring some of the producers to justice. Since the courts began to hear the fake milk powder cases in August 2004, 28 people have been convicted of manufacturing or selling fake milk powder and sentenced to imprisonment for six months to eight years.[75]

The media coverage on the Fuyang fake milk powder tragedy prompted much reflection on ways to enhance food safety regulation. Some commentators have noted that the SFDA lacks the power to effectively regulate food safety, and that its ability to coordinate policy is hindered by its lack of resources below the provincial level.[76] The State Council Development Research Center, in particular, released a report, *Study on China's National Food Safety Strategy*, which offers a series of recommendations to remedy the food safety problems. Among its suggestions is the establishment of a super-ministerial State (or National) Food Safety Commission (*Guojia Shipin Anquan Weiyuanhui*) that would be empowered to advise the central leadership on food safety policy and coordinate various government agencies in food safety regulation.[77]

---

[74] "Guangzhou shipin anquan shudi guanli zerenzhi yuanze tongguo" [Guangzhou Food Safety Jurisdictional Responsibility System Has Been Approved], *Xinxi shibao*, January 25, 2005, www.tech-food.com/news/2005-1-25/n0029425.htm.

[75] See the following news reports: http://news.sina.com.cn/c/2004-12-06/00214439946s.shtml; http://finance.sina.com.cn/money/x/20041208/08431209480.shtml; http://news.sina.com.cn/c/2005-01-02/17275403430.shtml; http://news.sina.com.cn/c/2005-01-07/07235453651.shtml.

[76] Tian and Wang, "Weilie naifen quanguo liutonglian"; Zhao and Fu, "Naifen jiagongchang: Yumu zahui hunzhu."

[77] See "Zhongguo Shipin Anquan Zhanlue Yanjiu Baogao — Zhengce Pian" [Study on China's National Food Safety Strategy — Policy Concerns], www.food-safety.cn/show_news.jsp?id=1326. The study is a collaboration of more than 150 researchers from 50 research and government bodies in China. See Qin Chuan, "Forum Focuses on Increasing Food Safety," *China Daily*, November 19, 2004.

In an era of administrative rationalization and with successive ministerial upgrading of all regulatory administrations and commissions, it may be difficult to persuade the national leadership to accept such a proposal. Nonetheless, the SFDA has actively promoted the establishment of local food safety commissions as levers to break down interdepartmental boundaries and promote regulatory coordination. As of July 2005, food safety commissions had been established in all provinces (except Tibet and Xinjiang), as well as major subprovincial cities such as Guangzhou and Shenzhen. The provincial (municipal) food safety commissions are invested with substantial powers and responsibilities: formulating food safety policy and general planning, handling major food safety incidents, establishing an emergency system to respond to serious food safety incidents, managing and disseminating regulatory information, and most importantly coordinating and solving major problems in food safety regulation. Led by the first deputy governor, a provincial food safety commission is composed of government agencies involved in food safety regulation. The commission's office is generally located in the provincial FDA building, and the head of the provincial FDA often serves as the commission's deputy chairman.[78] These arrangements reflect the substantial influence the local food and drug administration has on these commissions and allow it to invoke the authority of the provincial leadership to elicit cooperation and compliance from other agencies involved with food safety regulation.[79]

Meanwhile, the State Council has adopted measures to clarify the regulatory responsibilities of different agencies. In September 2004, the State Council promulgated the "Decision on Further Strengthening Food Safety." This decision directed the Ministry of Health to transfer the regulation of food hygiene in the production

[78] "Jiangsu sheng chengli shengzhengfu shipin anquan weiyuanhui" [Jiangsu Establishes Provincial Food Safety Commission], February 5, 2005, www.sfda.gov.cn/cmsweb/webportal/W4291/A64001544.html.

[79] "Guizhou jiaqiang jieri shichang shipin anquan zhifa jiancha" [Guizhou Strengthens Food Safety Inspection During Holidays], February 5, 2005, www.sfda.gov.cn/cmsweb/webportal/W4291/A64001582.html.

and processing stages to the GAQSIQ beginning in 2005. The Ministry of Health remains the regulator of the food retailing sector (including catering and dining halls), while the SAIC oversees the circulation arena. The SFDA is in charge of comprehensive supervision, policy coordination, and investigation of serious food safety incidents.[80]

Moreover, the Chinese government plans to institute a food recall system (*shipin zhaohui zhidu*) after a spate of food safety incidents involving multinationals KFC, Heinz, and Nestlé and domestic producers such as Guangming Dairy. The incidents showed that even the most reputable firms may not always put the interest of customers first.[81] Existing national laws relating to food safety did not have specific regulations governing the product recall and thus left a regulatory void that the food producers took advantage of. When it was revealed that Nestlé's best-selling infant milk powder contained too much iodine by Chinese government standards, the company initially refused to issue a recall. The company grudgingly pulled its product from store shelves only after mounting pressure from the Chinese media and officials.[82]

To fill the regulatory void, the draft Food Safety Law (*Shipin anquanfa*) reportedly includes a provision that requires food

---

[80] State Council, "Guowuyuan guanyu jinyibu jiaqiang shipin anquan gongzuo de jueding" [Decision on Further Strengthening Food Safety Work], September 29, 2004, www.tj.xinhuanet.com/shkj/2004-09/29/content_2957607.htm.

[81] In March 2005, a cancer-causing dye "Sudan-1" was detected in products sold by KFC (a fast food giant) and Heinz (an international sauce producer) in China. In May, the Guangzhou AQSIQ found that some brands of Nestlé milk powder contained excessive levels of iodine. The foodstuffs sold by these companies are circulated nationwide. For a detailed report on the development of these food safety incidents, see http://finance.sina.com.cn/nz/ycsdhyh/index.shtml and http://finance.sina.com.cn/nz/lnqcnfdhlcb/index.shtml.

[82] See Dwight Daniel, "Nestlé's Apology: Too Little, Too Late," *China Daily*, June 10, 2005; "Quechao Zhongguo qu zongcai xiang xiaofeizhe daoqian, xuanbu zhaohui wenti naifen" [President of the Nestlé Greater China Region Apologizes to Consumers and Announces Recall of Defective Milk Powder], *Xiandai kuaibao* [*Contemporary Express*], June 6, 2005, http://finance.people.com.cn/GB/1039/3444000.html.

producers to promptly recall defective products.[83] Some local authorities such as the Beijing municipal government have already made similar provisions in local food safety regulations.[84] These initiatives will contribute to a food safety credibility system (*shipin anquan xinyong tixi*) that national planners hope to build during the 11th Five-Year Plan period.[85]

Last but certainly not least, local authorities in parts of China have come up with a variety of initiatives to mitigate the vulnerability of rural China to food safety issues. The Decision on Further Strengthening Food Safety named the rectification of rural food markets as one of the critical tasks for the near future.[86] Zhejiang, one of China's most developed provinces, has taken the lead in devising new institutional mechanisms for improving food safety regulation in rural areas. Under a new program initiated in fall 2004, some 3,000 shops, most of which are household based and small in scale, are certified to have met government regulatory requirements and named "demonstration shops" (*fangxin shifan dian*) where customers may buy with assurance. These demonstration shops have reportedly attracted many rural consumers. Moreover, 32,000 wholesale food markets, small shops, shopping centers, and supermarkets have reportedly adopted food safety standards in their procurement processes. Additionally, there are about

---

[83] "Shipin anquanfa chugao chengxing, shipin zhaohui jiangyou fayi" [The Food Safety Law Has Been Drafted, Law Governing Food Recall Will Be Available], *Diyi caojing ribao* [*First Financial Daily*], June 27, 2005, http://chanye.finance.sina.com.cn/sp/2005-06-27/254888.shtml; "Shipin anquan tiaoli kaishi zhengqiu yijian, chanpin zhaohui wenti huo lieru" [Consultation on the Food Safety Law Begins, Issues of Product Recall Included], *Zhongguo xinwen wang*, June 28, 2005, http://news.sina.com.cn/o/2005-06-28/06256284451s.shtml.

[84] "Guojia gongshang zongju: zhongguo jiang dui qiye zhaohui wenti shipin lifa" [The State Administration for Industry and Commerce: China Will Legislate on Enterprise Food Recall], *Dongfang zaobao* [*Oriental Morning News*], April 26, 2005, http://finance.sina.com.cn/g/20050426/10031550873.shtml.

[85] "Dui shipin wenti chu zhongquan, xinyong tixi naru guojia shiyiwu guihua" [Putting Great Emphasis on Food Safety Problems, Credibility Network is Included in the State Eleventh Five-Year Plan], *Guangming wang* [*Illumination Net*], June 27, 2005, http://finance.sina.com.cn/roll/20050627/1050154930.shtml.

[86] "Guowuyuan guanyu jinyibu jiaqiang shipin anquan gongzuo de jueding."

12,000 rural consumer rights protection points (*weiquan jiandudian*) where consumer rights protection assistants may help residents seek redress from producers or sellers of fake or substandard products.[87]

The SFDA and the SAIC have also taken measures to boost information gathering in rural areas. By mid-2005, the SFDA in Hainan had recruited and trained about 300 voluntary coordinators (*xieguanyuan*) and monitors (*xinxiyuan*) to help monitor the food safety situation at selected townships and villages, respectively.[88] In the Huairou district of Beijing, the AIC established and trained a team of 610 voluntary food safety supervisors in early 2005. Each village has two supervisors who are responsible for reporting underground food producers (*heiwodian*) to law enforcement authorities such as the AIC and AQSIQ. These food safety supervisors so far have helped law enforcement authorities to ferret out 77 underground food producers.[89] Similar systems will be extended to all rural areas of Sichuan as well, following the completion of an experimental program at the end of 2005.[90]

CONCLUSIONS

By analyzing food safety regulation, this study has illustrated some salient issues and difficulties that China faces in building up an

[87] "Zhejiang luxian jianli sanzhangwang zonghe zhili nongcun shipin anquan" [Zhejiang Establishes Three Networks To Rectify Rural Food Safety], *Renmin wang* [*People's Net*], December 7, 2004, http://news.sina.com.cn/o/2004-12-07/14564457692s.html.

[88] "Hainan sheng nongcun shipin yaopin jiandu wangluo jianshe gongzuo zhashi tuijin" [The Construction of Food and Drug Regulatory Networks in Villages Is Proceeding Smoothly in Hainan], June 8, 2005, www.sfda.gov.cn/cmsweb/webportal/W4291/A64003123.html.

[89] "Huairou cuncun douyou shipin anquan jianduyuan" [Every Village in Huairou Has Food Safety Supervisors], *Beijing wanbao* [*Beijing Evening News*], May 17, 2005, http://news.sina.com.cn/o/2005-05-17/12545911384s.shtml.

[90] "Sichuan sheng zhaokai nongcun shipin anquan jianduwang jianshe shidian gongzuo xianchanghui" [Sichuan Convenes Meeting on the Experiment of Constructing a Regulatory Network of Food Safety in Villages], July 4, 2005, www.sda.gov.cn/cmsweb/webportal/W4291/A64003466.html.

effective regulatory state. First is the fragmented and ambiguous authority and responsibility among diverse regulatory bureaucracies, a situation that exists in other regulatory arenas as well. The cases show not only how ambiguous responsibilities may stymie regulation, but also why it is important to construct proper mechanisms to adjudicate conflicts among regulatory agencies. This study also points to the divergence in regulatory capability in urban vs. rural areas.

Second, this study shows that the government reform has tended to generate short-term uncertainty and a regulatory vacuum. The SFDA was built by expanding the former State Drug Administration and it was supposed to provide coordination among several government agencies in food safety regulation. Yet, the SFDA initially focused on pharmaceutical regulation, and this created a regulatory vacuum in the food sector. It was not until the Fuyang fake milk powder scandal that the SFDA began to put more emphasis on food regulation.[91]

Finally, the study demonstrates the conflict between the promotion of food safety regulation and employment generation, much like what has occurred in the coal mining sector. The market access system involves the closing down of numerous family workshops that do not have sufficient capital and expertise to help meet the official requirements regarding production conditions and facilities, and the quality of foodstuffs. The subsequent rise of unemployment contradicts another important policy objective: employment generation. This series of dilemmas raises serious questions about the appropriate role of the state in socioeconomic regulation.

[91] Dali Yang also examines how government reform led to short-term confusion and a regulatory vacuum in a number of other areas, such as workplace safety. *Remaking the Chinese Leviathan*, 54–55.

Chapter

6

Poverty Reduction, Decentralization, and Local Governance in China

Ran Tao and Mingxing Liu

INTRODUCTION

China's fast economic growth in the context of market-oriented transition has been accompanied by significant progress in poverty reduction. Real GDP grew at an average of 9.4 percent per year in the 1979–2003 reform period.[1] With strong economic growth and specific government poverty alleviation programs, China has been able to dramatically reduce large-scale poverty. In terms of the number of people escaping the absolute income poverty, China has made the single largest contribution to the global poverty reduction of any country in the last 20 years. Using the official poverty line ($0.7/day), the number of poor people is estimated to have fallen from about 200 million in 1981 to 28 million in 2002. Using the World Bank's $1/day income measure, the number of poor people is estimated to have dropped from about 490 million to 88 million over

[1] State Statistical Bureau, *Chinese Statistical Yearbook 2004* (Beijing: China Statistics Publishing House, 2004).

the same period, a decline in poverty incidence from 49 percent in 1981 to 6.9 percent in 2002.[2]

However, there are still great challenges ahead: the unbalanced regional growth in the process of globalization as well as intergovernmental fiscal arrangements without sufficient intergovernmental transfers result in enlarging regional inequality and marginalized poor regions; the overconcentration of still significant number of poor people in resource deficient areas, usually comprising entire communities located in upland sections of the interior provinces of northern and western China; the overrepresentation of minority people and the disabled in the remaining rural poor; and the lack of social services and deplorable educational, health, and nutritional status of these remaining rural poor in less developed regions.[3]

This chapter aims to give an overall introduction to China's area-based anti-poverty programs and examine how these poverty alleviation programs and other closely related development initiatives are associated with issues of local governance, decentralization, and intergovernmental arrangements. The first section briefly describes China's evolving spatial inequality since economic reforms starting from the late 1970s and the geographical incidence of poverty. The second section discusses the public responses to poverty, including the evolving strategy of China's anti-poverty policies, the designation of poverty counties, the allocation and the use of different anti-poverty funds. In the third section, we explore the relationship between poverty alleviation, decentralization, and local governance by looking at the incentives of local governments in poor regions as shaped by the political and fiscal arrangements and explore their impacts on the fund use efficiency and distribution within the locality. The last section concludes with lessons drawn from China's area-based poverty alleviation programs and policies implications for further improvement.

---

[2] World Bank, *China National Development and Sub-national Finance: A Review of Provincial Expenditures* (Washington, DC: World Bank, 2002).

[3] World Bank, *China: Overcoming Rural Poverty* (Washington, DC: World Bank, 2001).

SPATIAL INEQUALITY AND POVERTY DISTRIBUTION IN CHINA

From an international perspective, China's income inequality has worsened seriously; the national Gini index rose from 0.29 in 1981 to 0.45 in the late 1990s.[4] Spatially, inequality has also increased with the urban and the coastal regions growing fast while the rural and the inland regions lagging far behind. China's economic growth in economic transition is featured by an initial decline of the urban–rural as well as interprovincial inequality from 1978 to the mid-1980s.[5] Increased agricultural prices as well as rapid rural growth in the period account for most of such decline in spatial inequality. However, when China further decentralized, opened up, and experienced an explosion of trade and foreign direct investment in the mid-1980s, spatial inequality began to rise steadily and sharply right through the present.[6] The Gini index of provincial per-capita income declined from 29.3 percent in 1978 to 25.6 percent in 1984, but then rose to a historical high of 37.2 percent in 2000.[7] At the same time, the urban–rural average income ratio declined from 2.87 in 1978 to 1.86 in 1985, then rapidly increased to 3 by 2003 (SSB, 2004).[8] Along with the increasing regional income inequality, social inequalities in the distribution of illiteracy and infant mortality have also increased substantially across provinces and within provinces, between rural and urban and within rural and urban areas.[9]

[4] Li Shi, "A Survey on China's Inequality," Beijing, paper prepared for International Conference on Equity and Social Justice in China's Transition, 2002.

[5] Chen Shaohua and Wang Yan, "China's Growth and Poverty Reduction: Recent Trends Between 1990 and 1999," World Bank Policy Research Working Paper No. 2651, The World Bank. Washington, DC, 2001).

[6] Yao Shujie and Zhang Zongyi, "Regional Growth in China Under Economic Reforms," *Journal of Development Studies* 38 no. 2 (2001): 167–186.

[7] R. Kanbur and X. Zhang, "Spatial Inequality in Education and Health Care in China," The Center for Economic Policy Research, Discussion Paper No. 4136. Cornell University, December 2003.

[8] State Statistical Bureau, *Chinese Statistical Yearbook 2004*.

[9] R. Kanbur and X. Zhang, "Spatial Inequality in Education and Health Care in China."

Consistent with the significant urban–rural disparity, poverty is primarily a rural phenomenon in China, and China's war on poverty has thus far focused on the rural population. However, progress made so far has been uneven across regions largely because of spatially unbalanced growth patterns. Poverty reduction has been greatest in the coastal and central provinces where agriculture and rural industries witness stronger growth and rural–urban migration opportunities are plenty. In these regions, many farmers have shifted into higher valued non-agricultural enterprises, making decisions increasingly on market-oriented principles.[10] For many of the remote and mountainous inland regions, where agricultural productivity gains and migration opportunities are much more limited, poverty reduction has proven to be much harder to achieve.

As the interprovincial disparity has grown rapidly since the late 1980s, rural poverty has been mostly concentrated in places that suffer from severe ecological damage and below average irrigation facilities, fertilizer use, and general infrastructure. An increasing share of the rural poor now live in China's western areas with poor geographic location and at a disadvantage in terms of agricultural resources such as soil, rainfall, and climate, or other lands with limited potential for even subsistence levels of production.[11] Though the western provinces only accounted for about 25% of the nation's total rural population, their share of the poor rose from less than half of the national total at the beginning of the 1990s to more than two thirds in the early 2000s.[12] The remaining "poor" counties, generally better off among all poor counties, were located

[10] Zhang Linxiu, Huang Jikun, and Scott Rozelle, "China's War on Poverty: Assessing Targeting and the Growth Impact of Poverty Program," *Journal of Chinese Economic and Business Studies* 1, no. 3 (2003): 299–315.

[11] Tong Zhong, Scott Rozelle, Bruce Stone, Jiang Dehua, Chen Jiyuan, and Xu Zhikang, "China's Experience with Market Reform for Commercialization of Agriculture in Poor Areas," in *Agricultural Commercialization, Economic Development, and Nutrition*, ed. Joaqim von Braun and E. Kennedy (Baltimore and London: Johns Hopkins Press, 1994), 119–140.

[12] World Bank, *China: Promoting Growth with Equity*, World Bank Country Study, Report No. 24169–CHA (Washington, DC World Bank, 2003).

in less contiguous islands of poverty in the hills of eastern and central China.

Among the remaining poor, ethnic minorities are heavily represented. Ethnic minority groups make up less than 9 percent of the total population, but account for about 40 percent of the remaining absolute poor in China. They often live in the deepest poverty, because past anti-poverty programs have often not reached out to the most remote areas where they live and the obstacles to poverty relief are greatest.[13]

MAJOR PUBLIC POLICY RESPONSES

Poverty Alleviation Strategy

China's large-scale poverty reduction in the past two-and-a-half decades has been achieved mainly through rapid economic growth in rural areas. Half of the poverty reduction since the late 1970s actually occurred in the first half of the 1980s. However, when the potential of agricultural reform was exhausted in the second half of the 1980s, the central government found that the population remaining in poverty were stubbornly resistant to further reduction as rural income growth in inland provinces stagnated (World Bank, 1992). Prompted by the World Bank and the United Nations, China began to develop its area-based anti-poverty programs with a focus on regions with high poverty incidence starting from the Seventh Five Year Plan (1986–1990) period.

In 1986, the State Council's Leading Group Office for Poverty Reduction (LGPR) was established to provide greater coherence to the large number of poverty reduction initiatives and, in particular, to expedite economic development in the poor areas. Under the LGPR, the Poor Area Development Office (PADO) was set up as the

[13] Work sponsored by the State Ethnic Affairs Commission (SEAC) concluded that in the mid-1990s, minority autonomous counties accounted for three quarters of all nationally designated poor counties with per-capita incomes under CNY 400, and more than four fifths of the nationally designated poor counties with incomes under CNY 300. See World Bank, *China: Overcoming Rural Poverty*.

key agency responsible for coordinating the nation's funding for poverty reduction programs. Poor provinces, prefectures, and counties have all established LGPR and PADOs following the central model.

China's poverty reduction program comprises a wide variety of agencies, programs, and funding channels. The major programs that designated poor counties throughout the country for support include a *subsidized loan program* planned by the PADOs and administered by the Agricultural Bank, a public works program called *Food-for-Work* (*FFW*) run by the State Planning Commission (SPC), and a *budgetary grant program* managed by the Ministry of Finance (MOF). In addition, there are also nationwide welfare and disaster relief programs to provide direct consumption subsidies and disaster relief to poor rural households operated under the leadership of the Ministry of Civil Affairs. The Ministry of Education runs a *national compulsory education project* to support school construction in poor counties. The Ministry of Health is responsible for improving health care and facilities in poor regions. Although the PADO is the coordination agency for all poverty programs within a locality, most programs are administrated through the vertical chain of individual line ministries and departments outside the control of PADO.

In terms of overall strategy, China's poverty reduction policies have focused on building assets for and transferring assets to the poor to raise their income generating capacity. The idea is that that poverty alleviation should move beyond simply providing basic relief and be integrated with local economic developments. As a result, the emphasis of the poverty reduction strategy adopted since the Seventh Five Year Plan (1986–1990) has been on regional development programs in the poor areas. The actions taken since then have sought to enhance employment and income by improving the local infrastructure and expanding the local agricultural and off-farm capacity with a comprehensive input of capital, materials, technical personnel, and information into poor areas. Such orientation is most significant in China's ambitious National Plan for Poverty Reduction set up in 1993, also known as the "Eight-Seven Poverty Reduction Plan," i.e., to lift the remaining 80 million poor out of poverty within seven years. The objectives of the Eight-Seven Plan are to (1) assist poor households with land improvement, increase cash crop, tree crop, and livestock production, and improve access to off-farm employment; (2) provide most townships with road access and electricity, and improve access to drinking water for most poor villages; and (3) accomplish universal primary education and basic preventive and curative health care in poor rural areas.

The focus on production and infrastructure is also reflected in the sectoral distribution of poverty allocation spending. In the 1990s, almost 60 percent of the funding from the three major programs (subsidized loans, FFW, and MOF budget grants) went to agricultural and industrial development. Infrastructure development represented 30 percent of the total spending, while only 2–3 percent was spent on education and public health.[14]

Designation of Poverty County and Fund Allocation

Most of China's anti-poverty programs target at the nationally designated poor counties. In 1986, the LGPR designated 258 poor counties in 17 provinces across the country. The basic standard for selection was that the average rural net income per capita fell below CNY 150 in 1985. However, a higher poverty line of CNY 200 was applied to the counties in old revolutionary bases and to the counties with large minority populations. For some counties in key revolutionary bases and a few minority counties, the poverty line was raised to as high as CNY 300. By 1988, the area-based poverty alleviation program has expanded to include 378 counties.[15]

---

[14] World Bank, *China: Overcoming Rural Poverty*; Wang Sangui, Li Zhou, and Ren Yanshun, "The Eight-Seven National Poverty Reduction Program in China: the National Strategy and Its Impact," China country case study for Shanghai Poverty Conference, Shanghai, May 2004.

[15] Albert Park, Sangui Wang and Guobao Wu, "Regional Poverty Targeting in China," *Journal of Public Economics* 86 (2002): 123–153.

Complaints were soon heard from both policy advisors to the central government and the poor counties that had not been designated. First, no explanation was given to determine CNY 150 as the basic poverty line; second, the line was not uniformly set for all localities. Political criteria played an important role in the county selection as well as the subsequent allocation of poverty alleviation funding.[16] The inclusion of politically favored counties forced the exclusion of many counties with per-capita income levels well below the poverty line. At the same time, efforts to maintain balance among provinces in the number of designated poor counties hurt provinces in which the vast majority of counties were poor; third, because the incomes in more agricultural areas tend to be more heavily influenced by weather conditions, income data of a single year is not a good criterion for poor county selection; finally, the center had no set way to graduate those counties that developed rapidly or support those that fell into poverty during earlier years of implementation. Once a county was designated as a poor country, it retained the designation even when it was no longer poor.

Such problems finally led to the adjustment of both the poverty lines and poor county designations in 1993 when the "Eight-Seven Poverty Reduction Plan" was initiated. The State Statistical Bureau (SSB) was asked to calculate a new poverty line based on nutritional criteria. The adjustment was so made that all counties with annual rural net income below CNY 400 (current year) would enter the national poor county list, while those with annual incomes above

[16] Park et al. (2002) have noted that less than one third of the initial selection of 258 nationally designated poor counties met the lowest standard of poverty (that is, only 83 of the designated counties had average rural income levels of less than Y 150 per capita). Counties with favorable political credentials and strong supporters — most notably the old revolutionary base areas — were included under the roster of poor counties despite having per-capita income levels twice the level deemed to represent subsistence. Ibid.

CNY 700 would exit the list.[17] With such new criteria, national officials made a sweeping adjustment to the poor county designation. The new list included a larger number of poor counties in the very poor southwestern provinces of Yunnan and Guizhou, while the richer coastal provinces of Fujian, Guangdong, Shandong, and Zhejiang were net losers.[18]

Throughout the 1990s, the anti-poverty funds were allocated to each province, and local matching funds were required to reach 30–50 percent of the central funds (with poorer provinces putting up lower shares). The center claimed to allocate funds according to such factors as provincial poverty headcounts, the depth of poverty, the efficiency of anti-poverty funds use, the actual share of local matching funds, and local infrastructure conditions. However, no explicit formulas were ever provided. In practice, funding was related to provincial poverty alleviation proposals that were meant to reflect the poverty reduction target set within the provincial development plan. Within provinces, most provincial governments allocated the central transfers according to project-based anti-poverty plans proposed by poor county governments. At the same time, the poor headcounts and the fund allocation patterns in the past several years also mattered for the new fund allocation. Funding allocations based on local proposals usually left significant room for political negotiations

[17] Following a standard methodology, the SSB divided living expenditures into two parts — food expenditures and non-food expenditures. For minimum necessary food expenditures, the SSB assumed a minimum caloric intake level of 2400 kcal, the recommended daily caloric intake determined by the China Nutrition Association. The minimum expenditure for food was calculated using weighted prices. Non-food expenditures were calculated as a fixed percentage of total expenditures using an Engel's coefficient of 0.6. The coefficient was chosen for its comparability to that used in calculating poverty lines in other countries and was roughly equal to the average share of expenditures spent on food by Chinese rural households. Adding non-food expenditures to the food poverty line constituted the poverty line. See Wang, Li, and Ren, "The Eight-Seven National Poverty Reduction Program in China."

[18] Alan Piazza and Echo H. Liang, "The State of Poverty in China: Its Causes and Remedies," Paper presented at a conference on Unintended Social Consequences of Economic Reform in China, Fairbanks Centre, Harvard University, May 1997.

and local lobbying efforts. In practice, fund allocations became very political in nature and, to a large extent, were based on intergovernmental negotiations and political considerations such as maintaining balances across localities.[19] An empirical analysis carried out by Park et al. (2002) found that the fund allocation among designated counties was not progressive, i.e., there was no strong relationship between funding levels and income per capita. For both subsidized loans and *Food-for-Work* programs, richer counties usually obtained more funds, either because they had greater political influence or because fund allocated to them could generate higher returns. In contrast, budget grants for poor area development were highly progressive, consistent with the use of such funds to compensate for budgetary shortfalls correlated with lower incomes.[20]

While the 1993 new poor county list captured more of the poorest counties, it also nearly doubled the number of counties receiving central funding for poverty reduction activities. Despite a large reduction in the national poverty headcounts, the number of nationally designated poor counties reached 592 in 1993. This contributed to the spreading of the available poverty reduction program funding over a much greater population of 200 million.[21] Government estimates indicated that in 1997 roughly half (about 27 million) of China's remaining 50 million absolute poor population resided in its nationally designated poor counties; this means that only one in seven of these counties' rural inhabitants was absolutely poor.

The county-based targeting led to a severe dilution of available poverty reduction funding for the half of China's remaining poor population who resided in the nationally designated poor counties and the near complete omission of central government poverty reduction funding for the other half outside the poor counties. Moreover, the central poverty reduction funding was not specifically earmarked for the poor households or the poor townships within the poor counties. Instead, these funds were distributed both to poor and to non-poor townships within the poor counties on a

---

[19] Wang, Li, and Ren, "The Eight-Seven National Poverty Reduction Program in China."

[20] Park, Wang, and Wu, "Regional Poverty Targeting in China."

[21] Piazza and Liang , "The State of Poverty in China: Its Causes and Remedies."

more or less equal way. Given that 21 million absolute poor people resided in the poor counties in 1998, it is evident that assistance to the most needy was diluted by roughly 10-fold by the leakage of benefits to the non-poor, a very substantial leakage.[22]

Poverty Alleviation Programs

From 1994 to 2000, the total poverty spending on the subsidized loans, FFW, and MOF budget grant programs was RMB124 billion (US$14.9 billion), annually accounting for 5–7 percent of the central expenditures and 0.2 percent of the GDP. In administrative terms, different agencies were in charge of funding and management of different anti-poverty programs. Though the center repeatedly stipulated that different agencies bundle their funds for integrated development, in practice, such coordination was infrequent in place.[23]

Subsidized Loan Program

Subsidized loan programs to poor regions, viewed as the flagship of China's poverty alleviation efforts, include over half of all anti-poverty funds. The loans are provided to households or enterprises in poor counties at a subsidized annual interest rate of 2.88 percent. Subsidized loans are managed mainly by LGPR county offices and the county branch of the Agricultural Bank of China (ABC). By regulation, the choice of projects and households to be supported was left mainly to the care of LGPR county offices, while the ABC county branches were responsible for lending and loan recovery. With the commercialization of the state-owned banking system in recent years, ABC is gaining more independence in lending decisions.

Poverty alleviation loans were initially intended to provide basic food security to poor households. Therefore, policies during the second half of the 1980s required that 80 percent of the agricultural loans be allocated directly to poor households to develop cropping, animal husbandry, and agricultural processing.[24] However, after several years

[22] World Bank, *China: Overcoming Rural Poverty*.

[23] Wang, Li, and Ren, "The Eight-Seven National Poverty Reduction Program in China."

[24] World Bank, *China: Strategies for Reducing Poverty in the 1990s* (Washington, DC: World Bank, 1992).

of operation, the government concluded that much of the assistance was used to support consumption rather than spur income growth mainly because the poor lacked the technical or management skills necessary to make use of these resources. As a result, loan repayment rates were as low as 30–65 percent (Park et al., 2002).[25] By the late 1980s, local officials were asked to turn their attention away from loans to households in favor of industrial projects that would better promote local economic development. Consequently, much of subsidized loans went to county and township industrial enterprises with political and fiscal importance, usually regardless of their rates of return. In practice, loans usually reached the richer part of poor counties and areas with better infrastructure and natural conditions.[26] Worse still, most of the projects supported turned out to be failures due to lack of managerial skills and technological capacities in poor regions.[27]

Recognizing the problems of providing direct financial support to local industrial enterprises, the center in 1996 returned to the focus of lending to poor households. Seventy percent of the subsidized loans were to be directed to poor households and to agriculture. In response to past problems in targeting the poor and learning from successful micro-credit programs in China and abroad, the government began to experiment with using subsidized poverty loan funds for micro-credit activities in 1997. By the end of 2001, the amount of micro-credit issued by the ABC through the use of subsidized loans totaled CNY 3.8 billion, covering 2.3 million poor households and 10.6 million poor population.

---

[25] Park, Wang, and Wu, "Regional Poverty Targeting in China."

[26] Wu Guobao, "Goal Conflicts in Poor Areas: Growth, Budget Solvency, and Poverty Alleviation," in *Promoting Economic Development in China's Poor Areas: A Collection of Policy Briefs*, ed. Albert Park and Scott Rozelle (Beijing: China Poverty Research Association, 1994).

[27] In fact, the objectives of such subsidized loan program to reach the poor and promote local economic development are conflicting. For example, projects that will generate tax revenue have an obvious pull. Lower-level officials are aware that past performance will be a criterion for more future loans; so they tend to pick projects that they perceive as bringing higher financial benefits regardless of whether or not such projects will help reduce poverty.

Recent surveys in Yunan and Gansu have shown that by allowing households to independently select projects and introducing joint liability mechanism and peer screening, there were already a significant efficiency gain and higher recovery rates in government loan programs.[28]

Public Works Program (Food for Work)

The Public Works Program is to make use of the surplus labor resources in poor areas to build infrastructure facilities including roads, water conservancy, drinking water facilities, and farmland. By providing poor farmers with job opportunities and income sources, such programs aim to raise farmers' short-term income level as well as long-term development capacity in poor regions. The program originally made use of the left-over commodity stocks such as grain, cloth, and other daily necessities by state-owned enterprises. These commodities are firstly distributed to counties. The county project implementation agencies (such as the traffic bureau or the water conservancy bureau) then use a coupon system to pay for inputs and labor services provided by the poor households. The coupon could be exchanged for these commodities by the participating households. Beginning in 1997, the program has shifted from a coupon system to cash system with all funds directly coming from the government budget.

From the very beginning, the food/cash for work scheme was a multi-year program organized and implemented by the State Planning Commission at the central, provincial, and county level. Planning methods are top-down in nature that reflect political priorities and resource availabilities rather than locally defined needs or opportunities. The types of investment (for example, drinking water, road construction, irrigation) are determined by national and provincial governments. County governments then select the villages to participate in the program, and village committees decide the allocation of project investment and household labor contribution.

[28] Wang, Li, and Ren, "The Eight-Seven National Poverty Reduction Program in China."

Funding for the program in the early years went almost entirely to rural roads, drinking water, and agricultural land improvement projects. After spending increases in the early 1990s, the program diversified to investments in a much larger number of areas, including construction of water conservation projects, commerce (local market construction), and sometimes education and health facilities.[29] Available analyses indicated that the FFW program did a relatively good job in constructing infrastructure that benefited poor areas. Improvements in rural infrastructure, particularly in transport, irrigation, and flood control, indirectly contributed to the rural poverty reduction. At the same time, such programs also directly contributed to poverty reduction when farmers' work was paid by cash or by coupons that could be exchanged for grain, cloth, and daily necessities.[30]

Government Budgetary Grants

Government budgetary grants, accounting for 23 percent of the total poverty funds, are used to support investment in poor areas. Given the low level of fiscal capacity in poor areas, it is impossible for most poor counties to make any public investment. The purpose of the budgetary development funds is to support productive construction projects and investments by means of earmarked transfers. The fund is used to support promising industries that use an appropriate technology, promote infrastructure construction and agricultural structural adjustment. A small portion of the fund has also been used in primary education and basic health care, e.g., school and clinic construction. All budgetary development funds come from the Ministry of Finance and are managed by the finance bureaus. Matching funds from local governments (province, prefecture, and county) are also required, though they have rarely been fully provided.

[29] Zhang, Huang, and Rozelle, "China's War on Poverty," 2003.

[30] Zhu Ling, and Jiang Zhongyi, *Public Works and Poverty Alleviation in Rural China* (Nova Science Publishers, 1996).

Other Anti-poverty Programs and Rural Social Security

Besides the development programs mentioned above, China also has an independent rural relief system. Implemented by the Ministry of Civil Affairs, it offers special assistance to officially designated "poor counties," means-tested social relief to destitute persons and households as well as disaster relief. Such programs are need-based schemes directed to those considered truly destitute and lack any means or potential to support themselves, i.e., those with no children, no work ability, and no reliable sources of income, especially those enjoying the "Five Guarantees" (guarantees for food, clothing, housing, medical care, and burials). Funding for such welfare and relief system mainly comes from the local community fee collection as well as local government funding. Nonetheless, financial constraints mean that this welfare program is always limited in its coverage. Only 3 percent of the rural population are covered, with an average annual subsidy of CNY 16 per capita. In restricting the rural welfare coverage to minimum levels of assistance, the assumption is that the main sources of livelihood protection are to be self-provided.

The center also provides some budgetary funds for large natural disaster relief. Township level governments use funds to purchase necessities (including grain, clothing, and blankets) for relief recipients. In general, rural programs of relief and social assistances remain fragmented, limited in scope and coverage, and reliant for funding principally on local resources derived from collecting funds (township and village enterprises) or on fees raised from rural households.[31] With the ongoing rural tax reform that gradually phases out all fee charges starting from 2002, local governments in poor regions are having difficulties in sustaining such a system without sufficient transfers from upper level governments. For example, in Jiangxi Province, both the coverage of and the funding level of

[31] Sarah Cook, "From Rice Bowl to Safety Net: Insecurity and Social Protection during China's Transition," *Development Policy Review* 20, no. 5 (2002): 615–635.

the rural welfare system have declined in poor counties after the rural tax reform.[32]

With respect to social security, in contrast to the elaborate social security benefits enjoyed by most of the urban population, pension and health provisions in rural areas are sparse, highly variable, and dependent on local resources. Some locally organized old-age pension and co-operative health insurance programs have experimented with contributions either by the individual or from collective funds. All such schemes appear to work relatively well in more developed areas, particularly where payments are made directly from collective funds rather than being a direct cost to farmers. Farmers in poor regions generally have no access to such programs. Rural land and family resources are the major forms of old-age support for most farmers, and rural medical care largely takes the form of fee for service.

Overall speaking, then, what is the general impact of China's poverty alleviation programs so far? The available literature shows that household income and consumption in the officially designated poor counties grew significantly faster than in other counties. It was found that, during 1985 to 1990, living in a national poor county increased consumption by 1.1 percent per year, though this gain is more than offset by growing divergence in consumption due to other reasons.[33] Other scholars also found that household net income per capita increased 2.2 percent and 0.9 percent faster in the officially designated poor counties compared to the other counties during the period of 1986–1992 and 1992–1995.[34] The rate of return of poverty investment was estimated at 15.5 percent during the first period and 11.6 percent during the second period. However, the impacts of such programs on the number of poor people did not

[32] Yang Tuan and Zhang Shifei, "A Survey Report of the Rural Relief System in Jiangxi," Policy Report, Centre for Social Policy Research, The Chinese Academy of Social Sciences. Beijing, P. R. China, 2003.

[33] Jalan Jyotsna and Martin Ravallion, "Are the Poor Less Well Insured? Evidence on Vulnerability to Income Risk in Rural China," *Journal of Development Economics* 58 (1999): 61–81.

[34] Park, Wang, and Wu, "Regional Poverty Targeting in China."

appear to be very strong, suggesting that the non-poor may have enjoyed a greater share of the exhibited growth in household incomes. According to Zhang et al., economic growth appeared to be one of the major determinants of poverty alleviation, while there was no statistically significant relationship between poverty incidence and poverty investment. However, as the poverty levels fell, it became increasingly difficult to pull these people out of poverty by relying solely on economic growth.[35]

DECENTRALIZATION, LOCAL GOVERNANCE, AND POVERTY ALLEVIATION

Fiscal Decentralization, Un(der)-funded Mandates, and Poverty Alleviation

The success in reducing the large number of poor population in the 1980s was celebrated as an example of positive impacts from decentralization. Fiscal decentralization in the period was credited with hardening budget constraints for the local government and providing local incentives to promote economic development; thus it helped the coastal regions greatly in rural industrial development and contributed greatly to poverty alleviation in such regions.[36]

In the 1980s, the central–local tax relations were governed by a complex constellation of tax-sharing contracts, special exemptions, and provincial "loans" to the central government. In many instances, these revenue sharing contracts were regressive, because they allowed richer localities to keep a larger portion of collected revenue. The fiscal contracting system also favored richer localities with more local enterprises since local firms were the richest sources of extra-budgetary or off-budgetary revenues. Taking extra-budgetary revenue into account, poor regions with few local enterprises had to

---

[35] Zhang, Huang, and Rozelle, "China's War on Poverty."

[36] Ma Jun, "China's Fiscal Reform: An Overview," *Asian Economic Review* 11, no. 4 (1997): 443–458; Y. Qian and B. Weingast, "China's Transition to Markets: Market-Preserving Federalism, Chinese Style," *Journal of Policy Reform* 1 (1996): 149–185.

share an even larger proportion of the total collected revenue with the central government. As similar contracts were made between the provinces and sub-provincial units, the bias against poor localities extended to the grassroots levels.[37] By the end of the 1980s, fiscal decentralization, which tied budgetary expenditures more closely to local revenues, had created a budgetary crisis in nearly all poor counties. With limited help from the center and tight budget constraints, local governments in less developed regions had to cut spending on social development and let individuals share more healthcare and education expenses.[38]

In 1994, a fiscal reform was initiated to raise the central revenue share from around 35 percent of the general revenue to 60 percent along with a substantial increase in fiscal transfer without corresponding changes in expenditure responsibilities. On the expenditure side, the sub-provincial levels (prefecture, county, and township) face extremely heavy expenditure responsibilities that are out of line with international practice. This is true especially at the county and township levels, which together provide the bulk of vital public services, including 70 percent of budgetary expenditures for education, and 55–60 percent of those for health. Cities at the prefecture and county levels account for all expenditures on unemployment insurance, social security, and welfare.[39]

The center had originally planned to mobilize fiscal resources so as to channel more transfers from richer areas to poorer ones, but the promised transfers have not materialized. In order to satisfy the needs of coastal provinces that generate much of the revenues, a lump-sum transfer to guarantee them their pre-1994 income was

[37] Christine Wong, *Financing Local Government in the People's Republic of China* (Hong Kong: Oxford University Press, 1997).

[38] Loraine West and Christine Wong, "Fiscal Decentralization and Growing Regional Disparities in Rural China: Some Evidence in the Provision of Social Services," *Oxford Review of Economic Policy* 11, no. 4 (1995): 70–84.

[39] While these levels of government had always provided such services, they had previously provided them as agents of the central government, i.e., the center always subsidized the financial gap when necessary. See World Bank, *China: Strategies for Reducing Poverty in the 1990s*, 2002.

agreed. In addition, to permit each province to share in the growth of its lost tax base over time, the center committed to giving back 30 percent of its increased revenue from the newly created value added tax as well as consumption tax each year. Overall speaking, even though the central government returned a large proportion of its revenues to the provinces, the transfers were not equalizing. The tax rebates, the largest item in overall transfers, were highly correlated with incomes and disequalizing in nature. The *earmarked grants*, the second largest item of transfer, have been found to be mildly disequalizing because they were dominated by food and other consumer subsidies that favored urban areas. To offset this regressive effect, the government introduced an equalizing (general purpose) transfer to aid poor regions in 1996. It was rule based and relied on variables such as provincial GDP, student–teacher ratios, number of civil servants, and population density. However, these transfers have been under-funded since their inception, accounting for just 2 percent of the total transfers. For example, in 1998 the central government allocated CNY 2.2 billion to equalization transfers, compared to the estimated fiscal gap of CNY 63 billion produced by the formula. What each eligible province received was its estimated fiscal need multiplied by a coefficient of 0.035, which was derived from 2.2 divided by 63.[40]

With insufficient fiscal transfers, poorer regions experience difficulties even in paying basic salaries. In these regions, high nondiscretionary outlays for personnel on the government payroll, including local officials, teachers, health workers, and other social services personnel, generally account for well over half of local budgetary

[40] As a result, inequality in public spending across regions is significant. The combination of heavy responsibilities and inadequate transfers means that the levels of service provision vary across localities according to levels of local economic development. As regional growth rates have diverged during the transition, so have public expenditures. Among provincial level units, the ratio of the highest to lowest in per-capita budgetary expenditures (net of all transfers) has risen from 6.1 in 1990 to 19.1 in 1999. The coefficient of variation has grown from 0.55 to 0.86 (indicating growing dispersion among the provinces). Wong, *Financing Local Government in the People's Republic of China*.

revenues; educational spending alone, most of which goes for teachers' salaries, often accounts for 40–50 percent of the local budgetary revenues in poor counties. Poor county governments had to employ a range of creative mechanisms to cope with their persistent and accumulating fiscal deficits. These mechanisms include deferring wages, borrowing from the budgets of various local government bureaus, and borrowing against the next year's budgeted fiscal transfers from higher levels of the government.[41]

The difficult fiscal situation of poor counties has profound implications for the effectiveness with which central poverty funds are used. Given that all anti-poverty grants are channeled through provincial governments and ultimately are managed at the county level line bureaus, the central government usually has weak control over the county government agencies or offices that manage the poverty funds. Under pressing expenditure demands, including simply paying back wages to employees on the government payroll, revenue-starved county governments have strong incentives to divert poverty funds for other uses or use such funds in ways that quickly generate local fiscal revenues. In subsidized loan programs, lower-level officials are aware that past performance will be a criterion for more future loans; so they tend to pick projects that they perceive as bringing higher financial benefits regardless of whether or not such projects will help reduce poverty. When the central policy shifted its policy focus from lending to households to enterprises by the end of 1980s, local officials welcomed these changes and channeled significant share of loans to county-run enterprises regardless of the investment's projected rate of return. The infusion of cash allowed government officials to transfer funds to the county budget (through fees and remittances or tax payments) or to shift fiscal burdens to enterprises such as for hosting guests or paying travel costs. Even when the central government asked local governments to reorient the loans to agriculture and individual households in 1997, field investigations by many Chinese and

---

[41] Albert Park, Scott Rozelle, Christine Wong, and Changqing Ren, "Distributional Consequences of Reforming Local Public Finance in China," *The China Quarterly* 147 (1996): 751–778.

international researchers still indicated that large amounts of the agricultural lending continued to go to large agricultural production bases instead of to poor households.[42]

In a study of "Food for Work" projects in Guizhou and Sichuan provinces, Kang pointed out that some of the FFW investments included in the 1990s had no direct relation to poverty reduction and funds diversion was common practice. The manager of the FFW projects in the late 1980s and early 1990s, the local State Planning Commission, sold whatever materials they were allocated on the open market and used the funds to purchase cement, steel, and large equipment on their own.[43] These in-kind construction project investments were given to local companies and leaders under the close supervision of the local State Planning Commission. Such practices heavily dampened the effectiveness with which central poverty funds were used, and it was found that only through creative investment fund management, primarily dependent on keeping investment funds out of the fiscal system, could large investments be effectively made in remote rural areas.[44] Another study on the subsidy delivery of China's Sloped Land Conversion Program (Grain for Green) in three western provinces also found that almost all cash subsidies and significant shares of grain subsidies targeted for delivery to participating farmers had been skimped by the local governments.[45]

Insufficient transfer also led to un(der)-funded mandates that have negative consequences for the poor. With their low fiscal capacities, local governments in poor regions usually found it extremely difficult to fulfill the matching fund requirement. In the FFW program, this meant that central funds were mostly used for construction inputs, and the shortage in funds was offset by the use

---

[42] World Bank, *China: Overcoming Rural Poverty*.

[43] Kang Xiaoguang, "Commentary on China's Poverty Alleviation," Paper prepared for UNDP, Research Center for Eco-Environmental Sciences, Chinese Academy of Sciences. Beijing, 1998.

[44] Zhu and Jiang, "Public Works and Poverty Alleviation in Rural China," 1996.

[45] Xu Zhigang, Michael Bennett, Tao Ran and Xu Jintao, "China's Sloping Land Conversion Program Four Years on: Current Situation, Pending Issues," *International Forestry Review* 6, nos. 3–4 (2004): 317–332.

of mandatory non-paid labor contributions from villagers. It was estimated that 40 percent of the labor used for the FFW construction is free labor.[46] Apparently, the program would have benefited the poor more if all the work were paid, even if this would have reduced the total amount of infrastructure built.[47]

Unfunded mandates are closely related to heavy rural tax burdens that fall disproportionally on poor farmers. To fulfill various policy burdens imposed from above such as the Nine-Year Compulsory Education requirement, the local governments in poor regions frequently turned to farmers by levying various education charges. The fact that rural taxation became an increasingly acute issue in this period can be largely attributed to the rising rural income disparity and the uneven tax burdens biased against lower income groups in rural areas who were more vulnerable to agricultural-based taxes and fee charges.[48] By the late 1990s, the issue of rural tax burden became so serious that the poorest 20 percent of rural households were paying 50 percent of taxes collected in rural areas, and their tax burdens constituted over 20 percent of the net income.[49] As a result, fees paid for basic education and health comprised a very high share of their cash income in poor rural areas. Private expenditures on education often accounted for one fifth of the household net income and roughly half of many households' cash incomes.[50]

---

[46] Zhu and Jiang, "Public Works and Poverty Alleviation in Rural China."

[47] International experience has shown that public works schemes, using wage rates below the current wage, are very effective poverty alleviation measures. FFW would do well to experiment with such schemes in order to better reduce poverty and provide some insurance that those who have escaped poverty do not fall back below the poverty line. As such, using FFW as part of a public works scheme could form an important part of China's emerging social safety net. See World Bank, *China: Strategies for Reducing Poverty in the 1990s*. 2002.

[48] Tao Ran and Liu Mingxing, "Urban and Rural Household Taxation In China — Measurement, Comparison and Policy Implications," *Journal of the Asia and Pacific Economy* 10, no. 4 (2005): 486–505.

[49] Li Shi , "A Survey on China's Inequality."

[50] World Bank, *China: Overcoming Rural Poverty*.

Local Governance and Poverty Alleviation

The issue of local governance has figured prominently in China's anti-poverty action. Under a centralized political system and expenditure decentralization without revenue decentralization, local governments tend to be more responsive to the Party and higher-level government policies than they are to local needs. These officials are, after all, controlled from above both by tight hierarchical personnel arrangements and by fiscal transfer arrangements. Local governments in many regions are usually more interested in various show case projects that cater to upper-level governments rather than to local tastes.[51]

The problem is further complicated and aggravated by the fact that all levels of government in China are growth-driven in nature. The performance of individual government officials at every level is evaluated on a series of indicators imposed from above. These indicators usually include a number of economic targets such as the annual growth achieved in the local GDP, the amount of revenue collected and revenue contributions made to higher levels of the state, and the quantities of foreign investment attracted, as well as various "social" targets such as those for birth control, maintaining public security, raising school enrolments, and so on. Successfully reaching or exceeding the targets set up by higher-level governments is decisive for local officials seeking political promotion.

Such political and fiscal arrangements have led to a fairly top-down approach in anti-poverty policy formation and implementation. The major anti-poverty programs in China are almost invariably planned from above and reflect political priorities and resource availabilities rather than locally defined needs or opportunities. Usually they are not designed or implemented on the basis of consultation with intended local beneficiaries. One of the most prevalent complaints heard by farmers in poor areas that have received

[51] Liu Mingxing and Tao Ran, "Regional Competition, Fiscal Reform and Local Governance in China," Paper presented to a workshop on Paying for Progress. Public finance, Human Welfare, and Inequality in China, the University of Oxford, May 2004.

poverty alleviation investment funds is that they were not allowed the choice of what activities to do, and often are forced to participate even when they did not have the time, resources, or know-how to undertake the project. When households are given funds, provided with extension assistance, subjected to tight monitoring on their repayment, and offered participation in a sympathetic, supportive group, there is a very rapid increase in the household economic status and increased empowerment of farmers.

Under such a system, the center tends to dispatch earmarked transfers instead of general-purpose transfers. The center knows that local governments may easily divert the general-purpose transfers to bureaucratic expansion and staff wages rather than to public goods and services that reach to the villagers. Under these circumstances, earmarking the transfer and directing its use to designated purposes seem to be the only sensible alternative. However, given that funds are allocated from above and the performance are evaluated by certain "core" indicators that are relatively easy to monitor, earmarking transfers inevitably entails distortion in local incentives. This helps to explain why the center, being able to better control fiscal resources after the 1994 fiscal reform, did not increase its equalizing general-purpose transfer but instead dispatched more earmarked transfers. However, dependence on earmarked transfers usually translated into highly political intergovernmental negotiations over transfer allocation. Lack of rule-based formulas and transparency in transfer allocation has systematically distorted local incentives and drawn local governments in poor regions into unhealthy competition for more transfers and political performance. In China's case, such earmarked transfers easily degenerated into poorly targeted patronage-type programs.[52]

When the evaluation on poverty is conducted from above, local governments have a natural tendency to focus more on projects that can reduce poverty headcounts quickly but ignore the poorest people most in need. Since local officials are evaluated in no small part on the basis of concrete target such as the number of poor people that

[52] Liu and Tao, "Regional Competition, Fiscal Reform and Local Governance in China."

have been lifted out of poverty, officials have an incentive to direct the funds to the better-off households or areas with more advantageous location and natural resources to generate higher returns. Zhu and Jiang (1996) found that poor county governments usually omitted some of the poorest villages in the FFW projects based on evaluation of economic returns. Villages with favorable economic conditions were more likely to receive support.[53] In the subsidized loan program, local officials had strong incentives to direct funds toward industrial projects, not only because they could generate more fiscal resources, but also because local officials faced career evaluations in which the TVE output and profit count as major successful performance indicators even though these may not make much contribution to poverty alleviation.[54] All such practices have resulted in significant leakage of benefits away from the poor and undermined the effectiveness of China's anti-poverty programs.

Under the current system, there has been excessive focus on physical capital development such as agricultural production and infrastructure construction in anti-poverty programs. These projects are more visible and thus regarded as concrete progresses in poverty alleviation. Investment in human capital (education, labor training, and health), capacity building in agricultural extension, and social assistance lags far behind since such investments cannot engender an immediate success and promote short-term income growth. In the three major anti-poverty programs, funds for subsidized loans and FFW have all been used in agricultural production and infrastructure investment, only a very small part of the budget grants (2–3 percent) is used in education and health developments.[55] Although the Ministry of Education and the Ministry of Health have been running some programs to aid poor regions, the investment is still mainly on hardware investment such as construction of education and health facilities instead of providing the most

---

[53] Zhu and Jiang, "Public Works and Poverty Alleviation in Rural China."

[54] Jonathan Morduch, "Reforming Poverty Alleviation Strategy," in *Economic Policy Reform: The Second Stage*, ed. Anne Krueger (Chicago: The University of Chicago Press, 2000).

[55] Wang, Li, and Ren, "The Eight-Seven National Poverty Reduction Program in China."

needed operational costs for schools and hospitals. Consequently, farmers in poor regions have to pay high education charges, and ill-health has emerged as a major cause of poverty among vulnerable populations either due to excessive health expenditures or through the loss of labor as a result of illness. Lack of investment has led to a clear decline in access to health and education, and led to growing gender disparities in access to basic education in poor regions.[56]

Finally, such a system has led to lack of inter-sectoral coordination in poverty alleviation at the local level. Since each type of earmarked transfers is channeled through specific line departments, there is a general lack of coordination between different government agencies concerned with poverty alleviation, relief, health and education, as well as between government agencies, mass organizations, non-governmental, nonprofit, and other social organizations. Although the LGPR system is the coordinating agency for various anti-poverty projects, it has only limited access to data on the projects and activities undertaken through the FFW and MOF grant programs, and at best has only limited influence during the planning stage over the works and activities undertaken with subsidized loans provided through the ABC. This usually results in grants too small and dispersed to meet basic needs in poorer regions. Given that the remaining poor are usually those who are found to be most difficult to overcome, it is essential to enhance program coordination so that investment is directed to the poorest in an integrated manner.[57]

CONCLUSIONS

The Chinese experiences in anti-poverty programs confirm the view that regional targeting, though necessary, may be a rather "blunt instrument" for reaching the poor.[58] China's regional focus in its

[56] World Bank, *China: Overcoming Rural Poverty*.

[57] Ibid.

[58] Michael Lipton and Martin Ravallion, "Poverty and policy," in *Handbook of Development Economics: Vol. IIIB* ed. J. Behrman and T. N. Srinivasan (Amsterdam: North Holland, 1995).

anti-poverty strategy is based on the assumption that poverty is primarily a rural issue and is particularly associated with ecologically fragile and remote highland regions. This definition of poverty has led to a policy focus on raising average incomes in 592 designated poor counties through a variety of micro-economic interventions. However, such spatially defined strategy inevitably excluded significant groups of poor people outside the designated poverty counties and at the same time benefited some non-poor people within such poor counties. The evidence suggests that political constraints are likely to undermine regionally targeted programs when the level of targeting is at the county level or higher. In addition, a large section of the population, particularly rural residents, is exposed to new risks associated with market liberalization, but the collective welfare services that used to provide some minimum level of security have been eroded. Such groups highlight the need to look at the country as a whole rather than just to look at regions defined as "poor," and to disaggregate at the level of the individual and household rather than the locality. Starting from 2001, the central government began to shift its targeting unit from counties to poor townships, villages as well as poor households. This may help to benefit the poor who presently live outside the designated poor counties and thus currently receive no poverty assistance.

China's experiences in poverty alleviation also highlight the importance of keeping appropriate balance between expenditure and revenue decentralization as well as between political and economic decentralization. With increasing regional inequality following marketization reforms, sufficient equalizing transfers that are rule based and transparent need to be provided to poor regions in the short run. Lack of such transfer will not only reduce the level of general public service provision in poor regions, but also undermine the effectiveness of earmarked transfers allocated for poverty allocation. This is because local governments in poor regions have incentives to support revenue generating (rather than poverty reducing) activities, further limiting the resources available to poor localities for welfare expenditures or social sector investments. In a longer run, to hold local governments more accountable, political decentralization needs to go hand in hand with economic decentralization to engender higher local political and tax autonomy and wider participation. This will help to create an appropriate institutional framework for anti-poverty policy implementation in the future.

China's experiences in poverty alleviation also argue for the need of better inter-agency coordination in the overall campaign against poverty. Greater coordination has the potential to strengthen the multi-sectoral approach to regional development in poor areas, to consolidate the use of resources, and to develop a more comprehensive system of social protection and safety nets for the poor. Such a coordination mechanism necessitates a leading agency in poverty alleviation at all levels of the government. Such agency is to be responsible for planning, coordinating, and monitoring different programs within an integrated framework. This is important to pool resources from different departments to support a more integrated development of large-scale poverty reduction initiatives. The New Century Rural Poverty Alleviation Plan launched by the Chinese government in 2001, by strengthening the LGPR's role in pooling resources from different government agencies, can be viewed as a significant step forward.

Last but not least, the Chinese experiences also highlight the importance of balancing different anti-poverty programs. Though anti-poverty investment in local infrastructure and production capacity is essential for rural income growth, the importance in investing in the education, health, and social security for the poor cannot be exaggerated. Direct provision of basic health and education services to the poor is needed to address the broader dimensions of human poverty. After all, poverty reduction programs to increase income through productive employment will not benefit those without labor capacity due to age or disability. Direct income transfer or consumption support is the only way to address the poverty of such groups and ultimately forms apart of a social security or welfare system. Health, nutrition, and education interventions should be closely integrated with other components of a general anti-poverty program and be made essential components of multi-sectoral regional poverty reduction programs. Needless to say, such adjustments in poverty alleviation programs and policies necessitate fundamental reforms in the current local governance system and intergovernmental arrangements that shape the incentives of local government officials in poor regions.

Chapter

7

Grain for Green or Grain for Gain: An Empirical Evaluation of Sloping Land Conversion Program in China

Jintao Xu and Ran Tao

One of China's most pressing environmental problems is from land degradation. According to a World Bank report, "China has some of the worst water erosion problems in the world; the highest ratio of actually to potentially desertified land in the world; and rapidly degrading grasslands."[1] An estimated area of 3.6 million square kilometers in China has been affected by soil erosion, accounting for almost 38 percent of total land area; desertification occurs on 1.74 million square kilometers, some 18 percent of total land area.[2] China has 6 million ha (or 15 million acres) of fields with slopes greater

---

[1] World Bank, *China: Air, Land and Water, Environmental Priorities for a New Millennium* (Washington, DC. World Bank, 2001).

[2] Shuren Liu, "Description of Cropland Conversion Program," in *Workshop on Payment Schemes for Environmental Services: Proceedings*, CCICED Task Force on Forests and Grassland, ed. Jintao Xu and Ulrich Schmitt (Beijing: Beijing Forestry Publishing House, 2002).

than 25° (among which over 3 million ha are cultivated cropping land), with more than 70 percent in the relatively arid west of the country.

Having faced increasingly severe ecological pressure in the 1990s, the Chinese government initiated several large ecological restoration programs, such as the Natural Forest Protection Program, the Anti-Desertification Program in the areas surrounding Beijing and Tianjin Municipalities, and the remarkable Sloping Land Conservation Program (SLCP hereafter, or Grain for Green Program as commonly called). Stricken by an unprecedented 267 days of drought in the Yellow River in 1997, and the Yangtze River floods that led to huge financial loss and many causalities in 1998, the Chinese government claimed that it was necessary to take immediate actions to alleviate water and soil erosion. In this context, the SLCP was initiated as a pilot program in 1999 in the three western provinces of Sichuan, Shaanxi, and Gansu, all of which are located at the middle and upper reaches of the Yellow River Basin and upper reaches of the Yangtze River Basin. In March 2000, the pilot program was officially extended to 174 counties in Yunnan, Guizhou, Sichuan, Hubei, Shanxi, Henan, Shaanxi, Gansu, Ningxia, Qinghai, and Xinjiang as well as Chongqing municipality. In June 2000, another 14 counties in Hunan, Hebei, Jilin, and Heilongjiang were added, and the program was further expanded to include a total of 20 provinces, 400 counties, and 27,000 villages in 2001. By the end of 2001, 1.2 million hectares of cropland had been converted under the SLCP, as well as an additional 0.47 million hectares of barren land.[3]

According to internal government reports, the SLCP already covered a total of 1897 counties upon full implementation in 2002 and more than 2,000 counties across 25 provinces as of the end of 2003. By the end of 2003, 7.1 million hectares of cropland had been converted, and 4.92 million hectares of barren land had been

---

[3] Emi Uchita, Jintao Xu, and Scott Rozelle, "'Grain for Green' Policy in China: Cost-effectiveness and Sustainability of a Conservation Set-aside Program," Paper presented at AAEA 2003 Annual Conference, 2003.

afforested.[4] Figure 1 presents a graphical illustration of converted land area under the SLCP during 1999–2003. During the pilot phase, an average of 408,000 hectares of cropland was converted per year. Upon full-scale implantation in 2002, however, this jumped to 2.9 million hectares per year, a more than sixfold increase. The number of enrolled counties also jumped significantly, by 374 percent between the end of 2001 and the end of 2002.[5] According to the SLCP Planning issued by the State Forestry Administration (SFA hereafter),[6] by 2010 the total area of converted land would be 14.67 million ha.

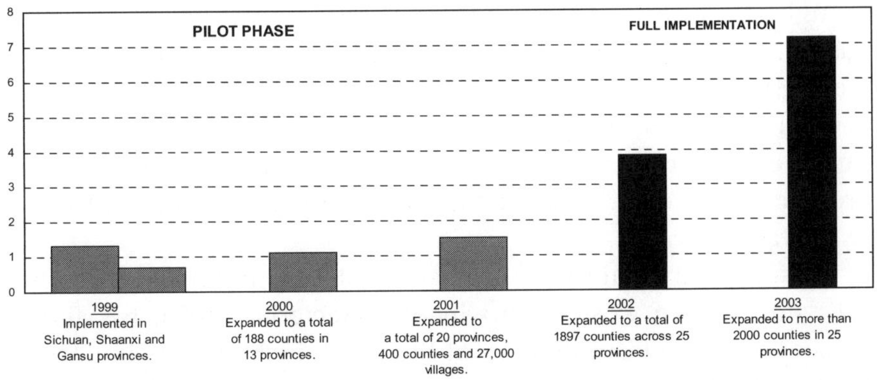

Fig. 1: SLCP Total Converted Area, 1999–2003 (million ha)
Source: Internal Chinese Government Reports.

---

[4] Zhigang Xu, Michael Bennett, Ran Tao, and Jintao Xu, "China's Sloping Land Conversion Program Four Years On: Current Situation, Pending Issues." *The International Forestry Review* (Special Issue: Forestry in China — Policy, Consumption and Production in Forestry's Newest Superpower) 6, nos. 3–4 (2004): 317–326.

[5] Zhang et al. (2005) find in a survey of investment projects during 1998–2003 in 2,459 sample villages across six provinces in China that SLCP is the second most common project being implemented, behind road and bridge investments, at the village level. See Linxiu Zhang, Renfu Luo, Scott Rozelle, and Chengfang Liu, "Investing in Rural China: China's Commitment to Modernization," Working Paper, Center for Chinese Agricultural Policy, Chinese Academy of Sciences, Beijing, 2005.

[6] State Forestry Administration, *Plan for Sloping Land Conversion Program (2001–2010)*, Internal Document, 2003.

If the program ends as planned, the total budget would reach CNY 337 billion (over US$40 billion). This would make it one of the world's largest conservation projects.

However, the fast expansion of the SLCP was suddenly turned around in December 2003 when the central government unexpectedly decided that the new quota for land conversion in 2004 be reduced from 3.33 million ha in 2003 to a mere 667,700 ha in 2004. Given that many local governments had begun to prepare cropping land for retirement during the fall of 2003, the center's decision came as a big surprise. Farmers who had been requested to prepare land for conversion earlier in 2003 had to recultivate their land even though the normal season for cropping operation was already passed. In the western province of Gansu, the local government had required farmers to prepare 249,000 ha of arable land for retirement in 2004. However, the central quota for the whole province in the same year was only 30,000 ha. This means around 88 percent of the prepared land could not obtain the state subsidy and had to be recultivated.

Based on an analysis of program evolution and utilizing empirical data in three western provinces collected in 2003, we aim to present a mid-term evaluation of the SLCP, including its impact on participant farmers' income, the problems existing in program implementation so far, and the potential risks involved in the near future. We believe such analysis not only helps to better understand the decision-making and policy formation process of the Chinese state both at the central and at the local level, but also enables us to assess the performance and sustainability of this largest land conversion/afforestation program in the developing world.

The rest of the paper is organized as follows. In the first section, we briefly introduce the operation of the SLCP followed by an assessment of the program cost-effectiveness based on a large household survey in three western provinces, where the SLCP was firstly carried out on a pilot basis from 1999 to 2002. The second section links the program's initiation and fast expansion to China's grain policy and local governance issue. There, we also argue that the radical program adjustment in 2004 was associated with a major turnaround in the country's grain market. After exploring the major problems in program implementation so far, we evaluate the program impact on participant farmers' income and the potential risks involved for different parties involved in the third section. The last section concludes with further discussions on policy options China is facing in its efforts to achieve sustainable development in ecologically fragile regions.

PROGRAM OPERATION AND COST-EFFECTIVENESS

Program Operation

The SLCP is an important departure from China's other water/soil conservations and forestry programs. It is one of the first, and certainly the most ambitious "payment for environmental services" programs in China. Most other large national forestry programs, such as the Natural Forest Protection Program (initiated in 1998) and the Northeast, North, and Northwest China Green Belt Program (initiated in the late 1970s), are directly implemented by either state-owned forest enterprises or local forestry agencies. In contrast, the SLCP uses a public payment scheme that directly engages millions of rural households as core agents of project implementation. Under this program, farmers are required to convert their sloping cropping land into forests and pastures. In return, they are compensated by the state for subsidy both in mind and in cash. As such, the program needs to be designed in a way that is incentive compatible for the participant farmers both during the subsidization period and after. During the subsidization period, farmers need to find state subsidy more than offset their opportunity costs to ensure program participation lucrative. In a longer run, if the central government's target is to have a permanent land retirement after the subsidization period, either farmers need to shift to more beneficial activities, or they can garner enough economic returns from the newly planted forest or pasture land. If such economic restructuring does not occur, farmers will have incentive to return the already retired land to cropping after the subsidization period.

To induce farmers to participate in the program and restore their lands for forests and pastures, the central government put forward a very generous compensation scheme. Farmers who convert degraded and highly sloped cropland back to either "ecological forests" (defined by the State Forestry Administration as timber-producing forests), "economic forests" (orchards or plantations of trees with medical value), or grassland will be compensated with (1) an annual in-kind subsidy of grain, (2) a cash subsidy, and (3) free saplings, provided to the farmers at the beginning of the planting period. To account for differences in regional average yields, the grain subsidy is set at 2250 kg/ha in the Yangtze River Basin, and 1,500 kg/ha (24 bu/acre) in the Yellow River Basin. The cash subsidy is CNY 300/ha of eligible land (US$36/ha or US$15/acre) per year. Both grain and cash subsidies are to be available for eight years if ecological forests are planted and for five years or two years if economic forests or grasses are planted, respectively.[7]

At the same time, realizing the potential risks of returning to cropping beyond the subsidization period, the central government clearly stated that the program was not only to conserve soil and water in China's ecologically fragile areas, but also to restructure the rural economy to enable participant farmers shift to ecologically and economically more sustainable activities such as husbandry, forestry, and off-farm work. However, no explicit policy, at least within the SLCP framework, has been designed to promote such economic restructuring. Thus, the implicit assumption is that retiring marginal land from cultivation is a prerequisite for, or at least serves to promote, rural economic restructuring.

The program is also designed to maximize local government incentives since the central government fully funds the program. Both the grain and cash subsidies are paid by the Ministry of Finance and are distributed to farmers through local government implementing agencies. The program to date has been run as partnerships

---

[7] Zhigang Xu, Michael Bennett, Ran Tao, and Jintao Xu, "China's Sloping Land Conversion Program Four Years On: Current Situation, Pending Issues."

between the central government, providing the overall vision and the funding, and the provincial and local governments, administering the programs on the ground.

Program Cost-Effectiveness

During the three-year (1999–2001) pilot period alone, the central government already poured CNY 7.68 billion (US$930 million) in grain and cash subsidy into the SLCP. By the end of 2003, the total government expenditures approached CNY 50 billion (over US$6 billion), of which 68 percent was spent on the grain subsidy. With such a huge fiscal expenditure, a cost-effectiveness analysis is essential for us to infer the room for cost saving in program implementation.

Our data come from a large sample household survey conducted by the Center for Chinese Agricultural Policy (CCAP) at the Chinese Academy of Sciences in 2003. The survey covers the three provinces of Shaanxi, Gansu, and Sichuan, where the program was firstly implemented on a pilot basis. In this survey, two counties per province, three townships per county, two participant villages per township, and 10 households per village were randomly selected. Therefore, a total of 36 villages and 360 households were covered. Given the fact that detailed information about land slots, households, and villages was collected for both 1999 and 2002, the survey provided a comprehensive and comparatively long window into program implementation. It is thus, to our knowledge, the best available data set for evaluating the SLCP.

We first compare the opportunity costs for all retired land slots and the real value of the state subsidy for these slots in each province. By opportunity costs we mean the loss of net benefits because of land retirement. This is approximated by the 1999 pre-program net income per unit of retired land. According to the compensation standards set by the central government, the cash equivalent of both grain and cash subsidies in the Yellow River Basin is CNY 2,400 per ha and that in the Yangtze River Basin is CNY 3,450 per ha (the grain expenditure here is set at CNY 1.4 per kg by the state). In Shannxi Province, the average opportunity cost was CNY 645 per ha, only around a quarter of the state subsidy of CNY 2,400 per ha. The average opportunity costs in Gansu and Sichuan were CNY 2,130 and 2,865 per ha, respectively, both lower than their state compensation standards of CNY 2,400 and 3,450 per ha. Table 1 compares the opportunity costs and state compensation standards province-wise. By deducting the participant 1999 net income from enrolled land from state compensation standards, we are able to calculate the room for cost saving for each province. As shown in Table 1, if all retired land slots were to be auctioned, there would be

Table 1: Participant 1999 Net Income from Enrolled Land Vs. SLCP Compensation Standards

	Net Losing Households	Net Gaining Households	All Participants
Shaanxi (n = 103)			
Number of households	6	97	103
Total converted land area (ha)	2.47	70.80	73.27
Compensation standard – 1999 net income (RMB)	–12,938	151,594	138,657
Average net gain as percentage of total compensation	–219	89	79
Gansu (n = 85)			
Number of households	31	54	85
Total converted land area (ha)	5.87	14.13	20
Compensation – 1999 net income (RMB)	–9,970	17,430	7,460
Average net gain as percentage of total compensation	–71	51	16
Sichuan (n = 76)			
Number of households	15	61	76
Total converted land area (ha)	5.13	17.60	22.73
Compensation – 1999 net income (RMB)	–15,037	37,871	22,564
Average net gain as percentage of total compensation	–95	68	32

Source: Authors' calculations.

a maximum cost saving of 79 percent in Shannxi, while the room for cost saving would also be 16 percent and 32 percent in Gansu and Sichuan, respectively.

Table 1 also compares the participant farmers' opportunity costs and the state compensation standards at the household level to examine whether there were households who incurred net loss from the program participation. On average, the participant rural households received a subsidy significantly higher than their opportunity costs. This is shown by the cost-saving percentages for each province in the last column of Table 1. However, there was still a significant number of net losers. Among the 103 participant households in Shannxi Province, 97 households gained from participation, while six households incurred net loss. In Gansu and Sichuan, there were 31 net losers out of 85 participant farmers and 15 net losers out of 76 participant farmers. The implication is that the subsidy scheme in the SLCP was over-simplified and could not match the huge heterogeneity in land productivity across households and regions.

However, it would be misleading to interpret the state compensation standards that were used for calculations in Table 1 (that of CNY Y 3,450 per ha in Sichuan and that of 2,400 per ha in Gansu and Shannxi) as the actual compensation for participant farmers. This is because the state compensation standards used in Table 1 were calculated by assuming a grain price of CNY 1.4 per kg. However, our field work in Gansu, Shannxi, and Sichuan indicates that grain prices were much lower in all the three provinces between 1999 and 2001. Table 2 presents grain market prices in

Table 2: Average Grain Prices in Surveyed Areas

	Wheat		Corn		Rice		Average	
	1999	2002	1999	2002	1999	2002	1999	2002
Shannxi	1.08	1.06	0.86	0.82	1.16	0.96	1.04	0.94
Gansu	1.24	0.96	0.94	0.9	1.16	0.96	1.1	0.94
Sichuan	1.18	1.06	1.12	1.02	1.16	0.96	1.16	1.02
Average	1.18	1.02	0.96	0.92	1.16	0.96	1.1	0.96

Source: Authors' calculations.

1999 and 2002 for the three provinces. As shown in the table, the arithmetic average price for wheat, corn, and rice in our surveyed regions was only CNY 1.1 per kg in 1999, and dropped further to CNY 0.96 per kg in 2002. Even if we use the CNY 1.1 per kg as the standard to estimate the cash-equivalent subsidy for participant farmers, the total subsidy per hectare was merely CNY 2,775 for Sichuan and CNY 1,950 for Shannxi and Gansu.[8]

In Table 3, we recalculate the real value of the state compensation for participant farmers using the actual local grain market prices and compare them with farmers' opportunity costs for each province; the picture of our cost-effectiveness analysis changes significantly. As shown in Table 3, the room for cost saving in Shannxi and Sichuan declines from 79 percent to 60 percent and from 32 percent to 10 percent, respectively. In Gansu Province, on average, participant farmers incurred net loss due to program enrollment. Furthermore, a significantly higher number of farmers incurred net loss because of program participation. In Gansu, for example, this is the case for almost 50 percent of the participants in the sample, with a total shortfall of CNY 13,139. In Sichuan, compensation standards fell below the 1999 net income of enrolled plots for around 29 percent of the participants in the sample with a total shortfall of CNY 19,439. In Shaanxi, where implementation appeared to be the best, the state subsidy was below the pre-program income for almost 7 percent of participants, comprising a shortfall of almost 45 percent of the average 1999 net household income.

In general, though the government expenditure on the SLCP was very generous even by international standards,[9] we find that for

[8] However, the central government indeed paid for the subsidized grain at the price of 1.4 per kg. Therefore, the difference was actually paid to the SGEs that delivered the grain subsidy to participating farmers. The second section deliberates on this.

[9] According to some scholars, the compensation standards in China are quite generous and in a majority of cases exceed the forgone incomes of converted land. A comparable case is the Conservation Reserve Program (CRP) in the United States with an average compensation of US$116 per acre, while the compensation standards in Yellow River Basin and the Yangtze River Basin are 1.5 times and 2.6 times higher, respectively. See Uchita, Xu, and Rozelle, "Grain for Green Policy in China."

Table 3: Participant 1999 Net Income from Enrolled Land Vs. Real Value of SLCP Compensation

	Net Losing Households	Net Gaining Households	All Participants
Shaanxi (n = 103)			
Number of households	7	96	103
Total converted land area (ha)	5.13	68.13	73.27
Compensation standard – 1999 net income (RMB)	–14,778	120,478	105,700
Average net gain as percentage of total compensation	–120	74	60
Gansu (n = 85)			
Number of households	40	45	85
Total converted land area (ha)	8.07	11.93	20
Compensation – 1999 net income (RMB)	–13,139	11,614	–1525
Average net gain as percentage of total compensation	–68	41	–3
Sichuan (n = 76)			
Number of households	22	54	76
Total converted land area (ha)	7.27	15.47	22.73
Compensation – 1999 net income (RMB)	–19,439	26,657	7,218
Average net gain as percentage of total compensation	–85	55	10

Source: Authors' calculations.

more than one fourth of the participants in our sample, the SLCP compensation falls short of the net revenue received from the plots in 1999 before conversion for a total shortfall of CNY 47,356. Although the total gain to the participant farmers in the sample exceeds the total loss by CNY 111,393, the differences between opportunity costs and compensation benefits vary greatly depending on regions and households. This highlights the fact that compensation standards are insufficiently graded to account for production heterogeneity. Net average gain per household for Shaanxi, for example, is CNY 1,026, compared with CNY 95 for Sichuan, and a net loss is CNY 18 per household for Gansu. This easily leads to a situation in which some participant farmers received a subsidy much higher than their opportunity costs, while there was still a significant number of net losers.

POLICY BACKGROUND AND LOGIC OF POLICY EVOLUTION

What are the factors, then, that can account for both the relatively low cost-effectiveness of the Grain for Green Program and the obvious mismatch between state compensation and participant farmers' opportunity costs? In this part, we argue that the program's relatively high and homogenous compensation standards, as well as its fast expansion in the earlier period, are related to the center's grain policy failure in the second half of the 1990s and its strong will to dispose of the huge grain stock accumulated in the state grain sector. Local governments, hoping to gain financially from the SLCP, also coordinated in pushing fast the program expansion. Finally, the unexpected radical program adjustment in 2004 was closely associated with a major turnaround in the country's grain market and various difficulties led by excessively rapid program expansion that rendered continuing fast expansion unsustainable.

Failure in State Grain Policy and Central Government Motivation

In the mid-1990s, China entered a period of grain surplus after the country's grain output hit a record high of 500 million tons in 1996 and remained at a similarly high level for several years. The high level of grain output and ensuing significant grain surplus in the second half of the 1990s could be partly explained by the center's grain policy in this period: Starting from the mid-1990s, the central government adopted a state grain procurement policy through which the state grain enterprises (SGEs hereafter) were required to purchase grain from farmers at protection prices (higher than the market prices).[10] The central government also installed a "Grain Bag Policy," which held provincial governors responsible for local food self-sufficiency (though the degree of such self-sufficiency varied province-wise). Unsurprisingly, these production-stimulating policies significantly raised grain output. As a result, the total grain stock held by the SGEs reached 200 million tons by the end of 1997 and was further increased to 250 million tons one year later.[11] The grain stock held by farmers also hit a historical high of 662 kg per capital by the end of 1998. This amounted to a surplus of 250 kg per capita after deducting farmer's own annual consumption and a national total of 225 million tons surplus grain held by individual farmers. All in all, China witnessed a huge grain stock of around 475 million tons by the end of 1998, something close to the nation's annual grain output.[12]

With fast growing grain stock and declining grain market prices, large financial loss emerged in the state grain sector that procured grain at protection prices. Between 1996 and 1998, the financial loss of SGEs grew by an astonishing CNY 100 billion, and this became the non-performing loans of the State Agricultural Development Bank, which dispatched loans to SGEs for grain procurement.[13]

---

[10] The agricultural reforms in the late 1970s and 1980s consisted of two transitional stages; initially decollectivization in the late 1970s followed by market liberalization in the mid-1980s. The Household Responsibility System (HRS) adopted since then has provided individual rural households with incentives by making them the residual claimants to farming returns once they fulfill state grain quota and agricultural taxes and fees. The full mandatory grain quotas were abolished in the early 1980s and replaced by grain procurement contracts in which every rural household needs to sell an amount of grain output at pre-determined procurement prices set by the state. With rare exceptions, the market prices are higher than the state procurement prices, and farmers thereafter could sell their produce to market. However, since the mid-1990s, the state began to procure grain at prices higher than the market prices.

[11] Feng Lu, "Three Grain Surpluses — Evolution of China's Grain Price and Marketing Policies (1978–1999)", Paper presented in International Agricultural Trade Research Consortium, China's Agricultural Trade and Policy: Issues, Analysis, and Global Issues, San Francisco, California, 1999.

[12] Ibid.

[13] Ibid.

Facing mounting financial pressures, the central government responded by installing a radical policy known as "Monopolized State Procurement" in 1998. This policy required the SGEs to procure all (rather than only part of) residual grain from farmers at state protection prices. By full procurement, the state hoped to exert firm control over the grain market. The idea was that state monopoly over the country's grain market could then make it possible for SGEs to sell its grain stock at prices that lower SGE's financial loss. However, such policy could only have worked if the SGEs had been able to exert full control over the country's grain market and higher grain prices would not have dampened grain demand. In reality, both conditions were not met. Since the state protection prices stimulated agricultural production and farmers themselves already held huge grain stock, local state grain enterprises were forced to, under the state policy, purchase all residual grain in 1998 and 1999. Many local SGEs soon found the central policies of full procurement and reducing loss making at the same time were in fact incompatible. Because higher sale prices necessarily dampened grain demand, many SGEs realized that following the central policies closely would only lead to further financial loss. Implicit resistance to the central policy emerged, and farmers' complaints against frequent IOUs issued by SGEs increased. Many farmers had to sell their grain to private merchants at much lower prices. The center's response was to push local governments to take administrative actions so that all private merchants be excluded from the grain market. However, this policy did not work very well since these private grain merchants were very mobile and difficult to monitor. What followed was greater grain stock in SGEs and even higher financial losses accumulated in 1998 and 1999.

The Grain for Green program was initiated against this background. By 1999, the grain stock in the state grain sector was even larger than the full storage capacity of the SGEs. The ever-increasing loss-making called for immediate and effective action to contain SGEs' grain stock. Apparently, the center had strong intention to dispose of the grain stock as soon as possible and as much as it could. The SLCP was then considered by the center as a way out.

Apparently, this program could not only contain the grain output, but also helps to consume SGE's existing grain stock. In practice, the central government purchased subsidy grain (used for the SLCP) from SGEs at a price of CNY 1.4/kg, a price much higher than current grain market prices of CNY 1.0/kg.[14] By doing so, the state clearly had an intention to reduce the loss-making of SGEs through fiscal expenditure on the grain subsidy in the SLCP. This not only explains why the central government set very generous grain compensation standards for the SLCP from the beginning, but also helps us to understand why the central government, under the request from local governments, agreed to expand the program so rapidly both during and after the program pilot period.

Understandably, state grain enterprises strongly supported the SLCP. Table 4 shows that by the end of 2003, the accumulated grain subsidy for the SLCP was as high as 2.45 million tons. Apparently, the difference between the grain market price and the price at which central government purchased the SLCP subsidy grain from SGEs

Table 4: Retired Land Area and Grain Subisidy

	Retired Area Current Year (Thousand ha)	Retired Area Accumulated (Thousand ha)	Grain Subsidy in Kind (Thousand tons)	Grain Subsidy in Cash (Million CNY)	Impliticit Subsidy SGE in Cash (Million CNY)
1999	381	381	698	980	280
2000	405	786	1,439	2,010	580
2001	420	1,206	2,207	3,090	880
2002	2,647	3,853	7,051	9,870	2,820
2003	3,338	7,191	13,159	18,420	5,260
1999–2003	7,191	13,417	24,553	34,370	9,820

Notes: The average grain price in China in 1999 was CNY 1.1/kg and declined to around CNY 1.0/kg afterwards. The implicit subisidy to SGE is calculated as the price difference CNY 0.3 times the total grain subsidy of SLCP.

[14] Ran Tao, Zhigang Xu, and Jintao Xu, "Grain for Green Project, Grain Policy and Sustainable Development," Chinese *Social Sciences* 150 (2004): 25–38.

was an implicit subsidy to the SGEs. Therefore, among the center's total grain subsidy of CNY 34.37 billion, 9.82 billion went to SGEs.

Simplified Compensation Standards, Fast Expansion, and Local Governance

The fast expansion of the SLCP since its initiation in 1999 could also be partly attributed to the financial incentives of local governments in China. As a matter of fact, local governments in many regions viewed the program as a chance of free lunch and made every effort to push for larger land conversion quotas. Given the generous state subsidy that went through the hands of local implementing agencies, local governments usually first overreached their land conversion quotas and then bargained for more subsidies.[15]

Local hunger for larger quota allotment, combined with the central target to lower the financial losses of the SGEs, helps to account for the sixfold increase in the converted land area in 2002 when the pilot period was ended. By obtaining a higher subsidy, local governments aimed to gain financially through fund diversion. Diversion of funds came as little surprise to those familiar with the complex institutional dynamics of rural China. Rather than granting localities the power to set the compensation standards, the central government settled on a simplified, two-tier compensation scheme in part to prevent local governments from exploiting their informational advantage by exaggerating estimates of the forgone incomes of converted land so as to inflate their subsidies.[16] Nonetheless, local governments

[15] Jintao Xu and Yiying Cao, "The Socioeconomic Impacts and Sustainability of the SLCP," in *Implementing the Natural Forest Protection Program and the Sloping Land Conversion Program: Lessons and Policy Recommendations*, CCICED-Task Force on Forests and Grasslands, ed. Jintao Xu, Eugenia Katsigris, and Thomas A. White (Beijing: China Forestry Publishing House, 2001).

[16] Diversion of upper level transfer has been a continuing and serious issue in China's local public finance system. It is due, in part, to significant shortfalls in local government finances, especially in the less developed regions due to serious lack of tax compliance and the decentralization of rural public finances. See Christine Wong, "Central-Local Relations Revisited: The 1994 Tax Sharing Reform and Public Expenditure Management in China," *China Perspectives* no. 31 (2000): 52–63.

usually could find other ways to milk the system by focusing their efforts on lifting the land conversion quotas, either through direct negotiation, or by first overreaching the quotas and then bargaining for more subsidies. Such behavior can be traced to the beginning of the SLCP. In 1999, the three pilot provinces of Sichuan, Shaanxi, and Gansu overshot their quotas by more than 100 percent within mere three to four months. This continued through 2000, when 312 counties initiated land conversions on their own initiatives despite the fact that the central government's plan was to implement the pilot program in only 174 counties in 2003 and 2004. The State Forestry Administration continues to receive numerous requests from local governments asking for higher land conversion quotas.

Table 5 details a comparison of the SLCP compensation both in kind and in cash with the actual subsidy delivery received by the participant households in our 2003 survey. For all six counties surveyed, the average compensation delivery in kind and in cash at the time of the survey fell significantly short of the state compensation standards. The average shortfall in cash compensation for the whole sample is CNY 105/ha, only around one third of the state compensation

Table 5: Average Shortfalls in Grain and Cash Compensation in Surveyed Areas, 2002

		Grain (kg/ha)[a]		Cash (RMB/ha)		
Province	County	SLCP Standard	Actual Delivery	SLCP Standard	Actual Delivery	Total Shortfall (RMB/ha)[b]
Shaanxi	Yanchuan	1,500	232.5	300	60	1,507.5
	Liquan	1,500	1,215	300	90	495
Gansu	Jingning	1,500	810	300	255	735
	Linxia	1,500	322.5	300	30	1,447.5
Sichuan	Chaotian	2,250	2,025	300	45	480
	Lixian	2,250	1,927.5	300	195	427.5
Average		1,763	810	300	105	1,148

Source: Authors' calculations-based on survey data.

[a]This is a sum of corn, wheat, and rise subsidies.

[b]This values grain at the national price of RMB 1/kg.

standard of CNY 300/ha. There was also huge heterogeneity in actual cash delivery across counties, ranging from a mere CNY 30/ha in Linxia County, to CNY 255/ha in Jingning County, both in Gansu Province. The average grain delivery was 810 kg/ha for the sample overall, around 46 percent of the state compensation standards. Again, significant heterogeneity in actual grain delivery across counties emerged, ranging from a minimum of 232.5 kg/ha in Yanchuan County, Shaanxi Province, to a maximum of 2,025 kg/ha in Chaotian, Sichuan Province. Moreover, numerous farmers in the 2003 survey also reported that the received subsidized grain was of poor quality.

Besides poor program budgeting and excessively fast expansion so that local agencies did not have sufficient staff and time to deliver subsidy, these shortfalls in the delivery of subsidy were also symptomatic of larger issues involving China's system of rural finance. Local governments in program areas retained significant subsidies to make up for expenditure shortfalls and tax arrears accumulated in the past. This was related to the recent rural tax reform that gradually deprived local governments of the power to levy various tax and fees on farmers. With the serious rural tax incompliance and high local government deficits in many regions, local governments had every incentive to expand the conversion program so as to obtain more resources to make up the tax arrears and budget deficits.[17]

Diversion of funds by local governments also occurred in other provinces. In our survey of one county in the southern province of

[17] Zuo gave anecdotal evidence that in a number of instances full compensation does not reach participating farmers for various reasons. In some cases, a portion is deducted by the village government either to pay laborers to plant trees on the farmer's converted land, or to pay back-taxes owed by the farmer. Xu and Cao (2001) find that in a group of 1,026 households, fully 49.5 percent received only partial compensation, 8.5 percent received only grain, and 17.6 percent received no compensation at the time of the survey. See Ting Zuo, "Part II. Chapter 3: Implementation of the SLCP," in *Implementing the Natural Forest Protection Program and the Sloping Land Conversion Program: Lessons and Policy Implications*, CCICED-WCFGTF, ed. Jintao Xu, Eugenia Katsigris, and Thomas A. White (Beijing: China Forestry Publishing House, 2001). And Xu and Cao, "The Socioeconomic Impacts and Sustainability of the SLCP."

Hunan in 2004, it was found that local cadres provided false reports to upper level governments by exaggerating retired areas to swindle upper level transfers. Serious cadre-mass conflicts emerged because local cadres retained the program subsidy to pay for tax arrears. In another mountainous county one of the authors visited, local governments required farmers to retire half of their arable land though the average land holding per capita was barely enough to produce grain for farmers' own subsistence and local soil erosion was negligible. Local governments apparently had the intention to retain at least a significant share of the subsidy to fulfill its tax collection targets.

Though the diversion of upper level funds in the SLCP was pervasive, the root of such activities sources back to the long-standing issues in China's local governance regime. In the late 1990s, the local government in agriculture-based regions usually over-charged farmers in the name of implementing upper level policy mandates such as grain procurement and birth control. In the early 2000s, when the center introduced the comprehensive tax reforms, revenue hungry local governments began to more frequently divert upper level transfers that are originally intended for farmers.

Grain Market Turnaround and Radical Program Adjustment

If the generous compensation standards and fast expansion of the SLCP is closely related to, as we have argued, the policy objectives of both the center and local governments, why did it happen that the central government in 2004 radically adjusted the program?

The major reason for this radical policy change is a major turnaround in China's grain market in 2003. The policy of protection price in grain procurement in the late 1990s led to huge grain stock and the state grain sector's fast growing financial loss. By late 1999 and early 2000, the central government found the policy of monopolized grain procurement to be financially devastating and had to adjust the policy by lowering the protection price and reducing the quantity of grain procurement. State policy changes and lower grain prices necessarily led to lower grain output. According to national data, grain output declined to 460 million tons in 2000 and further to 432 million tons in 2003, while the nation's annual grain consumption has stabilized at a level of 480–490 million tons since 2000 (Fig. 2). The difference between demand and supply was made up by the accumulated grain stock in the late 1990s. Using the CAPSIM simulation model developed by CCAP, we estimate that the national grain stock dropped by 110 million tons between 1999–2003 and the 2003–2004 national grain stock was only around 150 million tons (Fig. 3).

With the lower grain supply than the demand since 2000, the huge grain stock accumulated since the late 1990s was gradually exhausted, and grain price began to rise slowly since 2000 (Fig. 4). If the self-adjusting mechanism in the grain market itself tended to raise the grain price, the fast expansion of the SLCP helped to accelerate the turnaround in the grain market. The grain subsidy for the SLCP was about 7 million tons in 2002, but grew to 13 million tons in 2003 and 20 million tons in 2004. Under multiple forces, China's grain prices have begun to rise steadily since September 2003. Though the grain stock dissipated by the SLCP was not very high compared to the total national grain stock, it was no coincidence that a rapid grain price surge in the fall of 2003 fitted exactly the timing of the SLCP grain subsidy delivery, usually between September and November of a year. Therefore, it is perhaps no exaggeration to argue that the delivery of 13 million tons grain in 2003 at least constituted a trigger for the grain price surge in that year.

Overall speaking, the unsustainable state grain policy in the late 1990s led to declining grain prices and market self-adjustment in grain supply and demand. At the same time, as an important state policy to reduce the state grain stock and SGE loss making, the initiation and fast expansion of the SLCP accelerated the process of grain market turnaround, thus helped to exhaust China's grain stock and raise the national grain price in 2003. From this perspective, the initiation and fast expansion of the program planted the seed for its radical adjustment afterwards.

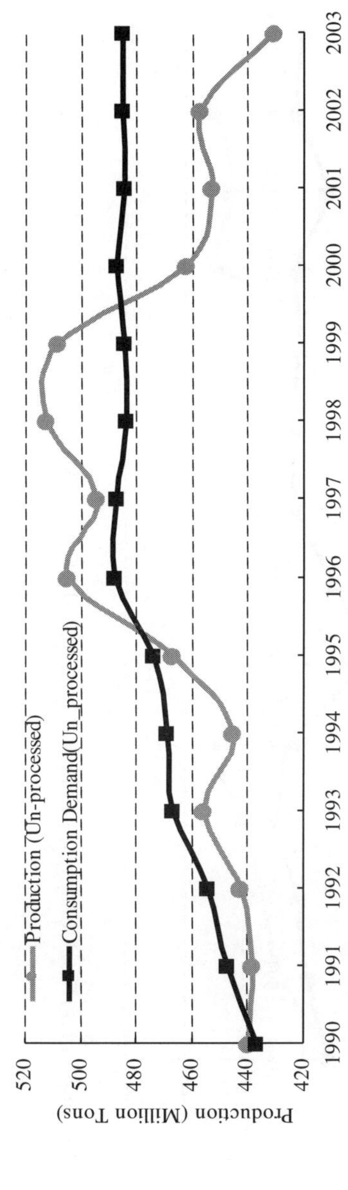

Fig. 2: Production and Consumption Demand of Grain in China from 1990 to 2003

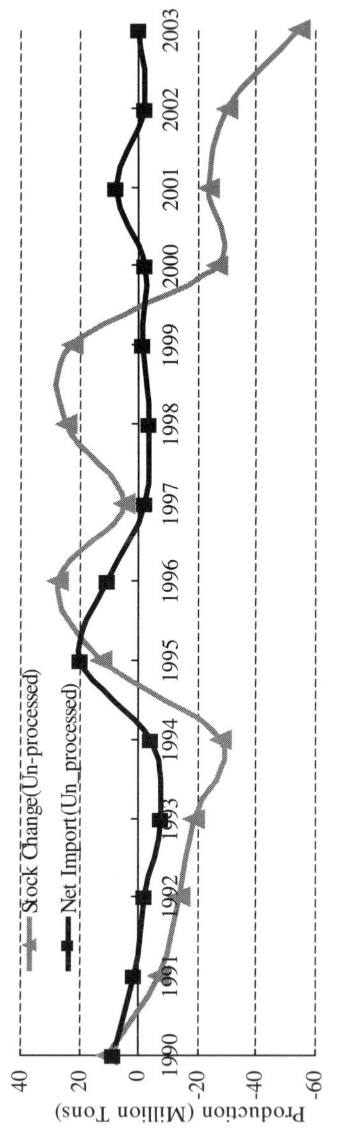

Fig. 3: Net Import and Stock Change of Grain in China from 1990 to 2003

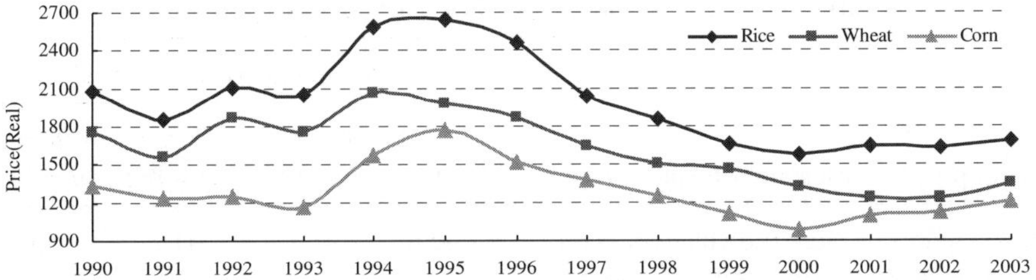

Fig. 4: Rural Grain Price in 1980–2003 (CNY/ton, 2003 price)

ISSUES IN PROGRAM IMPLEMENTATION AND IMPACT ON PARTICIPANT INCOME

Besides grain market turnaround and local diversion of funds, there were other problems emerging in program implementation that made it necessary for the center to make a radical program adjustment in 2004:

Farmers' Autonomy in Program Implementation

One of the most disturbing discoveries from the survey is the primarily top-down approach taken toward implementation. This is evident in the significant portion of sample households that reported that they had little or no choice of whether or not to participate.

Perhaps the greatest concern is the lack of respect for the principle of voluntary participation embodied in the program. In the 2003 survey, both participants and non-participants were asked questions regarding the degree of autonomy they had in deciding whether or not to participate. This was evident from informal discussions with households and local officials during fieldwork, as well as in the significant portion of households that reported that they had little or no choice of whether or not to participate. The responses to these questions are shown in Table 6. Only around 53 percent of the surveyed households felt that they could choose to participate (61.7 percent of the participants and only 25.9 percent of the non-participants). This ranged from 65.8 percent of households in

Table 6: Farmer Autonomy in SLCP Participation (n = 345)

Group	Measure of Autonomy	Percentage that said "*yes*"			
		All	Shaanxi (n = 103)	Gansu (n = 85)	Sichuan (n = 76)
Participants (n = 264)	Were the villagers asked their opinion about the project and how it could be best designed prior to its implementation?	42.8	41.7	41.2	46.1
	When your village began SLCP, did your household have autonomy to choose whether or not to participate?	61.7	72.8	43.5	67.1
	Did you have autonomy in choosing the types of trees to plant?	36.0	47.6	34.1	22.4
	Did you have autonomy in choosing areas to retire?	34.5	53.4	15.3	30.3
	Did you have autonomy in choosing plots to retire?	29.9	40.8	12.9	34.2
		All	Shaanxi (n = 11)	Gansu (n = 34)	Sichuan (n = 36)
Non-participants (n = 81)	Could you participate in SLCP if you wanted to?	25.9	45.5	29.4	16.7

Source: Authors' calculations based on survey data.

Shannxi, to 45.5 percent in Sichuan, to only 31 percent in Gansu Province. From fieldwork, we believe that these responses can be taken at face value; households were aware of the details of the program and cognizant of their choices. For example, respondents reported lower levels of choice for aspects of program implementation requiring technical expertise, and therefore more likely the purview of program officials; only 36 percent of the participant households said they could choose what kinds of trees to plant on their enrolled land, and only 34.5 percent and 29.9 percent of the participant households felt that they could choose areas and plots, respectively. Only 42.8 percent of participant households indicated that they had been asked their opinion about project design prior to implementation.

These results are clearly troubling for a number of reasons. Lack of household autonomy in participation choice runs counter to the program's explicitly stated principle of volunteerism. More importantly, use of market-based voluntary mechanisms of participation is key to the efficiency gains promised by payment for environmental services (PES) programs over traditional command-and-control approaches.[18] In the case of the SLCP, since no bidding mechanism exists to optimally match payer benefits with participant costs, participation should, at minimum, be voluntary. This could improve cost-effectiveness by ensuring that households with the lowest opportunity costs participate, and would minimize the possibility that program participation is having negative welfare effects on some participants. The survey data, in fact, provide some evidence that this second, adverse outcome has already occurred.

Lack of Administrative and Financial Resources in Program Implementation

Besides diversion of funds, one important reason for the subsidy delivery shortfall is the lack of administrative funds at the local level for SLCP implementation. Apparently, program coordination, inspection, and compensation delivery for millions of farmers are both burdensome and costly for local governments. Yet, it was only from 2002 that the central government allocated any administrative expenditure to provincial governments for SLCP implementation. These, however,

[18] Stafano Pagiola, Natasha Landell-Mills, and Joshua Bishop, "Making Market-Based Mechanism Work for Forests and People," in *Selling Forest Environmental Services: Market-Based Mechanisms for Conservation and Development*, ed. Stafano Pagiola, Joshua Bishop, and Natasha Landell-Mills (London, UK: Earthscan, 2002).

have also been inadequate, and are often in large part diverted by higher levels before reaching the county and township governments that carried out the major administrative work. The fast expansion of the program created even greater administrative needs, and thus shortfalls in required administrative funds, and in turn led to problems in implementation and subsidy delivery. In many cases, the program expansion was so fast that local government agencies responsible for the program supervision did not even have sufficient staff and time to check whether the converted land had reached the government requirements regarding tree types and survival rates. Therefore, the delivery of compensation had to be delayed. In a key project county in Shaanxi Province, for example, half of the participant plots were not inspected and compensated on time. In another township of the same county, many participant plots were yet to be inspected even three years after they had entered the SLCP. Although the county government recruited 30 additional staff to deal with these problems, manpower still fell far short of that required to inspect some 67,000 ha of converted land.

Low Survival Rates in Afforestation

According to the rules for SLCP implementation, tree survival rates after land retirement must reach at least 85 percent for the state subsidy to be delivered to the participant farmers. To facilitate subsidy delivery, local governments tended to over-report tree survival rates and mobilized farmers to replant trees on land plots with low survival rates before upper level inspection. In our survey of 18 townships across the three provinces, only five sample townships had survival rates consistently above the government standard (70 percent in Gansu and Shannxi, 85 percent in Sichuan). In Li County in Sichuan, survival rates were below the standard in all but one inspections in one township, and this has been declining in recent years. According to the farmers surveyed, survival rates were even below 40 percent in many places, and significant replanting has had to be done. Pervasive replanting has led to shortfalls in government seedling subsidies of around CNY 750 per ha according to our survey. Moreover, in many regions even replanting cannot guarantee survival rates due to lack of water, and in many cases is simply done to pass government inspections to obtain program subsidies.

Low tree survival rates and frequent replantation are worrisome since it not only significantly discounted program effectiveness, but also implied higher program implementation costs. Because of the need for frequent replantation to ensure higher survival rates before inspections, the state seedling subsidy of CNY 750 per ha is insufficient in many places. Local governments have bargained for more upper level fiscal transfers for seedling expenditure and also diverted more subsidy from farmers to make up for the shortfalls.

SLCP Planning

There was also a serious problem in the SLCP planning itself. According to the GIS data collected by the authors, China's total area of arable land with slope over 25° is 3.21 million ha and that with slope over 15° is 10.21 million ha (Table 7). However, by the end of 2003, the total area of land conversion through the SLCP was already as high as 7.19 million ha, of which land with slope over 15° was 4.42 million ha. This implies that around 38 percent of the retired land has slope lower than 15°, though the SLCP planning

Table 7: Land Types and Area in China (unit 10,000 ha)

Slope of Arable Land	North China	South China	Total
>25°	98	223	321
15°–25°	268	433	701
8°–15°	372	351	723
<8°	7,063	2,073	9,136
Total arable land area	7,801	3,080	10,881
Retired land area	405	314	719

Source: Authors' calculations through GIS data.

explicitly stipulates that the program need to focus on retiring arable land with slope over 25°. To make things worse, the total area of land retirement in the SLCP plan from 2001 to 2010 is as high as 14.67 million ha. This is not only much higher than the nation's total arable land with slope above 25°, but also higher than that with slope above 15°. Therefore, the SLCP plan itself is problematic, and some adjustment has to be made sooner or later.

Program Impact on Participant Income

Since the real ecological gains in the long run can only be realized if the program is carried out so that participants keep their land out of cultivation even after the program ends,[19] the key to the program's success in the long run is whether the participant farmers can adjust their production structure and benefit from other forms of agricultural production such as livestock-breeding or off-farm work, otherwise the possibility of return to cropping would be high and the program sustainability would be in question. Therefore, it is important to assess the impact of the program on participant farmers' income from sources other than cropping and government subsidies.

To assess the impact of the program on participant households, we utilize our data to analyze the change in real net incomes in 1999 and 2002 for both participant and non-participant households.[20] Table 8 presents 1999 and 2002 components of total income for both participant and non-participant households

---

[19] As a matter of fact, post-program land use decisions of the participating farmers have been one of the biggest concerns in conservation set-aside programs elsewhere. See P. N. Johnson, S. K. Misra, and R. T. Ervin. "A Qualitative Choice Analysis of Factors Influencing Post-CRP Land Use Decisions," *Journal of Agricultural and Applied Economics* 29, no. 1 (1997): 163–173.

[20] Real net income was calculated by subtracting the agricultural production cost from the total revenue. The total revenue was calculated by adding revenues from agricultural and non-agricultural activities plus the value of in-kind consumption, then converted into real terms using deflator.

Table 8: Per Capita Net Income of Participant and Non-Participant Households, 1999 and 2002

Region	Total Income[a] Income Component	Mean (Std Dev)			
		Non-Participant Households		Participating Households	
		1999	2002	1999	2002
Shaanxi	Total Without subsidy	940 (777)	1,335 (930)	986 (1,077)	1,325 (1,874)
	With subsidy received	—	—	—	1,394 (1,877)
	Cropping without subsidy	465 (521)	626 (429)	420 (672)	401 (622)
	Cropping with subsidy received	—	—	—	470 (628)
	Livestock	6 (23)	17 (63)	18 (78)	208 (916)
	Off-farm	388 (623)	590 (947)	401 (554)	525 (680)
	Other	82 (233)	101 (234)	147 (686)	191 (826)
Gansu	Total Without subsidy	1,803 (1,681)	2,021 (1,741)	1,287 (980)	1,287 (942)
	With subsidy received	—	—	—	1,317 (942)
	Cropping without subsidy	484 (350)	360 (246)	589 (523)	370 (320)
	Cropping with subsidy received	—	—	—	399 (345)
	Livestock	17 (53)	119 (220)	6 (30)	113 (222)
	Off-farm	1,192 (1,570)	1,346 (1,624)	633 (679)	681 (647)
	Other	110 (515)	196 (541)	59 (204)	124 (393)
Sichuan	Total Without subsidy	1,419 (1,425)	1,654 (1,271)	1,635 (1,195)	1,961 (1,524)
	With subsidy received	—	—	—	2,067 (1,514)
	Cropping without subsidy	721 (938)	506 (633)	829 (931)	472 (590)
	Cropping with subsidy received	—	—	—	577 (583)
	Livestock	33 (42)	202 (200)	49 (75)	459 (1,187)
	Off-farm	543 (953)	714 (987)	674 (897)	869 (971)
	Other	122 (295)	232 (476)	83 (251)	161 (375)

Source: Authors' calculations based on survey data.

[a]All units are in 1999 RMB, adjusted using the Rural Consumer Price Index.

province-wise.[21] These numbers suggest that the SLCP has indeed induced a restructuring of agricultural production, whereby participants have shifted relatively more of their inputs out of cropping and into husbandry. In Shaanxi Province, growth rates for cropping income were 35 percent for non-participants compared with only 12 percent for participants (including subsidies received). In Gansu, these were –26 percent and –32 percent, respectively, and in Sichuan cropping income declined by 30 percent for both groups. Conversely, growth rates for husbandry were higher for participants than for non-participants. In Shaanxi, average household per-capita husbandry income for participants increased more than 10-fold, compared to only 175 percent for non-participants. In Gansu, participants' husbandry income grew by 1,744 percent, compared with only 586 percent for non-participants, and in Sichuan these numbers are 845 percent and 514 percent, respectively. Differences between participants and non-participants in change of total income are less systematic across regions. In Shaanxi, total income (including subsidies received) increased by 41 percent and 42 percent for participants and non-participants, respectively. For Gansu, these numbers are 2.3 percent and 12 percent, respectively, and for Sichuan they are 26 percent and 17 percent, respectively.

Since such numbers could be the result of factors unrelated to the SLCP implementation, we use a first-differences model explaining change in household per-capita net income between 2002 and 1999 to more rigorously estimate the program impact on

[21] Cropping income consists of total crop production valued at an average village market price, net of materials, and hired labor costs. Husbandry income includes both sales income and own consumption, valued at market prices. Off-farm income includes all non-agricultural production activities, comprised mainly of sideline activities and wage labor income. Income from sideline activities is net of production costs and other business-related expenditures, while wage income includes both cash and in-kind income, valued at market prices. Other income consists of aquaculture, rental and interest income, gifts, pension income and government subsidies, and transfer payments. The SLCP subsidy is calculated as the subsidy received by the household for 2002.

income. A simple regression specification for explaining change in income is

$$\Delta y_i^k = \alpha_1 + \delta \cdot \text{prog}_i + \delta^{\text{L}} \cdot \text{pyrs}_i + \Delta x_i^{\text{H}} \cdot \beta^{\text{H}} + \Delta x_i^{\text{V}} \cdot \beta^{\text{V}} + d_i \cdot \gamma + \Delta\mu_i \quad (1)$$

where Δy_i^k denotes the change in farm household i's per-capita net income component k between 1999 and 2002, $\text{prog}_i = 1$ if household i is a participant (i.e., is in the treatment group), Δx_i^{H} and Δx_i^{V} are vectors of changes in household and village-level characteristics, respectively, between 1999 and 2002, d_i is a vector of provincial and county-specific time trend dummies, and $\Delta\mu_i$ is the difference in idiosyncratic disturbances across periods. We include in one specification the number of years household i has been in the SLCP before the end of 2002 ($pyrs_i$) to control for lagged program impacts not picked up in the first difference. Household characteristics included are the 1999 per-capita income, the 1999 per-capita number of plots affected by disaster, and changes in household population and labor share of population.[22] Village characteristics are included to instrument for changes in the village per-capita income not related to the SLCP implementation. These include changes in village population, in the number of village enterprises, in the number of daily long-distance buses that run through the village, in the share of village households that have a telephone, and in the share that have piped water.

Of interest for program evaluation is δ, generally referred to as the *difference in differences* (DD) estimator. This captures the difference, controlling for household and village-level factors, in the average income change between participants and non-participants that can be attributed to program participation. A central concern in the program evaluation literature is the impact of selection bias on the estimates of program impact. If selection bias is an issue, then the

[22] Neither variables capturing household per-capita land nor household program enrolled area were included due to concerns that participation effects would be confounded with impacts of changing per-capita land. Relatively little substantive change in the model results, and significance levels were found when these variables were included.

outcomes of non-participants cannot be used to estimate the counterfactual outcomes for participants were they not to have participated. In the case of our survey, we believe we can in large part control for the effects of selection bias due, ironically, to the predominantly top-down approach toward implementation observed in the survey. This gives us a subsample of households that have not self-selected to be participants or non-participants, allowing for empirical examination of selection bias in the sample.

Our baseline for comparison is the full sample of households. Model estimates for the subsample of non-autonomous households are presented for comparison, as well as to serve as our best estimate of program impact since these households are randomly selected for treatment and the selection can be viewed as exogenous. Though we argue that no self-selection bias exists in the non-autonomous subsample, another potentially important source of selection bias might come into play via the selection of certain types of individuals into the program by government officials and village leaders.

We test this by comparing the 1999 household characteristics between participants and non-participants in the full sample, and in the two subsamples of autonomous and non-autonomous households. We generally find in all three groups no statistically significant differences between the household characteristics of participants and non-participants, including characteristics likely to be the focus of selection, such as share of land that is highly sloping. The one important exception to this is already controlled for in the model: per-capita number of plots affected by disaster in 1999, which is significantly larger for participants than for non-participants in all three groups.[23]

Table 9 presents the results from the models. Note that estimates for the full sample are, in most cases, larger than for the non-autonomous

[23] This is found to be 0.26–0.32 larger for participants, significant at 0.1 percent. Total household land is also found to be significantly different, tending to be 0.24–0.27 ha larger for participant households, significant at between 1 percent and 5 percent, depending on the subsample. However, since differences in per-capita household land and total household population are insignificant, we do not believe that this is a concern.

Table 9: Program Impact on Participant Income

Income Component		All Households (n = 345)		Households w/o Autonomy (n = 161)	
		With Lag	No Lag	With Lag	No Lag
Program impact (δ)					
Cropping	Before subsidy	–8.15 (46.74)	**–98.87** (36.6)**	2.31 (57.87)	**–89.56** (42.25)*
	With subsidy	40.38 (48.67)	–33.63 (37.91)	53.38 (60.64)	–29.06 (44.07)
Husbandry		230.12 (126.18)	190.75 (97.47)	130.03 (79.99)	**127.84** (57.38)*
Total agricultural	Before subsidy	221.98 (133.07)	91.88 (103.12)	132.33 (98.52)	38.27 (71.13)
	With subsidy	**270.50** (134.74)*	157.12 (104.32)	183.41 (99.29)	98.77 (71.59)
Off-farm		–40.56 (75.97)	–40.15 (58.66)	–126.51 (118.57)	–102.23 (85.08)
Non-cropping		189.56 (146.7)	150.60 (113.31)	3.52 (144.78)	25.61 (103.88)
Other		0.73 (46.57)	–25.16 (36)	25.23 (71.17)	–30.69 (51.28)
Total	Before subsidy	182.14 (164.35)	26.56 (127.33)	31.06 (169.62)	–94.64 (122.15)
	With subsidy	230.67 (165.9)	91.80 (128.44)	82.13 (170.61)	–34.14 (122.79)

(*Continued*)

Table 9: *(Continued)*

Income Component		All Households (n = 345)		Households w/o Autonomy (n = 161)	
		With Lag	No Lag	With Lag	No Lag
Program lag (δ^L)					
Cropping	Before subsidy	**−58.43** (19.08)***	—	**−61.35** (26.83)**	—
	With subsidy	**−47.67** (19.87)**	—	−55.06 (28.11)	—
Husbandry		−25.36 (51.52)	—	−1.46 (37.08)	—
Total agricultural	Before subsidy	−83.79 (54.33)	—	−62.81 (45.67)	—
	With subsidy	−73.02 (55.02)	—	−56.52 (46.03)	—
Off-farm		0.26 (31.02)	—	16.22 (54.96)	—
Non-cropping		−25.09 (59.9)	—	14.76 (67.12)	—
Other		−16.67 (19.01)	—	−37.35 (32.99)	—
Total	Before subsidy	−100.20 (67.1)	—	−83.95 (78.63)	—
	With subsidy	−89.43 (67.74)	—	−77.65 (79.09)	—

*Significant at 10 percent.
**Significant at 5 percent.
***Significant at 1 percent.

subsample, providing evidence that selection bias is inflating the full-sample estimates of program impact.[24] Overall, these results provide evidence that the program is indeed inducing participants to shift their structure of agricultural production (i.e., toward husbandry and away from cropping). At the same time, however, they provide mixed results regarding program impact on total income. To begin with, impact on cropping income is significant in all specifications. Using as a basis for comparison the average 2.8 and 2.6 years that full-sample and non-autonomous subsample households were in the SLCP, respectively, results from the model controlling for program lag indicate that participation has induced a reduction in per-capita net cropping income (without subsidy) of CNY 94 based on the non-autonomous household sample and CNY 92 based on the full sample. For the model with no lag, the reduction is CNY 87 and CNY 81, respectively. Change in husbandry income associated with participation is weakly significant in three of the four specifications. The model with a program lag effect estimates that the SLCP has induced an increase in husbandry income of CNY 130 using the non-autonomous sample, and CNY 186 using the full sample. The model with no lag estimates an increase of CNY 129 and CNY 194, respectively.

Estimates of program impact on total income are statistically insignificant. As our best estimate of program impact, however, the results are informative. The model with program lag effects estimates that SLCP participation has induced an average decrease in total household per-capita net income of CNY 69 based on the non-autonomous sample, and an increase of CNY 35 based on the full sample. In the model with no program lag effect these estimates

---

[24] We have ruled out the existence in the sample of reporting bias that is systematically related to household autonomy, wherein non-autonomous participants report inflated estimates of their 1999 income due to dissatisfaction with the program. As mentioned, we find no statistically significant difference in household per-capita income between autonomous and non-autonomous households. Added to this, we also find no statistically significant difference between the 1999 (i.e., pre-program) per ha net income of enrolled plots between these two groups.

are a decrease of CNY 60 and an increase of CNY 57, respectively. The lack of statistical significance might simply be because it is yet too early for impact on total income to have clearly emerged. The program could also be having systematically different impacts on different subgroups in the sample — beneficial in some cases, harmful in others — resulting in large standard errors for the estimates.[25] This would not be surprising given the large diversity of economic, natural, and institutional conditions encompassed by the sample, as with the program in general.

Overall speaking, the general lack of strong results regarding program impact, though not surprising given the relatively short time period being evaluated, is counter to government claims regarding the SLCP's impact on the rural welfare. Not only did we find no significant impact on the total income, we also found, not surprisingly, no impact on the non-agricultural components of income. Though the results weakly suggest that participants are shifting inputs into other activities (i.e., husbandry) as a result of participation, they also indicate that the effect of this is not significant. Part of this is likely due to the large amount of time farmers in the sample reported they had to spend planting and caring for trees on enrolled land so as to guarantee that they received subsidies. This means that an additional cost of program participation has been the opportunity cost of labor spent in managing retired land, in this case in terms of the foregone crop income on remaining plots or other activities. Viewed in this way, foregone income on retired plots might, indeed, be a reasonable estimate of total opportunity cost to farmers. Furthermore, though production risk might be a significant concern for households in the sample, participation in the SLCP might simply be replacing one type of risk for another. Specifically, program stipulations requiring a minimal survival rate of trees or grass planted on retired land in order for subsidies to be

[25] A version of the model was examined that interacted program participation with the disaster-affected number of plots and with total income. Program impact on total income remained statistically insignificant in this model, as were the interactions.

delivered, combined with the uncertainties and lag time involved with implementation and inspection by village and higher-level authorities, suggest that participation itself entails a form of non-negligible income risk. Given this, it is very possible that participants are adjusting their consumption, savings, and investment choices to cope with this risk, resulting in reduced program impacts on income.[26]

Income Risks and Grain Security for Program Participants

Income risks for participant farmers actually go far beyond the household survey data have suggested. Though the SLCP itself did not promote restructuring from cultivation to other farm and off-farm sectors, restructuring across sectors indeed occurred in the regions surveyed. As shown in Table 8, income from off-farm and livestock breeding grew in this period for all households, and such growth was more significant for non-participant farmers. However, our field surveys found that much of the off-farm income growth came from employment opportunities generated by large-scale state investment in the same period when the center implemented a "Western Development Strategy" to boost domestic demand in a period of deflation. When the Chinese economy walks out of deflation and the center's budget constraint becomes harder, it is unlikely such investment will continue to grow as fast. This tends to dampen the growth of off-farm incomes in the future, especially when we take into account the relatively low education level and limited off-farm employment opportunities in regions covered by the SLCP.

[26] See Deaton (1992) and Besley (1995) for a review of the theory and evidence regarding this. Angus Deaton, *Understanding Consumption* (Oxford: Oxford University Press, 1992) and Timothy Besley, "Savings, Credit and Insurance," in *Handbook of Development Economics, Volume 5*, ed. Jere Behrman and T. N. Srinivasan (Amsterdam: North-Holland, 1995).

Potential income from forestry is also not optimistic due to the low tree survival rates, the slow timber growth in many SLCP covered regions with low rainfall, uncertainties in the state logging policy, and potential oversupply of economic forestry products because of large-scale economic forestry plantation following the SLCP implementation. Most trees planted on the converted land are ecological in nature with very limited perspective economic returns. Most parts of northwestern China are semi-arid or arid areas ecologically unsuitable for timber trees (as shown by the low tree survival rates from our survey in these regions). In south China where there is more rainfall, relatively tight logging policies will also hamper farmers' interest in planting and maintaining timber trees. For "economic forests" (such as bamboo, chestnut trees, tea shrubs in south China, and jujube and apple trees in north China) whose subsidy lasts only for five years, the fast expansion in the SLCP led to a situation in which many regions in the SLCP planted very similar types of economic forests, and it is highly likely that their economic value will decline with oversupply.

With regard to income from livestock breeding, much of its growth came from the grain subsidy that farmers received from the SLCP which then was used as livestock feeds. Though the government encouraged domestic husbandry that had minimum adverse impact on the local ecology, such approach will be threatened after the eight-year subsidization period. As a matter of fact, significant surge in the grain price since 2003 not only put pressures on the central budget and may push the government to replace its grain subsidy with cash subsidy, but also threatens the feed supply and puts an end to enclosure stock-raising in the program. If feed price continues to rise to the extent that it is unprofitable to follow the government mandate of enclosure stock-raising, farmers may resort to pastoral grazing that undermines the original program goal of soil protection.

Finally, grain security for participant farmers may also arise as a serious issue in the near future. Our field survey showed that the converted land as a share of total household land holding was

Table 10: Per-Capita Arable Land Holdings Before and After the SLCP (ha)

	All Farmers		Participant Farmers		Non-participant Farmers	
Sample	1999	2002	1999	2002	1999	2002
Sha'anxi	0.229	0.098	0.241	0.091	0.144	0.147
Gansu	0.164	0.131	0.176	0.129	0.135	0.135
Sichuan	0.182	0.134	0.165	0.099	0.217	0.207
All sample	0.192	0.121	0.198	0.105	0.171	0.167

Source: Authors' calculations using CCAP survey data.

very high in many regions, which led to excessive drop of per-capita arable land for participant farmers. As shown in Table 10, on average, per-capita arable land in the surveyed regions dropped by more than one third. In Shannxi Province, it dropped from 0.24 ha to 0.09 ha per capita, a decline of 60 percent. If we consider the adverse climate conditions and frequent natural disasters in these regions, retaining a relatively large area of land for cultivation and keeping sufficient number of land plots for each household are essential for farmers to avoid risks across time and land plots. Our field survey in Shannxi and Gansu found that on average a "normal" year for agricultural production is usually followed by two to three years of drought. Therefore, farmers tend to save one year's harvest for two to three years of consumption. Even if the SLCP will not lead to the national grain security issue, it may still threaten the food entitlement of program participants after the subsidy period and thus undermine program sustainability.

CONCLUSION

Overall, the Sloping Land Conversion Program, a program used in a period of grain surplus, was expanded too fast given the center's intention to dispose of grain stock in SGB and local governments' intention to gain more transfers. Based on our survey, we found evidence of systematic problems in implementation, and no evidence that the program has — contrary to government claims — had any significant positive impact on participants income. Most troubling is the finding that, though on paper a payment for environmental services scheme, the SLCP appears to be, in practice, just another top-down, campaign-style program. The importance of farm households as the key long-term actors in implementation makes the participant's willingness and choice key conditions for the program's success. Otherwise, in the absence of significant gains in the development of sources of non-cropping income, participants who originally did not wish to participate, or who are not being adequately compensated for their opportunity costs of participation, will simply return land to cultivation upon the end of the subsidy period. And results from the survey indicate that this is not a small share of participants.

This paper at least demonstrates that government claims about the success of the pilot phase of the SLCP have been, at minimum, inflated. Given that claims made by the government about the huge success of the pilot phase have served to justify the break-neck speed of expansion seen during full implementation, these results are important. Excessive speed in program expansion led to significant fiscal risk for governments, income risks for participants, and ecological risks for program covered areas. To reduce such risks, officials need to significantly scale back program expansion and profoundly reexamine program design and implementation. Although the government's growing largesse toward environmental initiatives is encouraging, large-scale campaign-style programs are not the way to reverse adverse environmental outcomes stemming from a complex combination of factors. Only by positioning the SLCP within an array of policies focused on the rural economy can the dual goals of environmental amelioration and poverty alleviation be realized.

Policymakers also need to halt the expansion in order to seriously reevaluate program design and implementation. Combined with improvements in program design that allow for greater local initiatives, flexibility and the use of more market-based instruments could also help to improve program cost-effectiveness by better matching participant opportunity costs with program subsidies, thus increasing the possibility of long-term program success. Program cost-effectiveness could also be improved by allowing land-rich villages with better developed off-farm employment to — as they are much more willing to — enroll more land. In addition, if authorities are serious about realizing the long-term ecological goals of the program, the subsidy period should be extended. Though five years might be sufficient for orchard forests, the eight-year period for timber forests is far too short. Most trees planted on the converted land are ecological in nature (i.e., are not orchard trees) with limited potential economic returns in terms of their value for timber.

Our analysis also implies that the longer-term sustainability of the program might be related as much or more to off-farm income-generating opportunities as to on-farm structure of production. An underlying assumption of the SLCP has been that retiring land from cultivation is a prerequisite for rural economic restructuring, not vice versa. Therefore, in the fast and large-scale expansion of the program, neither the central nor the local governments have taken sufficient action to promote participants' income restructuring within and permanent migration out of the regions targeted by the program. Under such circumstances, it is not surprising that there was no significant program impact on incomes from sources other than cultivation. Restructuring rural economy first to reduce ecological pressures on rural land is particularly important given evidence in the literature of regional poverty traps in China, since many of the targeted areas for the SLCP are in relatively inaccessible and ecologically fragile regions wherein farm households have low average levels of education and social capital. This would suggest that in the longer term, general investment in agriculture balanced with development of non-agricultural sectors of the rural economy, and permanent migration out of ecologically fragile regions, might do as much or more to relieve pressure on sloping, marginal cropland than a campaign-style government program advertised as the final solution to high soil erosion. Given that such measures can only be realized gradually, the fast-paced expansion, rather than an indication of success, is more likely a harbinger of failure.

Last but not least, in addressing ecological problems in China, the government should pay more attention to the issue of cost-effectiveness in program selection and design. In the arid and semi-arid north and northwest areas in China, retiring sloping land from cropping to forestry may not work well since local rainfall and soil conditions are not suitable for timber trees. As a matter of fact, timber tree plantation would indeed hamper the water conservation function of soil or even lead to further land desertification because timber trees need much more water than grass or shrubs. The low survival rates of timber trees have been very apparent in China's other ecological programs implemented in early periods, such as the Northeast, North, and Northwest China Green Belt Program. One example is Mingqin County, Gansu Province, where the area of government afforestation was as high as 87,000 ha, but only 20,000 ha survived.[27] In reality, land degradation and desertification due to excessive irrigation in the upper stream of river basins (in Xinjiang and Gansu, for example) and over-grazing (in Inner Mongolia, for example), rather than soil erosion, are more urgent ecological challenges that need to be dealt with immediately. These usually constitute ecologically irreversible processes that may lead to disasters such as sandstorms with impacts going far beyond the source regions. With limited government allocation for ecological protection, ecological programs to address land degradation and desertification need to be prioritized. As to soil erosion in the Yellow River basin, the existence of the Loess plateau itself constitutes by far the most important reason for the serious soil erosion issue in North China. Since

[27] Gaoming Jiang, "More Emphasis on Plantation Than Conservation: Ecological Protection Is Not Equal to Tree Plantation," *China Youth Daily*, September 24, 2003.

current engineering technology to consolidate riverbanks in the lower streams can significantly reduce the hazardous impact from soil erosion, retiring cropping land in the upper stream is perhaps a less urgent issue. As argued, such reduction can only be achieved gradually as more non-cropping or off-farm job opportunities are created.

Chapter

8

Elections, Governance, and Accountability in Rural China

Fubing Su and Dali L. Yang

INTRODUCTION

Village democracy has attracted considerable attention in recent years. Nowadays, millions of villagers head to voting stations in the countryside and elect their leaders according to the Organic Law of Villagers' Committee. By the end of June 2005, nine provinces had already completed their elections. Seven provinces were in the middle of this process, and five more would launch their own in the second half of the year. By the end of 2005, all villages would have completed two rounds of elections since the law was formally enacted in 1998.[1]

While competitive elections are a crucial aspect of village democracy, they are only one means to the end of good governance. In this chapter we consider village elections in the broader context of improving governance in China. We argue that the promotion of

[1] "Chinese Villagers' Committees Elections Have Three Clear Features and Many Institutional Innovations." See http://news.tom.com/1988/20050712-2297178.html.

village democracy should be complemented by simultaneous institutional improvements in a number of other non-electoral areas that enhance the accountability of public officials. These other areas clearly were on the minds of the drafters of the Organic Law. According to the document, the ultimate goal of village democracy is to achieve self-governance in the Chinese countryside. The law states that there are four components of village democracy: democratic elections, democratic decision making, democratic management, and democratic supervision. To hold village leaders accountable, all these institutions need to be in place. In fact, improvement in three other areas tends to help improve the chances for sustaining sound electoral practices. In contrast, the introduction of elections in an inhospitable environment may ruin the reputation of elections, give democracy a bad name, and thus harm the consolidation and further expansion of democratic governance.

The chapter is organized as follows. We first review Chinese village self-governance in the past two decades. The next section provides some theoretical arguments as to how elections may and may not improve governance. Drawing on insights from the literature into institutional design, we discuss some basic principles in facilitating control and accountability. This is followed by an analysis of a number of non-electoral institutions in recent years. The chapter concludes with some remaining issues.

VILLAGE SELF-GOVERNANCE AND ELECTIONS IN CHINA

At least for the past century, there has been a long-running debate on whether the trappings of democracy, or the competition in the political marketplace, can sink roots in China. The travails of the past century have in turn added to the pessimism of many China observers. As Steven Mosher, one of the most persistent critics of China, recently wrote:

> There is no Chinese tradition of respect for human rights, indeed, no notion of inalienable rights at all. There is no ghost of a suggestion that government in any way derives its just powers from the consent of the

> governed. From the beginning of Chinese recorded history, the emperor has been an absolute despot. In this regard, there is little to distinguish Qin Shihuang, who ruled from 221–206 B.C., and Mao Zedong, who ruled from A.D. 1949–1975, China's autocratic traditions provide no roots, and precious little foothold, for the foreign shoots of democracy.[2]

For writers such as Mosher the apparent willingness of the Chinese people to tolerate the current birth planning policy reflects a deep passivity in the national character and suggests that the Chinese are culturally unfit for democracy. Such conclusions have led Mosher and others to argue for treating China as an enemy.[3]

Obviously, Mosher is extreme in interpreting China's history. Other distinguished scholars of Chinese history and thought, such as William Theodore De Bary of Columbia, have produced studies that suggest China's historical tradition was not one of a monolithic autocracy.[4] For contemporary China, leaving the village elections aside, survey research by Tianjian Shi, Zhong Yang, and others have revealed much popular political participation in urban areas. It is within this context, and in a decade when democratization has captivated several social sciences disciples, that the village elections have become a major topic in studies of China. Until recently, various members of the elite, both within the ruling circles and even among the anti-regime dissidents, have argued that China is too backward and simply has too many "farmers" for democracy.[5]

Article 111 of the 1982 Chinese Constitution provided for the establishment of villagers' committees (VCs) and specified that the residents elect the chairman, vice chairmen, and members of residents' or villagers' committee. This provision became legally executable with

[2] Steven Mosher, "Are the Chinese Ready for Liberty & Self-government?" *The American Enterprise* 9, no. 4 (July–August 1998): 50–53.

[3] Steven Mosher, *Hegemon: China's Plan To Dominate Asia and the World* (San Francisco: Encounter Books, 2000).

[4] William Theodore De Bary, *The Liberal Tradition in China* (New York: Columbia University Press, 1983).

[5] Daniel Kelliher, "Keeping Democracy Safe from the Masses: Intellectuals and Elitism in the Chinese Protest Movement," *Comparative Politics* 25, no. 4 (July 1993): 379–396.

the passage of the Organic Law of Villagers' Committees (for trial implementation) by the National People's Congress (NPC) in 1987. At the time, Peng Zhen, chairman of the NPC and one of the more orthodox party politicians, strongly supported the enactment of the Organic Law, whereas Zhao Ziyang, the party general secretary who would be ousted in 1989, was less enamored of it.[6] In a reflection of the somewhat uncertain political status of the village elections, the Organic Law was promulgated for trial implementation only — a strategy Chinese leaders had skillfully used in the rural reforms of the late 1970s and early 1980s.

Formal implementation of the Organic Law of Villager's Committees began in 1989–1990 — not the most auspicious circumstances. Yet, armed with the imprimatur of the Constitution and the national law, a small number of bureaucrats in one department of the Ministry of Civil Affairs (MCA) took their mission seriously and steadily promoted the village elections province by province.[7] In fact, under the constraints of limited personnel and travel limitations, the MCA officials first worked with provinces closer to Beijing and gradually fanned out spatially. As a result, Yunnan (an ethically diverse but less developed province in the Southwest) and Guangdong (Canton, the economic powerhouse adjacent to Hong Kong) were the last two provinces to jump on the bandwagon of popular village

---

[6] Tianjian Shi, "Village Committee Elections in China: Institutionalist Tactics for Democracy," *World Politics* 51, no. 3 (1999): 385–412.

[7] There is a growing number of studies on the village elections, notably Kevin J. O'Brien, "Implementing Political Reform in China's Villages," *Australian Journal of Chinese Affairs*, vol. 32 (July 1994): 33–67; Kevin O'Brien and Lianjiang Li, "The Struggle over Village Elections," in *The Paradox of China's Reform*, ed. Roderick MacFarquhar and Merle Goldman (Cambridge: Harvard University Press, 1999), 129–144; Melanie Manion, "The Electoral Connection in the Chinese Countryside," *American Political Science Review* 90, no. 4 (1996): 736–748. For recent overviews of the issues, see Robert Pastor and Qingshan Tan, "The Meaning of China's Village Elections," *China Quarterly* no. 162 (2000): 490–512; Tyrene White, "Village Elections: Democracy from the Bottom Up," *Current History* 97, no. 620 (September 1998): 263–267; Jean Oi and Scott Rozelle, "Elections and Power: The Locus of Decision-Making in Chinese Villages," *China Quarterly* 162 (June 2000): 513–539.

elections.[8] By the late 1990s, the village elections had become an accepted practice nationwide; they were seen as a major accomplishment of China's political reforms and socialist democracy. Building on this record, the PRC Organic Law of Villager's Committees was formally enacted by the NPC in November 1998.

Given the relatively small size and homogeneity of villages and the close proximity between village residents and the candidates, elections (in 1999) for the 801,000 village committees in China provided an excellent setting for a basic-level political participation, if not the direct democracy that theorists such as Rousseau would desire. Although the villages are not formally a part of the state apparatus, the very fact that meaningful elections are taking place in such a multitude of villages (and, in the future, in urban neighborhoods) is a signal political achievement. Moreover, over time the conduct of village elections has improved. The 1998 Organic Law of Villager's Committees specifically stipulated that the elections be conducted using secret ballots, direct nominations, and the number of candidates be more than the number of positions available. Scholarly studies have demonstrated that the village elections have become a meaningful mechanism of accountability for village governance.[9] Some analysts have suggested that the village elections are becoming the training ground for further democratization.[10]

By building democracy from the bottom up and among China's less educated, the successful popularization of village elections offers a powerful counter-argument against those who see agrarian China as unsuited for democracy. Yet, while the procedures for village

---

[8] There is a strong statistical correlation between a province's distance from Beijing and the time taken by the province to approve a regulation for village elections.

[9] See especially Manion, "The Electoral Connection in the Chinese Countryside." See also Melanie Manion, "Democracy, Community, Trust: The Impact of Elections in Rural China," *Comparative Political Studies* 39, no. 3 (April 2006): 301–324.

[10] Jamie Horsely, "Village Elections: Training Ground for Democratization," *China Business Review* 28, no. 2 (March–April 2001): 44–52. For an example of township level elections, see Melanie Manion, "Chinese Democratization in Perspective: Electorates and Selectorates at the Township Level," *China Quarterly* no. 163 (2000): 133–151.

elections have seen a steady improvement over time, there is also no denying that elections per se are no panacea for rural China's difficulties, including lagging incomes and corruption. Moreover, some of the village elections have been plagued by problems that are found in elections in other countries, including vote buying and various forms of manipulation.

DEMOCRACY, ELECTION, AND GOOD GOVERNANCE

From Election to Governance

The idea of democracy is to minimize the arbitrary exercise of domination and ameliorate asymmetries of power. Public-office holders should be responsive and accountable, and the rights and interests of ordinary citizens should be protected. In the Western democratic theory, there has been a long-standing debate on the meaning of democracy. Formal (or minimalist) representative democracy and civic-participatory substantive democracy are the two major strands of thinking on this topic.[11] They offer different answers to the following question: Is reelection sufficient for holding public officials responsive and accountable? While the minimalist tradition answers on the positive note, the civic tradition argues that more direct participation by citizens and constant vigilance are needed to protect citizens' rights.

Most scholars of democracy today work with the minimalist definition propounded by Joseph Schumpeter that democracy entails periodic competitive elections.[12] From a theoretical point of view, there are two mechanisms for elections to improve the responsiveness

[11] John McCormick, "Machiavellian Democracy: Controlling Elites with Ferocious Populism," *American Political Science Review* 95, no. 2 (June 2001): 297–313.

[12] Joseph Schumpeter, *Capitalism, Socialism, Democracy* (New York: Harper, 1942). See also discussions in Fareed Zakaria, "Illiberal Democracy," *Foreign Affairs* 76, no. 6 (November–December, 1997): 22–43, and Philipper Schimitter and Terry Lynn Karl, "What Democracy Is . . . and Is Not," in *The Global Resurgence of Democracy*, ed. Larry Diamond and Marc Plattner (Baltimore, MD: Johns Hopkins University Press, 1996), 49–62.

and control of the public-office holders.[13] The forward-looking one focuses on voters' ability to select good politicians with similar policy orientations. Since every individual may have pieces of information about the candidates (especially in the village community with typically one thousand or so people), popular elections are the best mechanism to make use of that decentralized information and pick the most capable or ethical leaders. In order to get elected, candidates need to listen to the public and try to propose policies that best serve the majority of the community. This is a mechanism for aggregating scattered information and producing sound public policies. Generally speaking, capable people with sound policy platforms will win the competition. The backward-looking mechanism emphasizes rewarding or punishing politicians depending on their behavior in office. If politicians renege on their campaign promises after taking office, they will be thrown out in the next election. Therefore, politicians have incentives to stick to their campaign promises.

But for several reasons, the electoral mechanism alone may not be sufficient to keep politicians in check. First, information asymmetries between candidates and voters may seriously undermine the reputation mechanism. One crucial assumption of the minimalist argument is that information about the candidates and their track records are readily available in the society; so, voters can reward or punish the candidates accordingly. For citizens only with bounded rationality, however, the above assumption requires too much cognitive capability from the voters. In addition, public-office holders have an advantage in this reputation game. Without proper checks, they can create more noise in the information dissemination process or even mislead the voters by bending information in their favor. Some supporting institutions need to facilitate the flow of information and

[13] James Fearon has a more formal treatment of this subject. See his "Electoral Accountability and the Control of Politicians: Selecting Good Types versus Sanctioning Poor Performance," in *Democracy, Accountability, and Representation*, ed. Adam Przeworski, Susan Stokes, and Bernard Manin (Cambridge: Cambridge University Press, 1999), 55–97. Also important is John Ferejohn, "Incumbent Performance and Electoral Control," *Public Choice* 50, nos. 1–3 (January, 1986): 5–25.

ensure its authenticity; otherwise, deviations are not likely to be promptly detected and punished.

Second, democratic elections are inherently uncertain.[14] Even though in the long term and on average, good and capable people will prevail through competition in the political marketplace, voters may make mistakes or evil politicians can successfully mimic good persons. This is especially problematic for newly democratized countries. It usually takes time for voters to learn the rules of the game and vote responsibly. In addition, the time horizon of politicians varies greatly. While future reelection may be enticing enough to keep some politicians honest and responsive, others may have a shorter time horizon, due to idiosyncratic personality or a dim prospect of reelection. The reelection mechanism will not deter these latter kinds of officials, in which case it is dangerous to entrust much power to them.

Third, and closely related to the above point, there may be institutions to correct these problems, but post-facto correction can be too costly in certain instances. Stokes has demonstrated how some Latin American leaders adopted policies that went against their mandates after being democratically elected. Of course, in her cases, the politicians were believed to be fighting for the long-term economic welfare of the country.[15] But it is conceivable and commonplace to see democratically elected public officials do something contrary to the majority interest. There are mechanisms such as impeachment and votes of no-confidence to throw them out of office. But resorting to such mechanisms requires much time and cost. By the time the process is initiated, the harm is already done. Sometimes, the damage is irreversible: Investments go sour, public funds are squandered, and human lives may be lost. Moreover, it is costly to overcome the collective action problem and initiate these processes.

[14] Przeworski even defines genuine democratic election with uncertainty. See Adam Przeworski, *Democracy and the Market: Political and Economic Reforms in Eastern Europe and Latin America* (Cambridge: Cambridge University Press, 1991).

[15] Susan Stokes, "What Do Policy Switches Tell Us about Democracy," in *Democracy, Accountability, and Representation*, ed. Przeworski et al., 98–130.

One way of avoiding these problems is to build checks and balances in the decision-making process, and make sure that no one, whether appointed or democratically elected, can determine the fate of public policies without going through proper scrutiny. This is based on a skeptical view of human nature, but it is precisely the nature of democracy.

Therefore, good governance needs not only periodic competitive elections but also supporting institutions that provide oversight and check on the public-office holders. A parallel can be drawn from the marketization of the former socialist economies. Before the reform, it was generally believed that privatization and competition would automatically lead to a free-market economy. The events afterward, especially in Russia, have reminded scholars of the importance of other institutions for a competitive market system. In the case of democracy, theorists recognize that seeking reelection alone may not be sufficient to make politicians responsive and accountable.[16] They realize that "accountability agencies" may be needed to supplement the electoral mechanism and control politicians. These agencies include independent electoral commissions, independent accounting offices, and independent statistical agencies. These institutions, in combination with electoral processes, make up the tapestry of modern democratic governance.

In the real world, plenty of examples support this claim. The United States, despite a century of democratic elections, found itself in a deep crisis by the latter half of the 19th century. Governance was in a shambles, and rampant corruption, gang violence, irregular markets, and major accidents plagued the society. This provoked a series of institutional innovations and started the state-building processes that are now known as the Progressive Era. As a result of these efforts, a regulatory state emerged.[17] These developments saved its democracy from collapsing.

---

[16] Ibid.

[17] Steven Skowronek, *Building a New American State: The Expansion of National Administrative Capacity, 1877–1920* (Cambridge: Cambridge University Press, 1982).

Likewise, many new democracies have found themselves "haunted by old demons that they had hoped to exorcise with democratic rule: violations of human rights, corruption, clientelism, patrimonialism, and the arbitrary exercise of power."[18] As we look around the world in the early 21st century, Russia has become a basket case of corruption and bad governance. The democratically elected president of the Philippines was forced to resign for corruption, while the Indonesian president, who came to power democratically following the overthrow of the Suharto regime, was charged with corruption. And it is not just new democracies that must confront the scourge of corruption. India is caught in a massive corruption scandal concerning defense procurements. There are major corruption probes in Germany and France. The list goes on and on.

With respect to village elections in China, we find that a worrisome sign is already emerging in rural areas. In some villages, elections without proper institutional support have indeed ruined the reputation of democracy in some places. Even in a widely publicized model of democratic election, Lishu County of Jilin Province, villagers are cooling down and some have become suspicious of the electoral process. When asked why he had lost interest in elections, one villager responded, "it is meaningless. Whoever gets elected will cash in their power."[19] As a result, election turnout has moderated and even declined in some areas.

From Theory to General Principles

Democratic theory provides philosophical underpinnings but falls short in supplying concrete proposals for the institution building. For this purpose, we turn to the institutional design literature. Growing out of transaction cost theories in economics, this literature finds the most fruitful applications in the international political

[18] Andreas Schedler, Larry Diamond, and Marc Plattner, ed., *The Self-Restraining State* (Boulder, CO: Lynne Rienner, 1999).

[19] Zhang Jing, *Problems of Rural Level Governance in China* (Hangzhou: Zhejiang People's Press, 2000), 209.

economy and American politics, especially studies of the American congressional structure and legislature–bureaucracy relations.[20] Scholars in this tradition place their emphasis on oversight and control problems in a hierarchical setting. The most standard setup is a principal-agent model, which is complicated by control problems arising from the information asymmetry and interest divergence. Scholarly analyses have sought to identify institutional mechanisms that will not only keep agents in compliance but also improve overall efficiency. Therefore this literature seems to be particularly relevant to governance.

Some basic principles that emerge from the institutional design literature include ex ante control, ex post control, cost-efficiency, transparency, professionalism, and checks and balances. As we will now discuss, these concepts and principles are useful for understanding the rationale as well as the weaknesses of some institutional innovations in the Chinese countryside. While monitoring and punishment can deter agents from shirking, it is also very costly for the principal since the harm is already done when punishment is meted out. A more effective control is to stamp out possible deviations ex ante. Specifically, scholars argue that administrative procedures, such as appointment, budgets, and operating rules, achieve precisely this goal.[21] Principals can control agents because these procedures have either screened out agents with different ideological preferences or narrowed the discretion exercised by the agents. Operating rules, in particular, stipulate as clearly and with as much detail as possible what each agent should do and should not do under different situations. The U.S. government owns and manages hundreds of acres of forests employing thousands of forest rangers. As part of the control method, forest rangers are required to follow

---

[20] For some standard references, see the works of Douglas North, Margaret Levi, Kenneth Shepsle, Barry Weingast, and Matthew McCubbins.

[21] The most cited piece is Matthew McCubbins, Roger Noll, and Barry Weingast, "Administrative Procedures as Instruments of Political Control," *Journal of Law, Economics, and Organization* 3 (1987): 243–277. In the American context, scholars are divided as to whether the president or the Congress really controls the bureaucracy.

the manual (two volumes containing thousands of pages) strictly, and to keep a diary of their daily activities. As a result, despite the tremendous centrifugal forces in the bureaucracy, the level of compliance is remarkable.[22] These administrative procedures have in essence reduced the agents' discretion, leaving little room for abuse.

While administrative procedures can mitigate the control problem significantly, monitoring and punishment are nevertheless necessary. Screening cannot be perfect, and "bad" persons may successfully fool the superiors. Moreover, the operating rules (like sunshine provisions) make defections more visible; but some enforcement is needed to ensure adherence by the agents. These mechanisms include self-reporting by the agents, inspecting, rewarding the loyal, and punishing the deviants. Control mechanisms should be constantly in place to make them effective.

Any control comes at a price, and good institutional design should try to minimize the costs associated with the monitoring. One clear alternative to monitoring by the principal is to shift the burden to a third party. Ideally, the principal will spend very few resources in monitoring the agents, and only respond to complaints filed by an injured party. The specific example that receives most academic attention is the fire alarm mechanism.[23] A truly independent media can also serve that purpose. For a principal with very limited resources, this is an attractive alternative.

The fundamental problem with effective control is the information asymmetry. If the principal knew what the agents had done, the control problem would simply disappear. Therefore, information disclosure is essential to control, and it is necessary for both electoral and non-electoral mechanisms to function. As discussed earlier, for the electoral mechanism to work, public officials should develop

---

[22] Herbert Kaufman, *The Forest Rangers: A Study in Administrative Behavior* (Baltimore, MD: Johns Hopkins Press, 1960).

[23] For an application to the Chinese context, see John Brehm and Emerson Niou, "Police Patrol vs. Self-Policing: A Comparative Analysis of the Control Systems Used in the Former Soviet Union and Communist China," *Journal of Theoretical Politics* 9, no. 1 (January, 1997): 107–130.

a reputation or generate a track record of their past activities. Many institutional rules, such as revealing the voting records in the legislature, just provide such valuable information for the voters.[24] By facilitating information flows, transparency can also significantly lower the costs for the monitoring efforts by the principal or by third parties.

While the material incentive of agents can be shaped by various control mechanisms, people are also susceptible to non-material controls. Lindblom argues that persuasion is one of three means to control humans, the other two being power and exchange.[25] Recently, more material-oriented scholars have argued for the usefulness of ideology and corporate cultures in obtaining compliance within organizations. Professionalism not only utilizes material incentives but also appeals to human beings' psychological needs. Through training and various symbols, agents can be assimilated into the profession with which they are associated. They take pride in being a member and try to stick to the ethics of the community. Material losses aside, non-compliant agents also develop a great deal of shame if they are caught.

No human is perfect, and no rules will operate flawlessly all the time. Therefore, good governance should avoid placing too much power in any one institution and create a government with human weaknesses in mind. This point was always close to the hearts of the drafters of the U.S. constitution, particularly James Madison, who was also one of the authors of the Federalist Papers. Those men deliberately divided the state apparatus into three branches, endowing each with the authority to counterbalance the others. Such an arrangement entails significant institutional costs, but it is worthwhile as an attempt to guarantee vital public interests. In the case of governance at the village level in China, the problem is further complicated by the fact that most village committees consist of only

[24] Based on this logic, John Ferejohn argues that legislators in the U.S. Congress opted for disclosing the voting records of all legislators. Ferejohn, "Accountability and Authority: Toward a Theory of Political Accountability," in *Democracy, Accountability, and Representation*, ed. Przeworski et al., 131–153.

[25] Charles Lindblom, *Politics and Markets: The World's Political-Economic Systems* (New York: Basic Books, 1977).

three to seven members. That means they can easily collude to infringe on the villagers' interests, especially in financial matters.

The principles discussed above will not lead to foolproof strategies, but they offer a perspective that we can use to evaluate the design of various institutions. They can also shed light on possible institutional remedies.

NON-ELECTORAL INSTITUTIONS AND ACCOUNTABILITY IN RURAL CHINA

The Chinese central government is now putting more emphasis on promoting non-electoral institutions. The most recent policy regarding village democracy (No. 17 [2004]), for example, specifically clarifies issues related to transparency and democratic management. It also tries to standardize rules and practices in the country.[26] As in previous policy changes in rural China, the top leadership has been fairly open-minded so far: It is willing to allow local governments and officials to experiment with alternative ways of rural governance. The Central Party School and the Central Editing and Translation Bureau (*Zhongyang Bianyi Ju*), together with Beijing University, have even set up a prize for institutional innovation by local governments, and some prize-winners have created new village governance models.[27] Despite its official status, this prize is judged by university professors and therefore has a high degree of independence and credibility. The central government's tolerance is a clear indication of its flexibility, which will encourage further local experiments. Of course, the central leadership is not entirely passive in this process. It listens carefully and promotes good innovations while vetoing others. These choices can enhance village self-governance in the countryside but also reflect the party's own political interests. Undoubtedly, these dynamic

---

[26] General Office of the CCP Central Committee and General Office of the State Council, "Opinions on Promoting and Perfecting Village Affairs Publicity and Democratic Management" (June 22, 2004), http://news.xinhuanet.com/zhengfu/2004-07/12/content_1591421.htm.

[27] A full list of prize-winning institutional innovations is available at www.chinainnovations.org. The third round of competition is currently under way.

interactions between central intervention and local innovations will determine the evolutionary path of rural governance.

Tax-for-Fee Reforms and the Abolishment of the Agricultural Tax

No other area is more prone to official abuse than village finance. And this is indeed the major source of rural instability.[28] Even though closely related, revenue collection and public expenditure can be treated somewhat differently in the analysis. We will mainly focus on revenue collection in this section and discuss some institutional solutions.

Many peasants are complaining about the widespread collection of illegal fees by village cadres. In fact, peasants' burdens have increased quite rapidly since the early 1990s. This has led to an increased number of visits to local Letters and Visits offices (*Xinfang*) by disgruntled peasants and, in some cases, large-scale violent confrontations.[29] The causes of the peasants' burdens are many, but the central government is partly to blame. In 1994, China overhauled its old fiscal system and adopted a separate-tax system (*fen shui zhi*). There were two major goals of this change. The first was to increase the percentage of government revenue in total GDP, and the second was to allocate more revenue to the central government. The reform was reasonably successful, but it also led to a fiscal crisis at the local level.[30] Faced with a tight budget and increasing public expenditures mandated by the central government, many local governments felt a financial pinch. County and township governments in poor areas were especially hard pressed to find new sources of income, and that usually meant creating new categories to collect money from peasants. The central government found itself

[28] For more analysis of this phenomenon, see Thomas Bernstein and Xiaobo Lu, "Taxation Without Representation: Peasants, the Central and the Local States in Reform China," *China Quarterly* 163 (September 2000): 742–763.

[29] See ibid. for some examples.

[30] For more discussion, see ibid. and Ran Tao and Mingxing Liu, "Regional Competition, Fiscal Reform and Local Governance in China" (working paper, 2004).

in an awkward position. If it wanted to get things done locally, it had to tolerate this local practice. Of course, like most public officials worldwide, local government officials, especially township and village cadres, abused their discretionary power. They created many new ways to raise revenues and wasted the money on extravagant wining and dining, entertainment, and luxury cars. Because of their *assumed* discretion, local cadres, regardless of whether they were appointed or popularly elected to their posts, all faced a strong temptation to misuse their power. The central government has been experimenting with policy measures in the past few years, one thrust of which is to curb local cadres' discretion.

One such major change is the *tax-for-fee reform*. In the early 1990s, the Ministry of Agriculture, in response to the problem of peasants' burdens, proposed a unitary tax in rural areas. Peasants who were affected expressed strong support for the idea.[31] According to this plan, local cadres would not have the discretion to levy fees on peasants but could only collect one nationwide agricultural tax from peasants. But the proposal was put on hold because the country was caught in the growth euphoria that followed on the heels of Deng Xiaoping's celebrated southern tour in 1992. As the growth began to slow down, however, some rural localities began to experiment with tax reforms. Beginning in 1995, Wugang (Hubei Province) was authorized to experiment with tax-for-fee reforms in rural areas. By standardizing fees into taxes, Wugang's experimental townships were able to reduce burdens on farmers as well as reform public finance.[32] In Anhui Province, one of the pioneers of rural reforms in the post-Mao era, officials in Taihe and Woyang counties initiated a similar experiment in 1994 with the approval of provincial authorities.[33] Taihe officials sought to rein in arbitrary

---

[31] Dali Yang, *Calamity and Reform in China* (Stanford, CA: Stanford University Press, 1996), 210.

[32] *China Economic Times*, June 24, 1999.

[33] The practice was started in 1993 in Xinxing Township of Anhui's Woyang County, against the express prohibition of the county people's congress. The Xinxing leadership fixed the amount of farmer taxes and fees at 30 yuan per *mu*. For details of this case, see *China Economic Times*, February 24, 2001.

levies on peasants who were caught between stagnant prices for farm products and rising costs. By 1999, 15 counties (cities) had adopted rural tax reforms.

Based on local trials, the central government chose Anhui to experiment with the tax-for-fee reform province-wide. For the first year of the reforms, the financial burdens on peasants in Anhui were reduced by 1.7 billion yuan, or 31 percent. With the implementation of the reforms, per-capita tax and levies decreased to 75.5 yuan. To boost the transparency of the reforms, the counties also set up supervision stations staffed by the members of the county people's congresses. Tax administrators also set up stations to answer queries from peasants and thus ensure that farmers paid taxes with a full understanding of what they were paying for, thereby reducing the chances of local officials collecting unauthorized levies.[34] In 2001, Jiangsu and Zhejiang joined the experiment, and the program further expanded to 20 other provinces in 2002.

In 2003, the central government decided to promote the tax-for-fee reform nationwide.[35] Under this new system, local governments were allowed to collect only one agricultural tax from peasants, and no fees were allowed to be charged. Legal charges for township governments, such as the so-called *wu tong* (for rural education, family planning, militia, support for veterans, and road construction), were incorporated into the agricultural tax. The *san ti* in villages (for collective investments, welfare, and cadre compensations) was added as a surcharge. As a result, the agricultural tax rate was raised from 3 percent to 7 percent, and a 20-percent surcharge was added for village-level finance. In total, peasants would pay no more than 8.4 percent of their income. Additionally, tax collectors from local taxation agencies would be in charge of the collection, and township and village cadres could help but were not in direct control.

In early 2004, Premier Wen Jiabao announced at the NPC's annual meeting that the state was planning to phase out the agricultural tax

---

[34] CCTV, January 24, 2001.

[35] "State Council's Opinion About Promoting Rural Tax-for-Fee Reform Trial Work in the Country," March 27, 2003, www.China.org.cn/Chinese/Pl-c/331156.htm.

in three years.[36] This may be based purely on a cost-benefit analysis of tax collection. Many officials acknowledge the high cost of collecting taxes in vast and remote rural areas. By February 2005, 26 provinces had already abolished the agricultural tax, and by 2006 this tax category will finally disappear in China.[37]

From the perspective of controlling local officials, the tax-for-fee reform will clearly lead to better governance. In essence, this reform has curbed the discretionary power of township and village cadres. By centralizing revenue collection in tax agencies in higher-level governments, the central government is signaling its unwillingness to tolerate "creative" fee collection. While holding local cadres more accountable, this policy change does impose more financial hardships on local governments and villages, and it compromises their ability to provide public services. Abolishing the agriculture tax, in particular, may cause already heavily indebted local governments that were previously financed largely by agricultural surpluses to crash. For example, with the introduction of the tax-for-fee experiment in Anhui, township governments in Anhui Province had a budget of 4.6 billion yuan in 2000, but the payroll alone amounted to 4.95 billion yuan. An additional 2.28 billion yuan was needed to fund rural education.[38] To partly address this shortfall, the central government has pledged to subsidize about 10 billion yuan annually to agricultural counties and townships.[39]

---

[36] In addition to alleviating peasants' burdens, there is also a simple reason for abolishing agricultural tax: It makes economic sense. Because of China's highly scattered population, it is very costly to collect taxes from many individual households. Local governments often employ extra manpower to collect taxes, but the revenues can barely cover the costs. For some concrete examples, see Yang Weijun, "A Study of the Impact of Abolishing Agricultural Tax on Grassroots Governments," http://guancha.gmw.cn/showaspx?id=3066.

[37] "Abolishing Agricultural Tax Nationwide and Lifting the Curtain for Comprehensive Reform in the Countryside," March 11, 2005, www.lianghui.org.cn/chinese/zhuanti/2005lh/808939.htm.

[38] *China Economic Times*, March 6, 2001.

[39] "Abolishing Agricultural Tax Nationwide and Lifting the Curtain for Comprehensive Reform in the Countryside," March 11, 2005, www.lianghui.org.cn/chinese/zhuanti/2005lh/808939.htm.

Some provinces also began holding provincial and municipal governments responsible for financing rural education.[40] Despite these efforts, it is still possible that cash-strapped township or village cadres may fall back on fee collections again.[41] The State Development and Reform Commission completed a sixth round of inspection in mid-2005 and disclosed 13,000 cases of violations in the rural areas, most of which were illegal fees for education.[42] On the positive side, the tax-for-fee reform has tied local cadres' hands and forced them to downsize bloated local governments. To raise funds, village leaders in particular must seek consent from villagers and go through villagers' assemblies (*cunmin dahui*) or villagers' representative assemblies (*cunmin daibiao dahui*).

Accounting and Auditing Reforms

It is clear from various reports on peasants' petitions (*shangfang*) and other media investigations that the most contentious issue in peasant–cadre conflicts in the villages is financial mismanagement and corruption. Peasants have accused village cadres of corruption, embezzlement, and misuse of public funds to support lavish lifestyles. Some surveys further disclose that most villages do not follow basic accounting practices. According to one survey, 90 percent of the villages in the sample do not have formal accounting rules and regulations and have no accounts for collective assets. Seventy percent of village accountants are unclear about their responsibilities and the limits of their discretion, and half of the accountants also serve as cashiers. Indeed, 20 percent of villages do not even have accounting books, and 30 percent of accountants refuse to pass their books on to their successors.[43] In some cases, the village leader

---

[40] An interview with Wang Chaowen, deputy director of the Finance Research Institute, Ministry of Finance, www.cncitizen.org/article.php?articleid=1416.

[41] Ray Yep, "Can 'Tax-for-Fee' Reform Reduce Rural Tension in China? The Process, Progress, and Limitations," *China Quarterly* 177 (March, 2004): 42–70.

[42] *Zhongguo qingnian bao* [*China Youth News*], August 5, 2005.

[43] *Zhongguo shenji bao* [*China Auditing News*], November 21, 2000.

(either the party secretary or villagers' committee director) also serves as the accountant and the cashier. More often the accountant is either a relative or close ally of the village leader.

The backwardness of village financial management has made village-level finances a hotbed of corruption and mismanagement, but it also means that certain basic reforms, such as the popularization of sound accounting practices, could generate large payoffs. One institutional development entrusts the management of village accounts to township governments (*cunzhang xiangguan* or *cuncai xiangjian*). Under this arrangement, the township government establishes an accounting service office and is responsible for hiring the accountants. All villages in the jurisdiction transfer their accounts to the accounting office and pay fees for its services. Every village still needs one cashier and has to have full control of the collective funds in its accounts. This approach has been widely adopted in Hanzhuang Township of Pinggu County in Beijing and several counties in Zhejiang Province.[44] One variation of this mechanism has been practiced in localities such as Jiuguan Township of Nintai City, Shandong Province.[45] It is called the accountant secondment system (*kuaiji weipai zhidu*), which means the township government is responsible for recruiting accountants through competitive exams. The accountants are then dispatched to the villages but supervised directly by the township operations station (*jingying zhan*) rather than the village leaders.

These arrangements have different names in other places, but they all share two features. First, by aligning the interest of the accountants more closely with township governments, they make it more difficult for village leaders and the accountants to collude. Second, the township intervention may help isolate accounting from village politics and may breed a sense of service and professionalism through more training and better pay. Both are helpful in checking the corruption and misuse of the public funds by village leaders.

[44] *Zhongguo gaige bao* [*China Reform News*], November 11, 2000; *China Economic Times*, July 19, 1999.

[45] *Fazhi ribao* [*Legal Daily*], October 8, 1999.

Besides centralization and professionalization of village accounting, some localities have begun to allow more public involvement in matters of financial management by forming villagers' financial management small groups (*cunming licai xiaozu*). The small groups consist of representatives elected through the villagers' representative assembly and are empowered to supervise the details of village finances. They examine original receipts submitted for reimbursement, verify changes in collective assets, determine the salaries of the village leaders, and monitor contract enforcement and cash flows.[46] For example, every village in the previously mentioned Hanzhuang Township established the village financial management small group in 2000. Members range from six for big villages to three for small ones. They verified all the expenses village leaders submitted for reimbursement to the township accounting office. Such financial oversight helped curtail dining and entertainment expenses and administrative expenditures.[47] In the past, village party secretaries monopolized the power of village spending. With the introduction of these financial management groups, spending in the village will be reviewed by the small groups.

Interestingly, this institutional design was not in the Organic Law in 1998. After local experiments, the central leadership decided to promote this institution in 2004. According to the "Opinions on Promoting and Perfecting Village Affairs Publicity and Democratic Management" (No. 17 [2004]), villagers' financial management small group members are to be elected in the villagers' assemblies or villagers' representative assemblies. The small groups are directly responsible to the assembly not the villagers' committee or the party committee. The intention of creating checks and balances is very clear.[48]

Rules quickly become meaningless if violations go unpunished. Frequent monitoring is an integral part of any properly functioning institutional design. In the financial realm, audits play this important role. Ideally, an independent third party should be invited to audit

46 Zhang Jing, *Problems of Rural Level Governance in China*, 157–158.

47 *Zhongguo gaige bao*, November 11, 2000.

48 "Opinions," June 22, 2004, http://news.xinhuanet.com/zhengfu/2004–07/12/content_1591421.htm.

the village accounts regularly. It was reported that Liji villagers in Weishan County, Shandong Province, hired an accounting company, Weishan Xingheng Ltd., to audit the accounts of their village leaders in 2000.[49] However, this may not be feasible for most villages. While some accounting and auditing services are licensed to practice in the metropolitan areas, their reach to the rural world remains limited. In their stead, township governments have filled the void and played an active role. Baodi County of Tianjin has ordered township governments to audit village accounts on a regular basis, making the first week of every January and July the "auditing week." The county party disciplinary organization and auditing bureau were authorized to issue "auditing notice."[50] By the end of 2000, 79.3 percent of villages in the county had been subjected to such audit.[51] The 2004 "Opinions" also mandates auditing of village leaders before elections. County and township governments are held responsible for this task.

From a control perspective, entrusting village accounts to accounting service offices under the township government and auditing villages by township governments are only second-best institutional solutions. They should be replaced by more independent third parties in the future. After all, it may be difficult to convince villagers that township governments are truly neutral in village affairs. Moreover, these institutional designs, though technical, have more fundamental political implications. If villages are truly self-governing, should township and county governments manage village affairs? Opinions seem to be particularly divided on the issue of "*cunzhang xiangguan*." Some scholars regard this practice as a violation of village self-governance and therefore should be banned. Zhan Chengfu, a senior official in charge of village self-governance in the Ministry of

---

49 *Nanfang zhoumo* [*Southern Weekend*], Internet version, February 22, 2001. Of course, the interesting twist of this story is that the township government interfered in the disclosure of these auditing results, and the villagers finally had to take the problem to court.

50 *Renmin ribao* [*People's Daily*, Beijing], August 15, 2000.

51 *Economic Daily*, November 20, 2000.

Civil Affairs, publicly endorsed this view.[52] But other government agencies, such as the Ministry of Finance, are more motivated by corruption control and actively promote county governments' managing township accounts (*xiangcai xianguan*).[53] Many local governments seem to be willing to sacrifice self-governance for the sake of financial control. At least two provinces, Fujian and Zhejiang, and some local governments in Henan and Hubei Provinces have promoted *cuncai xiangguan*.[54] This may be a worrisome sign for many people with village self-governance in mind, but it does reveal that improving accounting practices is a high priority among current leaders.

Transparency and Cunwu Gongkai

While centralizing accounts and intensifying auditing can control village cadres, these are very costly practices, and village cadres still enjoy information advantage. An alternative way is to take advantage of villagers' information about local conditions and invite them to monitor their own cadres. Typically, villagers know best about the public works needed, real cost of materials, and whether or not cadres live a luxurious lifestyle. In addition, there are village affairs other than financial spending, such as the implementation of family planning policy, distribution of emergency and poverty funds, allocation of housing land, and renting and selling of collectively owned land. All these issues are of great concern to villagers and are vulnerable to the abuse of power. Forcing village cadres to disclose all the information can empower villagers to monitor their leaders, which improves transparency in village governance.

The central government started to promote village affairs publicity (*cunwu gongkai*) nationwide in April 1998. In a key policy directive, it asked all villages to disclose major issues relevant to the interests of villagers, including new projects, collective assets and finance, land

[52] Zhan Chengfu, "Be Cautious in Promoting *Cuncai Xiangguan*," *Gaige neican* no. 18 (1998).

[53] *People's Daily* (Internet ed.), July 13, 2005.

[54] *Xinanjiang nongwang*, June 3, 2003; *Renmin ribao*, June 28, 2005; *Zhongguo jijian jiancha bao*, June 8, 2005.

uses, family planning, fees and levies, contracts, and cadres' salaries. The emphasis was on full disclosure of village finances.[55] Following a major promotion drive, about 80 percent of the villages across the country had adopted the village affairs disclosure system by the end of 1999.[56] Some places have produced specific operational rules governing such disclosures. For example, Laiyang City in Shandong Province directed every village to publicize village affairs twice a year (June 25 and December 25) and financial affairs four times a year (at the end of each quarter). Every village was required to set up publicity boards (one for villages with fewer than 200 people and two for those with more than 200). The information was also disseminated via broadcasts, village meetings, and flyers (*mingbai zhi*). Cadres were required to respond to questions within two days.[57]

The expectation that spending will be publicized tends to moderate spending by village cadres and to reduce wasteful expenditures. By the end of 1998, 93.2 percent of the counties in Anhui Province had adopted village affairs transparency. According to one estimate, village expenses decreased by 25.8 percent that year.[58] In Zhejiang Province, where 98 percent of the villages had achieved financial transparency, entertainment and dining expenses by village cadres dropped by 10–40 percent.[59] The promotion of transparency also has the added benefit of exonerating village cadres from unfounded charges, thus easing strained cadre–farmer relations. One of the reasons for villagers to petition officials at upper levels is lack of transparency. Not infrequently villagers' suspicion and discontent feed on the secrecy surrounding the village decision making and financial management. Some cadres have thus welcomed the drive toward transparency and claimed that it cleared their names of suspicions and innuendoes of misdeeds.[60]

---

[55] *Economic Daily*, June 11, 1998.

[56] *Renmin ribao*, November 25, 1999.

[57] *Nanfang zhoumo*, December 25, 2000.

[58] *China Economic Times*, November 23, 1998.

[59] *Renmin ribao* (Huadong Xinwen), November 8, 2000.

[60] *Zhongguo gaige bao*, November 23, 1998; *Renmin ribao*, June 22, 1999 and July 19, 2000; *Guizhou ribao*, October 7, 2004.

On the basis of initial successes, the central government formed the coordination group for village affairs publicity and launched nationwide campaigns to implement this change in recent years. More specific details were added to this policy in the 2004 "Opinions" cited previously. Most notable is the introduction of one institution: the village affairs publicity supervision small group (*cunwu gongkai jiandu xiaozu*). All members are to be elected in the villagers' assemblies or villagers' representative assemblies. Like the villagers' financial management small group members, they are directly responsible to the villagers' assembly and supervise the villagers' committees. In many places, the membership of these two small groups overlaps.

While the transparency measures mainly serve as an ex post control mechanism, with some modifications it can also control the village cadres' behavior ex ante. For example, Shandong's Jiaonan City inaugurated the "housing land approval disclosure system." Villagers who want to build houses need to get approvals from both village cadres and village residents. Decisions by the cadres are not final until three days after the public disclosure. Within three days, villagers may file complaints with the city land resources bureau. Such ex ante control involves villagers in the decision-making process, which will be further discussed below.[61]

Transparency and village affairs disclosure can be a powerful tool in facilitating information flow and control. But there are also some serious weaknesses in the current design of this policy. One key problem remains in the shape of the information asymmetry. How can villagers verify the truthfulness of the disclosed information? The village affairs publicity supervision small group is intended to empower villagers institutionally and allow them to access the same information as village cadres. In reality, researchers and field workers discovered that in many places group members either were close associates of village cadres or soon colluded with them.[62] Second, even when group members exercise their power, there is

---

[61] *Renmin ribao* (Huadong Xinwen), March 27, 2001.

[62] *Fazhi ribao*, January 12, 2002.

no institutional guarantee of satisfactory results. When village cadres refuse to disclose information, or doctor the records, group members report this to the township governments according to the Organic Law.

But the township party committees and governments are hardly neutral third parties in rural governance. They have incentives to side with village cadres, rendering this institution still very weak. The supervision small group should be able to issue a more credible threat to non-compliant village officials. For example, it should be given the power to call a representative meeting of the villagers to impeach the leaders. Even this authorization may encounter problems, since the party is still strong in village governance and is not subject to villagers' consent. This is a more fundamental challenge, and we discuss it in the next section. Because of the weaknesses in the institutional design, the national campaign has made only moderate progress. In its first national meeting in 2003, the coordination group for village affairs publicity admitted that, among about 680,000 villages in China, 95 percent had promoted publicity and only 60 percent had followed the central government's instructions.[63] That number does not say anything about the quality of disclosure. In one study, only 27.7 percent of villagers said they could trust the content of the publicity boards.[64]

PARTICIPATORY DECISION MAKING

Bringing villagers into decision-making processes serves two main purposes. First, the village as a whole can take advantage of the superior local information of the residents and make efficient economic and social policies. Many people, including some scholars, believe that peasants are not sufficiently educated to make good policy choices, and that the elites (party members and village

---

[63] *Xinhua Net*, June 13, 2003.

[64] It was conducted by the State Council Development and Research Center in the late 1990s. More information can be found in Zhao Shukai, "Dilemmas Facing Village Organizations," www.chinaelections.org. The numbers reflect conditions in the late 1990s.

cadres) should take the lead. This is probably reasonable under certain circumstances, but when it comes to understanding local conditions, each resident has some useful information, and the villagers as a whole have far more knowledge than a handful of elites from out of town. Second, villagers' participation, adopted widely and routinely, can put some kind of ex ante institutional checks on village cadres. By making villagers' participation and majority votes a necessary part of a decision-making process villagers are given a veto right. Unlike the ex post control mechanism of public disclosure, greater villager participation gives villagers a direct voice in the content of policies, thereby putting an effective control over village cadres, especially in the domain of public spending. Ideally, wasteful spending or public policies that hurt the majority interest will be vetoed at the decision-making stage.

As in other areas, the specific institutions where villagers can exercise their decision-making power have evolved in the past two decades. In the trial version of the Organic Law of Villagers' Committee, villagers should participate through villagers' assemblies (*cunmin huiyi*), consisting of all villagers of age 18 or above. This is feasible for small villages whose population is only in hundreds, but for large ones with thousands of villagers, this institution is quite clumsy. In addition, as a result of economic reform, many peasants migrated to cities to find jobs so that meeting the minimum number of participants was a challenge for some villages. In response to this practical problem, some places experimented with villagers' representative assemblies (*cunmin daibiao huiyi*), where five to 15 households elected one representative to the assembly. This institution improved the effectiveness of village democracy and was adopted by the central government in the Organic Law in 1998.[65] Now, all major issues in the village, such as renting collective land, raising debts, and determining the salaries of village cadres, must be discussed in the villagers' assemblies or villagers' representative assemblies. The majority will prevail in the development of policies.

---

65 Cheng Tongshun, *Studies on Village Political Development in Contemporary China* (Tianjin People's Press, 2000), 186.

Public involvement can lead to better policies and more checks on cadres' discretion. For example, leaders at Nanlou village in Zhengding County, Hebei Province, wanted to invest 650,000 yuan and build a business center next to the highway passing by the village. When the proposal reached the villagers' representative assembly, representatives pointed out that trucks would not stop for this isolated building if no other supporting services were around. Instead, they suggested an oil-extracting plant, which could take full advantage of the rich sideline products in the neighboring areas. This counter-proposal was finally accepted, and villagers even volunteered their labor for this project, which was quite unusual. The plant turned out to be profitable.[66] Lishu County of Jilin Province pioneered the open ballot election (*hai xuan*) in village elections. Villager participation in decision making in this county had also been active. Villagers not only vetoed proposals that lacked sound economic justifications, but also exercised moderate checks on the fees and levies from higher-level governments. Village cadres cannot collect those fees without the assembly's authorization.[67]

The tax-for-fee reform and the abolishment of agricultural taxes have created more demand for functioning assemblies. As a result of these changes, village cadres can no longer raise funds for public projects. But it is also important that local communities do have the financial resources to provide basic public goods, such as the paving of roads and the construction of necessary irrigation facilities and infrastructure. According to the new rules from the central government, village leaders must request permission from the villagers' assembly or villagers' representative assembly. These permissions may be granted on a case-by-case basis (*yishi yiyi*). In He County of Anhui Province, 309 villages have used this mechanism to raise money for public works such as irrigation stations, roads, bridges, and broadcast networks. The county leaders admitted that, before the tax-for-fee reform, the county had 11.22 million yuan in public accumulated funds (*gongjijing*), or about 22 yuan per peasant.

[66] *China Economic Times*, July 6, 1998.

[67] Zhang Jing, *Problems of Rural Level Governance in China*, 206–207.

But very little money was actually spent on peasants. With the case-by-case approval process, 7 million yuan was raised, and villagers were generally satisfied with this change.[68] In June 2001, Jiaoshanpo village of Shandong Province raised 1,500 yuan per villager to bring the nearby river under control. The party secretary of the village noted that, if not for public participation in decision making, such an undertaking would have been unimaginable.[69] Similar positive developments are also reported in other villages. Villagers vetoed either over-active cadres or public consent led to speedy collection of funds.[70]

Of course, all these developments depend on one condition, namely, that the villagers' assembly or the villagers' representative assembly can indeed function as a decision-making body. While positive cases are certainly numerous, many researchers report a large number of negative examples. Many villagers' assemblies did not work or villagers' representatives were controlled or coopted by village cadres.[71] Currently, scholars and policy makers are debating the causes of this problem and looking for possible solutions. In a way, this touches a fundamental issue in village governance, i.e., who should control village lives in rural China? Should it be the communist party, democratically elected leaders, or villagers themselves? Institutionally, how should these three institutions (the party committee, the villagers' committee, and the villagers' assembly or villagers' representative assembly) be organized? Traditionally, the party committee was in absolute control, and only in recent years have the villagers' committees begun challenging the party's authority. In fact, the conflict between these two committees has been one

[68] *Xinhua Daily News*, February 21, 2001.

[69] *Banyuetan* [*China Comment*, Internet ed.], June 24, 2001.

[70] *Nongmin ribao*, April 19, 2003; *Fazhi ribao*, April 7, 2004; *Xiangzhen luntan*, April 2003.

[71] *Zhongguo shehui bao*, January 13, 2004; *Xiangzhen luntan*, November 2003; *Renmin ribao*, October 22, 1997. Lily Tsai also reported that some traditional institutions have played an important role in providing local public goods. "Cadres, Temple and Lineage Institutions, and Governance in Rural China," *The China Journal* 48 (July 2002): 1–27.

major concern for many people since the implementation of the Organic Law.

There have been some institutional innovations to solve this conflict.[72] The "two-ballots-rule" (*liang piao zhi*) requires that all villagers, both party members and non-party members, vote for candidates for village party committees, and candidates who get half of the votes will be formally nominated by the party for village party committees. In the second round, all party members in the village cast a ballot to select party committee members. Another solution is called "carrying on one shoulder" (*yijian tiao*), where the party will nominate party committee members to run for villagers' committee positions. If they are elected, the same group of people will effectively control both committees. These two institutional innovations have the potential of solving the conflict and have been endorsed by the CCP's Department of Organization. But the danger is also clear: in both cases, the party becomes stronger and replaces the villagers' committee. Even though they work through the democratic process, these changes may harm the village self-governance in the long run. Moreover, in order to get their candidates elected, higher-level party organizations have strong incentives to intervene and manipulate the election. In both cases, the villagers' assembly or the villagers' representative assembly is marginalized.

One recent innovation was started in Qing County, Hebei Province, and was widely praised by scholars and policy makers.[73] Unlike the last two solutions, this "Qingxian model" centers on the villagers' representative assembly. The assembly is reinforced and becomes a permanent institution. The representatives elect a chairperson. At the same time, the party committee stops micro-managing village affairs and concentrates on macro issues. More specifically, the party secretary must seek election for the assembly chair position.

---

[72] For interesting discussions, see Xu Fuqun, "Solutions to the Conflict Between Two Committees," October 7, 2004, www.chinaelections.org; Jing Yuejing, "Villagers' Self-governance, Two Committees' Relations, and Chinese Political Transition," *China Reform Forum*, June 15, 2005, www.chinaelections.org.

[73] Xu Fuqun, "Solutions to the Conflict between Two Committees." More analyses can be found at www.chinainnovations.org.

Secretaries who fail must resign. The villagers' committee is the operational arm of the assembly, and all major policies are decided in the villagers' representative assembly. Among these new innovations, the "Qingxian model" is closest to the Western-style democracy, where parties are only vehicles to power. But, from the CCP's perspective, this may come too close to yielding the party's leadership position in the rural area. Therefore, despite the praise for this approach, the CCP has not endorsed this innovation. In the latest document (No. 17 [2004]), the party committee is still in a leadership position even though the villagers' assembly or the villagers' representative assembly has formal power. This will certainly compromise villagers' ability to determine their own affairs. Until the CCP is willing to give up its dominance, this kind of political struggle is likely to continue in the future.

CONCLUSION: IMPROVING GOVERNANCE IN RURAL CHINA

The popularization of village elections in China is a major achievement of China's political reforms and democratic development. Nevertheless, sound rural governance is far more than the periodic holding of elections. On the one hand, greater popular participation in village affairs translates into greater demand for better governance and is believed to have resulted in improvement in local administration, including greater transparency. On the other hand, corruption and misrule by elected village officials have undermined popular trust in democratic institutions in some localities. In this chapter, we have discussed some mechanisms for governance that have evolved in the rural areas during the past few years. Evidence indicates that these non-electoral institutions can improve the function of the democratically elected village committees and facilitate a healthier development of good governance in rural China.

Having said that, however, is not to dismiss the value of elections. It should be reiterated that both electoral and non-electoral mechanisms are important parts of good governance. Given the small size of the village committee, it is important to institute regular monitoring and checks and balances in the management of village affairs. A functioning villagers' assembly, villagers' representative assembly, active financial management small group, and village affairs publicity supervision group should serve as balancing forces against the elected village committee members. They should be responsible for drafting village budgets, overseeing their implementation, calling for outside auditing, and initiating no-confidence processes, when appropriate. In a word, they should help solve the collective-action problem in the village and constantly check on the village committee and its handful of members. This improvement can also mitigate vote buying and bribery as reported in recent years. One major concern for vote buying is that people who spend their own money to get elected will abuse their power and pocket collective assets. Instead of electing good leaders, vote buying can send entrepreneurs, people more interested in making money and advancing their own interests, into village leadership positions. Institutional innovations discussed here, on the other hand, can decrease the prospect of power abuse and thus discourage this type of candidate from seeking public office.

Given the amount of information available, we are unable to analyze each institution in great detail. How do different regions respond to these opportunities? Why are some regions more active than others? What factors can explain the level of economic development, the degree of conflict in the villages, the local leadership, and the dependability of the connection to the central bureaucracy? These are certainly important and interesting questions, and more empirical research is needed. Regardless of the success or failure of particular institutions, however, the dynamic interaction between the local innovation and central intervention shapes the future trajectory of village self-governance. Both electoral and non-electoral institutions count.

Index

About the Contributors

Ashley Esarey, Assistant Professor of Political Science, Middelbury College.

Bobai Li, Assistant Professor of Sociology, Northwestern University.

Mingxing Liu, Associate Professor, School of Government, Beijing University.

Fubing Su, Assistant Professor of Political Science, Vassar College.

Yanfei Sun, Ph.D. candidate, Department of Sociology, the University of Chicago.

Waikeung Tam, Ph.D. candidate, Department of Political Science, the University of Chicago.

Ran Tao, Shaw Research Fellow, the Institute for Chinese Studies, University of Oxford and Research Fellow, Center for Chinese Agricultural Policy, the Chinese Academy of Sciences.

Fei-Ling Wang, Professor of Political Science, Sam Nunn School of International Affairs, Georgia Institute of Technology.

Tianfu Wang, Assistant Professor of Sociology, Qinghua (Tsinghua) University, Beijing.

Jintao Xu, Professor and Deputy Director, Center for Chinese Agricultural Policy, the Chinese Academy of Sciences.

Dali L. Yang, Professor and Chairman, Department of Political Science, the University of Chicago.

Dingxin Zhao, Associate Professor of Sociology, the University of Chicago.

About the Editor

Dali L. Yang is Professor and Chairman in the Department of Political Science at the University of Chicago. Among his books are *Remaking the Chinese Leviathan: Market Transition and the Politics of Governance in China* (Stanford University Press, 2004); *Beyond Beijing: Liberalization and the Regions in China* (Routledge, 1997); and *Calamity and Reform in China: State, Rural Society, and Institutional Change since the Great Leap Famine* (Stanford University Press, 1996). He is also co-editor and contributor to *Holding China Together: Diversity and National Integration in Post-Deng China* (Cambridge University Press, 2004).